LIMERICK CITY LIBRARY

ıone: 40751?
ebsite:
ww.li? ?ick?

The Granary,
Michael Street,
Limerick.

CHAPLIN'S
GIRL

Fiction
The Stones of Maggiare
Daughter of Darkness
Count Manfred
The Goddess
Medea
Madonna of the Island: Tales from Corfu
Carrying On
The Reluctant Devil: A Cautionary Tale
The Telling

Non-fiction
A Ring of Conspirators: Henry James and his Literary Circle
Ottoline Morrell: Life on the Grand Scale
Robert Graves: Life on the Edge
Mary Shelley
The Bugatti Queen: In Search of a Motor-Racing Legend
In My Father's House: Elegy for an Obsessive Love

Children's Books
Mumtaz the Magical Cat
The Vampire of Verdonia
Caspar and the Secret Kingdom
Pierre and the Pamplemousse

Miscellaneous
A Brief History of Thyme, and other Herbs

In memory of Father Virgil Cordano
(1918–2008)

CONTENTS

CONTENTS

PART FOUR
WARTIME

For a moment the last sunshine fell with romantic affection upon her glowing face; her voice compelled me forward breathlessly as I listened – then the glow faded, each light deserting her with lingering regret, like children leaving a pleasant street at dusk.

F. Scott Fitzgerald, *The Great Gatsby*

PROLOGUE: A SONG AT TWILIGHT

Montecito, Santa Barbara, California
(1992)

Propped against the pillows in her Santa Barbara bedroom, her cheeks reflecting the glow of her quilted pink jacket, Virginia Cherrill – if we make an allowance for the more temperate climate – might still be living in England, the country she adopted as her home in 1935. The Californian garden in which she is no longer strong enough to walk is filled with roses; her bed is surrounded by relics of her English life. The curved dressing-table once stood in the showroom of a house in Brook Street, Mayfair, presided over by the decorating team of Sybil Colefax and John Fowler. The fine-bristled hairbrushes and gold-topped cosmetic bottles that rest upon its half-moon surface came from Asprey; hanging in the shadows of a half-open cupboard are two cocktail frocks from the Thirties, their flared chiffon hems brushing a pair of green-and-ivory embossed satin sandals. Casual snaps of London friends compete for position upon the crowded table-tops against the more formal photographs of Virginia's mother, grandparents, a cherished nephew – and other, less easily identifiable figures: the swarm of godchildren that attempts to compensate for the lack of any descendants of her own.

A cat, springing through the open window, alights upon a table and picks its paws among the silver frames, tracking a familiar route towards the bed.

'Get out, damn you! *Out!*'

The old lady is concerned, not from any reason of intrinsic value, but because, among these ranks of photographs, so many represent past companions. She can't bear to think of losing one. An ocean and a continent offer too great a challenge, by now, for even the fondest of old friends to negotiate; the few octogenarians who have survived maintain their contact with occasional letters and the tender, empty promises of the cards they send at Christmas.

'You were saying,' prompts Teresa, the friend and neighbour who has recently decided to create a record of Virginia Cherrill's life, 'that you hated seeing the tigers shot when you were out in India.'

The old lady seems more interested in twisting a pointed stub of red wax up from its gilt cartridge case and – lips pursed before the oval compact-mirror – in refreshing the scarlet bow of her mouth.

'Isn't it time that Father Virgil was here?' Virginia asks, and then: 'Is Florek back yet?'

She sounds anxious; instinctively, she reaches down beside the bed to touch the tapered fingers of a hand, a bronze, cast from the slender arm of a young maharani, a friend from the Thirties.

On the near side of the bed, Teresa keeps the tape recorder held low, well out of range of visibility. Flicking it off, she waits for the rasp and roar of a vacuum cleaner to subside; she tries not to wince as the machine's plastic carapace whacks against the spindle legs of a gilded chair, bumps off and out of view along a wall. She knows better than to call attention to the maid's clumsiness; Virginia's faith in every person she knows to perform always to the best of their ability permits no criticisms.

Now that they can hear themselves speak again, Teresa flicks her machine back into recording mode and offers reassurance. Father Virgil will be along in an hour; Florian Martini, Virginia's Polish husband, should be back any minute now from his daily afternoon stroll along the sleepy Montecito lane.

'You know he's always home by six. But you were going to tell me about how you first met Cary Grant . . . or shall we go back to the tiger-shoot?'

'I worry about Florek,' the old lady murmurs (the machine can hardly catch her voice). 'If we'd had children . . . I can't help it, Teresa. I do worry. Who's going to care for Florek when I've gone?'

Her friend puts the recorder away and leans over the bed. She kisses the old lady's soft cheek, straightens the collar of her quilted jacket, and tells her not to fret. Going towards the door, Teresa sees the husband coming slowly down the path, a dog padding at his side. She calls to him that Virginia's getting anxious; he'd better hurry along.

And so, she thinks, had she: there's so much still to be told, so many snippets and anecdotes from a life she can't bear to think will one day be forgotten. Teresa isn't yet sure what to do with the recordings that she's made, whenever Virginia had fallen into the mood to chat, over the past year. For the present, all she's doing is storing the cassettes away and keeping up the flow of questions.

The project is not, as Teresa explains to friends, any kind of an ordeal; Virginia Cherrill has, after all, led a charmed and extraordinary life. Teresa, who has known the old lady since her own Polish family reached London in the early Forties, remains captivated by the personality of a woman who has inspired adoration – and broken hearts – without ever perceiving herself for what she seems to be: a true *femme fatale*.

Teresa can't bear to think of Virginia Cherrill being forgotten after her death. The tapes are her first step towards ensuring that something of an uncommon spirit will endure. A book, perhaps, will one day be written. The tapes will offer, then, both a record and the sense of a personality that letters (Virginia Cherrill was never an enthusiastic correspondent) can never quite convey.

★

I had never heard of Virginia Cherrill before the winter evening in 2005 when I first watched *City Lights* and fell in love with her performance as the blind flower-seller who wins the heart of Charlie Chaplin. I could not believe that this mythic performance was the first screen role of a 21-year-old girl, an untrained, untested newcomer. I could not stop talking about her. Everybody knew about the beautiful blind flower-girl. Nobody could tell me about Virginia Cherrill. One of the most celebrated actresses of her time, following the worldwide success of *City Lights*, a silent film made in the age of talkies, she had vanished from view.

Serendipity – dining with relatives during that same winter, I learned that my cousin's husband, William Ducas, had been the godson of Virginia Cherrill, and that a biography was planned – brought about the next step. I reminded William that I myself was a biographer. I begged for an introduction to Teresa MacWilliams, the loyal friend who, so William told me, had recorded Virginia's extraordinary story during the old lady's last years. (Virginia died, aged eighty-eight, in 1996.) He promised to do his best.

In April 2006, I travelled to California. Sitting beside Teresa MacWilliams in her Santa Barbara home, I pored over Virginia Cherrill's elegantly monogrammed blue scrapbooks.

'It's all here,' Teresa said. 'I haven't done much cataloguing, but I didn't throw anything out. Everything to do with Virginia is right here, in this room.'

I liked Teresa, a slender, quick-witted woman with high cheekbones and bright, girlish eyes. I wondered if she, too, had been a film-star.

'No chance,' she said, laughing. 'Although, Virginia, bless her heart, did do her best, took me along for an audition with Hal Wallis when I was eighteen years old, set everything up. She loved to do things like that.'

Together, the two of us worked our way through the big cardboard boxes brimming with old letters, cards and discarded snapshots, all saved from the modest Californian house in which Virginia had spent her last years. But it was when Teresa allowed me to listen to the tapes that I first felt the presence of a vivid, funny, entirely unpretentious personality.

'Virginia never cared about fame, or wealth, or power,' Teresa said, as we began sorting papers into piles for me to borrow from her collection. 'She wasn't interested in making an impression, or even in making a career in films. Things happened to her, but she really never cared if things went wrong. She *did* care about her friends. She wanted the best for everybody.' She glanced at me. 'You'd have loved her.'

The tapes were made when Virginia Cherrill was frail and bedridden; according to Teresa, they had been undertaken without the old lady's knowledge.

'Or maybe she did know. We never discussed it.'

What the tapes communicated as their new auditor sat, rapt and attentive, was the story of a woman whose exceptional life had been governed almost wholly by the impulses of an affectionate heart. Listening to these crackling monologues and sudden spurts of laughter, I envied Teresa the experience of having been the first to savour the old lady's memories of another world, reminiscences of a life that was rich in glamour and adventure, but that – it was clear – had been embraced, by Virginia herself, simply as it came to her.

The cassette tapes provided the voice and personality of a woman I never knew, but to whom I have become shamelessly attached. Teresa's recordings are neither technically perfect nor professionally organised. Virginia, in her eighties, often repeated herself, jumped directly from one startling episode in her life to another, leapfrogging whole decades without the slightest break in her sentence. I've taken liberties with the order of conversations;

I've edited the loose syntax of the spoken word; I've filled in the story and corrected dates and locations when – such occasions were rare – Virginia's memory let her down. But the voice that speaks from these pages, is true – I believe – to her own.

Charisma, meaning the power to communicate happiness, is neither a definable nor a conventional quality. Virginia Cherrill had it in spades.

PART ONE

Growing Up

1

BACK THEN

(1840–1908)

'We're talking about two respectable families back there in the Midwest, remember.'

The key to Virginia Cherrill's exceptional lack of pretentiousness, a natural sincerity that was in evidence throughout her life, lay in her childhood and early upbringing. Unlike many of her contemporaries in the competitive film world of the early Thirties, this young woman had not suffered hardship or deprivation during her adolescence. She never felt the temptation to sell her body for favours. She had never starved.

Consistently and inaccurately described later by reporters as a product of upper-class Chicago, Virginia's roots were in the countryside that she loved. When she informed startled European interviewers that her idea of bliss was drinking a glass of milk under an apple tree, she wasn't making it up. The rustic girl she evoked was who she remained, the heir to two settler families who first reached frontier territory back in the early 1840s, when Chicago was home to a mere 6,000 inhabitants, and the State of Illinois itself remained largely untamed prairie.

★

The Cherrills, her father's family, had travelled out from England. They brought with them a library of books and an iron sword from the Civil War, a weapon that Elizabeth (Wood) Cherrill had inherited as an heirloom and which – fearing both bears and natives in an alien land – she was ready to employ. Life back then, among a group of pioneer farmers in western Illinois, just south of Carthage, offered no immediate need for such defensive measures.

The newly arrived Americans liked to give classical names to the places in which they made their settlements: Carthage, Illinois, was one among several towns to bear the name. Today, revisiting the life of the town's most celebrated citizen, the word Carthage sounds prophetic: to those who are familiar with her life, it seems apt that Virginia Cherrill should have emerged from a place connected by its name to the beautiful Queen Dido.

The lustre surrounding the town's name always outshone its appearance. Still, by the time that Elizabeth and Adolphus Cherrill reached western Illinois in the early 1840s, the modest cluster of brick and timber-framed houses had already established itself as the seat of government for tiny Hancock County. For the settlers who had travelled so far, Carthage presented itself as the goal for their aspirations.

Today, this mythic sense of the town is hard to imagine. Carthage stands upon what once was the frontier's boundary; the edge of the wilderness; the tranquil back of beyond. It still is. Walk out from Carthage Square for the length of three streets in any direction; nothing greets your eyes but trackless fields of corn, stretching out to small, scattered clumps of trees along the broad rim of the horizon.

Adolphus Cherrill, tilling his portion of prairie land with scant enthusiasm (he was a city-born man), retained Carthage as his goal, offering a chance to move up in the world. A talent for playing the flute, exquisite penmanship – Adolphus had worked as a warehouse clerk back in London – and the totem of his wife's historical sword (no visitor to the Cherrills' rural home escaped the duty to admire it) helped to give the impression that this cultivated couple derived from eminent stock. Their proper place in this new world was apparent; all they had to do was to achieve it. Elizabeth, while disheartened by the featureless landscape, the savage climate and the simplicity of their coarse farmer neighbours, was cheered by her husband's promises of a red-brick town house, a garden of her own, and a new, brightly painted buggy in which to go calling. She had only, Adolphus reassured his wife, to be patient. The means to attain their golden future in Carthage would be found.

Elizabeth was still biding her time in 1844, when word began to spread that Joseph Smith's 20,000 Mormon followers, established in the nearby and self-governing town of Nauvoo, planned to overthrow Carthage and add it to their empire. The rumour caught fire and flared. Nauvoo maintained a private army of 5,000 men, loyal only to Smith, their leader. Carthage, with a population of just 300 citizens, could never compete. How could the little town hope to survive? What would become of the cherished aspirations of Adolphus Cherrill?

Luck proved to be upon the side of Carthage. Joseph Smith, infuriated by criticisms of his autocratic regime in a local newspaper, ordered all copies of the offending rag to be destroyed, together with its printing press. By employing his home-grown army for this act of vandalism, and by further declaring that his Mormon militia would defend Nauvoo against all invaders, Smith opened himself to the charge of treason.

On 25 June 1844, trusting in the promise of safe conduct issued to him by the Governor of Illinois, Joseph Smith and his brother Hyrum rode into Carthage and surrendered themselves to the authorities. Escorted to the jailhouse, a pleasant, comfortably furnished building on the square, they were led in and promised the protection of a troop of guards until the time of their trial.

Adolphus Cherrill was among the mob of 200 masked and armed men who, two days later, stormed the Carthage jailhouse and murdered the Smith brothers. (Joseph, captured after his desperate leap from a window, was propped against a well-head and used for target practice.)

Old Carthage jail, in which the Mormon leader was ambushed by a mob that included Virginia Cherrill's forebear.

Many of the Mormons, fleeing Nauvoo, took refuge beyond the Great Plains in the more remote territory of desolate Utah. Adolphus, fearful of reprisals from those of Smith's followers who remained in Illinois, spent the next three years hiding out in the house of a friend who lived outside the state border. Returning to Carthage in 1847, he gradually transformed himself into a prominent and lauded citizen, stately as a carp in a goldfish bowl. His elder son, Edward, would co-found the little town's chief bank. His younger son, Alfred, married July Edmunds (whose singular name honoured her birth month), the pretty daughter of a local judge. James, the son born to Alfred and July in 1886 – one of five children, the indulged bad boy of a sober brood – would one day become the father of Virginia Cherrill.

★

It isn't clear that Virginia connects her forebears to the murder of Joseph Smith, but the man she describes could – just as easily as his grandfather, Adolphus – have ridden into Carthage Square and helped shoot the Mormon leader down.

'My father wasn't like the rest of the Cherrills,' Virginia tells her friend, Teresa, who sits listening beside the bed, holding her tiny tape recorder down and out of view. 'Jim's brothers, Arch and Syd, were handsome men, and my aunts were pretty and sweet, but he – well, he was *wild*! Imagine this. James Cherrill – I don't like to think of him as "father" – was just twenty when my mother crossed his path; he'd already set himself up as a livestock broker, buying cattle outright and selling them in the stockyards in Chicago. It was a dreadful place to work, right beside the slaughter-houses. You've read *The Jungle*, haven't you? Upton Sinclair wrote it back in 1906, just after my – after Jim Cherrill started out in that business. It's about his world, all blood and violence. That's what he chose for his career. My father was a cattle-trader for his entire life. He dealt in flesh.'

Virginia, evidently, wants to sound disapproving, but it's clear that she understands exactly why her mother was so charmed by a tall young man with blond hair, scorching blue eyes and thick eyelashes as black as his dark brows.

'Jim Cherrill was handsome as any movie-star,' she boasts. 'He could get any woman he wanted. And he did. He was terrible!'

And just why, if that was the case, would a boy with a roving eye and a free spirit choose to marry Blanche Wilcox, a woman who was shy, overweight, and nearly eight years older than himself? It's a difficult question for Teresa to put to the old lady; nobody, in all the time they've known her, has ever heard Virginia Cherrill breathe a word against the mother she never deserted. Loyally, she insists now that Blanche's beauty was a matter of personality. Why shouldn't Jim Cherrill have been charmed by a woman so gentle-hearted, so trusting and affectionate?

'Look at her! It's all there!'

The sepia-tinted photograph, always kept in a drawer close to Virginia's bed, has been posed in a professional studio. It presents Blanche upon her eighteenth birthday, nine years before she met Jim Cherrill. To me, the sitter looks closer to thirty. Her mouse-brown hair is tucked up in a bun; her chin tilts up to mask the

Blanche Wilcox, Virginia Cherrill's mother, aged eighteen.

first signs of a fleshy undertow. Her flounced dress manages to be both smart and dowdy; had she borrowed it from her mother's wardrobe? But an expression of rare sweetness does indeed illuminate the face of young Blanche Wilcox. Her mouth is full; her soft eyes meet the photographer's lens with an apprehensive gaze. Her vulnerability is poignantly apparent. She looks as though she desperately needs to be loved.

'And here's the man who broke her heart,' Virginia comments to Teresa. 'She never got over him. And he really was not worth it, that's what's so sad about it all.'

Jim Cherrill, photographed in 1911, when he was twenty-five, is lean and swaggering [plate 1]. A low-brimmed cap shades the hot, appraising eyes; a velvet-collared coat drapes jaunty shoulders. He has the look of a man who is used to being admired. It is clear that he is striking a pose for the photographer – his wife? – on that chilly day, in long-ago Chicago. But what strikes me most about the informal snap is Jim's evident detachment from the radiant child who stands beside him. She's dressed in her smartest winter clothes, her tiny person is all wrapped up and glowing. Among all the photographs of Virginia Cherrill's early years, no other communicates such joy. But Virginia declines to bestow any credit for her expression upon the company of the father who looks to be oblivious of her presence. She was, she says, simply happy to be taken out for a stroll. She concedes, nevertheless, that the effect Jim Cherrill had on every female who came near him – including his daughter – was uncommon.

'He was like catnip. And boy! Did he know how to use it! All the girls fell for him. But only my poor mother got pregnant. We're talking about two respectable families back there in the Midwest, remember. Jim Cherrill was told he had to do the right thing. It was a shotgun marriage. No question.'

Blanche Wilcox's grandparents had formed part of a group of pioneer families from New England who travelled in covered wagons west to Illinois. They reached Durham, a mere handful of farm-homes out on the prairie, during the early 1840s, back at around the same time that the Cherrills settled near Carthage. Linus Wilcox built up enough money from the manufacture of an agricultural chain pump to erect a handsome clapboard house, the finest home in the new settlement. Grange Farm possessed broad verandas, a pillared porch and expansive views across the plains of rich black farmland that Linus's son Ed – Blanche's father – began ploughing when he was fourteen. (Fieldwork suited Ed Wilcox better than sharing the family home with his own father's second wife, a widow from a local settler family.)

Blanche was a child at Durham when she first heard tales from her parents of the runaway slaves, escaping up from the South to freedom in Canada, who had been given refuge at Grange Farm; the local town, LaHarpe, was a well-known stopping point along the famous Underground Railroad. Blanche, in her turn, passed the stories on. When Virginia first saw the subterranean cells in which the slaves were sheltered at the farm, she saw a bundle of bones in a shadowy lair, and shrieked for rescue. All that fuss for nothing, the family scolded her. Couldn't a big girl of five recognise a simple heap of sticks, stockpiled for winter fuel?

Grange Farm, Durham, Illinois, Virginia's favourite childhood home, owned by her Wilcox grandparents.

Blanche was born in 1879, the year that her father married Gertrude Ketcham, a local girl. Blanche's sister, Jess, arrived ten years later; her brother, Ted, was born in 1900.

'Twenty-one years between them!' Teresa exclaims. 'So Blanche was old enough to have been Ted's mother!'

Virginia gives a wry little laugh: 'Or his nurse!'

Perfunctorily educated at a school in LaHarpe, Blanche Wilcox was soon put to full-time work at Grange Farm. By the age of twenty-one, her life revolved around keeping house for her parents, making clothes for her younger sister, and taking care of baby Ted.

Ed and Gertrude Wilcox, Virginia's grandparents.

'My Wilcox grandmother was terribly selfish,' Virginia comments. 'Tiny little woman, tough as a walnut. She wouldn't let my grandfather lift a finger. She even buttoned up his shirts for him! Caring for Grandpa Ed was her province. Everything else in the house had to be done by Blanche. My poor mother. She had a hard time.'

Many years later, Blanche told her daughter about a relationship – there had been just one – before she came to meet Jim Cherrill. She had made friends at the Union Church of LaHarpe with a quiet and pale young man who begged her, several times, to become his wife. Virginia never learned this suitor's name, only that her Wilcox grandmother had opposed the marriage. The reason was transparent: she didn't want to lose the services of her free cook and children's nurse.

'And my mother,' Virginia ruefully adds, 'was such a good little mouse that she just gave in and turned her beau down. I'm sure she never complained. It wasn't in her nature.'

In 1904, the year Blanche turned twenty-five, her father was appointed Circuit Clerk to Hancock County. The connection to Durham was retained, but from then until Ed Wilcox retired in 1929, he and his family spent most of the year at the seat of local government, in Carthage.

It seems probable, within such a small community, that two of the leading families in Carthage struck up a friendship; all Virginia knows is that her mother, then aged twenty-seven and in despair of finding herself a husband, fell in love with a wild and handsome boy of twenty whose family lived just across the street from the Wilcox home.

Entertainments back then weren't plentiful in a rural town; Jim Cherrill may have fondled his new girlfriend into submission in the flickering darkness of the nickelodeon on Carthage Square. He may taken her for a walk out at Wildcat Springs and allayed her fears with reckless promises as he laid her down and raised her skirts. Seductive as catnip, in Virginia's pithy description, the young man found an easy prey in Blanche Wilcox – and promptly left her.

Blanche became pregnant; apprised of the situation, the Cherrills summoned their errant son home from his work in the Chicago stockyards and ordered him to do his duty. A wedding, arranged in haste and conducted without witnesses, took place in the front room of the Wilcox house. In December 1906, just under nine months later, Blanche gave birth to a daughter she named Sydney Rose.

'My sister,' Virginia states. 'Pretty as a picture, so I've heard. My mother was over the moon.'

Jim didn't relish fatherhood any more than his forced marriage. While Blanche nursed the new-born baby at the home of her parents-in-law, her young husband returned to his bachelor life in Chicago, 250 miles off along the railroad from sleepy little Carthage. Virginia does not deny that her father worked long, hard days as a livestock trader in the city's great sea of stockyard pens (where 500 million dollars' worth of cattle flesh were traded every year). She does, however, wonder how Jim spent his nights.

I'm curious, myself, to know more about Jim Cherrill's relationship with women, given the exceptional fear of physical violence that Virginia would show in later life. She describes his second wife (they met just once, and briefly, after Jim's death), as a loud and lively woman, well able to fight her own corner. Did Blanche's docile nature madden Jim? Could he have hit her, or threatened her with blows? Might this explain why neither the Cherrills nor Blanche herself objected to the length and frequency of her young husband's absences from home? Was life less frightening for a woman who was pregnant with her second child, when her husband kept his distance? These questions are not raised during Teresa's recorded interviews with Virginia. They represent only my own speculative thoughts.

Jim was off at the stockyards in March 1908 when Blanche, a month away from the birth of their second child, noticed worrying developments in the health of their first, Sydney Rose. The little girl lost her appetite. Refusing food, she became increasingly comatose. Alerted to Blanche's fears, the Cherrill family tried – and failed – to locate Jim in Chicago. The Carthage doctor, annoyed at being summoned from table in the middle of a supper-party, proved dismissive. The child had been fed too much rich food, he opined; nothing was amiss that could not be righted by his usual prescription: a dose of quinine. A few days later, learning that Sydney Rose's condition had worsened, the doctor changed his diagnosis to food poisoning and prescribed a light diet of toast and beef jelly.

The symptoms changed once more. Lethargic no longer, the child stiffened, writhed, and shrieked, all through the night and day, for forty-eight hours. On the morning of 9 March 1908, she died.

'Her appendix burst,' Virginia says. 'It was nobody's fault. They didn't understand, but my mother took the blame. She felt Sydney Rose's death could have been prevented. She couldn't forgive herself.'

Virginia's first appearance in the Press.

Virginia was born on 12 April 1908, just one month after her sister's death.

Miss Luella Worthen, on that same day, won praise from Carthage for her spirited performance at the opera house as 'Mrs Wiggs of the Cabbage Patch'. Virginia's arrival attracted less interest. Her birth announcement was overshadowed by reports in the local press that the palm of a fisherman's hand had been pierced by a catfish horn, and that one 'coloured' factory worker had been murdered by another, in a fight over a woman.

Jim Cherrill was out of town on the weekend of his daughter's birth. 'Womanising, so I later heard,' Virginia comments in a dry tone. 'Other than trading livestock, that was what my father did best. I don't mean to put him down. He just wasn't cut out to be a family man. It took my mother a long time to accept the truth of the situation, that fact.'

2

GROWING PAINS

(1908–1924)

'Carthage was where I had my schooling, but the farm was always my home . . .'

Virginia on a winter day, outside what may have been her parents' home in Chicago, 1911.

Virginia was still a baby when Blanche, spurred on by anxious love for her husband (or driven away by the painful memories of her elder daughter's death), elected to join Jim Cherrill in Chicago. For five years, Virginia and her parents lived with Jim's brothers, Arch and Syd, at an apartment on East 67th Street, between Blackstone and South Dorchester Avenue. A couple of photographs offer the only clues to their style of life. In one, the three tall Cherrill brothers range themselves like a guard of honour behind a tiny, beaming Virginia. A bleak set of cold-water apartments can be seen in the background; viewed on a wintry day in 1911, this area looks like a wasteland. Another snapshot shows baby Virginia sitting in an open carriage driven by her grandfather. The house that forms the background here hints at a better class of area, but the location of the Cherrill's own abode was not, at the turn of the century, good.

Virginia remembers nothing of this city childhood. It seems likely that she has chosen to blot out memories that it might grieve her to recall. A harsher interlocutor might have forced the old lady to relive old traumas, buried fears; fortunately for her, Teresa feels no such compulsion.

No hint survives of how Virginia's uncles treated her or her mother while they all shared a home (Syd died young; Arch has been dead for many years), but Jim Cherrill's behaviour must have been flagrantly bad, in order for a kindly woman, already in her mid-thirties and without independent means, to react in the way that his wife did.

In the spring of 1913, Blanche Cherrill left her husband and began taking steps towards a divorce. These actions constituted courageous behaviour in an era when a wife, however ill-treated, was expected to stand by her man. In leaving Jim Cherrill – whom she had married, as Carthage gossips must have whispered, with indecent haste – Blanche painted a mark upon her forehead as vivid as Hester Prynne's scarlet letter. The woman who gave up on a marriage was always in the wrong. Blanche Cherrill was disgraced.

Blanche once spoke to Virginia, years later, about their return from Chicago, first to a lonely homestead which they briefly shared with one of Jim Cherrill's sisters, and then to the Durham farmhouse where the Wilcox family continued to spend their summers. Here, as Blanche was willing to admit, she hoped to resume her connection with the pale, unnamed young man who had once been so eager to marry her; the house that her former suitor still shared with his mother lay only ten miles away from Grange Farm, the Wilcox family home. Months went by, and Blanche heard nothing. Attending a service with her parents at the local Union Church in LaHarpe, where they had first met, she saw her former suitor conduct his mother to her pew. As he passed by, he glanced once at Blanche, and turned away. It was, she told

Jim (left), Arch and Syd Cherrill with Virginia in Chicago, 1911.

Virginia, as if he feared to meet her eye. She never saw him again.

Possessing neither an income nor a spouse, Blanche Cherrill was forced back into her old role of her parents' housekeeper, shuttling with them between their home in Carthage and the farmhouse out at Durham. Her sister Jess had married and moved away; life with the Wilcoxes revolved around fourteen-year-old Ted, Blanche's youngest sibling, and Virginia's persecutor. The stories of his bullying ways, as she relates them to Teresa, sound insignificant.

She speaks of being roped to a gnarled apple tree, of being hoisted atop the tall casing of a rickety upright piano and left with no way of climbing down, locked up for half a day in the chilly parlour of an empty house. A note of uncharacteristic distress in the old lady's voice, just here, makes me wonder if these events were the worst that took place in a household where Ted Wilcox evidently enjoyed asserting his power.

'He didn't treat me nicely,' Virginia states, before her voice drops to a whisper. The tape continues to record her, but it picks up nothing but sputters and crackles.

'She certainly never liked her uncle,' Teresa says, when I ask her about these blurred recollections. 'I do know that. But she didn't say much about those early times.'

By 1917, Blanche had gained herself a little freedom; census forms establish that she took rooms for a time in a modest clapboard house in Carthage, and that her nine-year-old daughter had begun to attend the local grammar school.

A studio photograph from this period displays a solemn little girl with a bow perched like a taffeta sausage atop a puritan crop of fine

Back in Carthage in 1917, without Jim Cherrill.

blonde hair. Blanche must have used a mail catalogue to procure her daughter's full-skirted tartan frock with its deep satin collar: Emrick and Owslie, the only dress store on Carthage Square, did not run to such elegant items of clothing. The dress appears splendid, but the child looks wan and resigned. Virginia, at this point in her life, did not have much choice.

Carthage, around 1908, in the town centre. With the kind of carriage called 'a Surrey' at the left.

It's easier to find photographs of the town in which Blanche's daughter was being schooled than of Virginia herself; these old pictures show that Carthage, at the beginning of the twentieth century, remained surprisingly primitive. The roads leading into its central square hadn't changed since the Smith brothers, in the summer of 1844, came trotting through the dust to their doom. The town's sparsely placed streetlamps were fuelled by kerosene; an indoor lavatory remained as rare a commodity as piped water. The arrival of the town's first automobile agency made headlines in the local – and sceptical – press; by 1918, there were just six cars in Carthage.

'We made our own fun' is how the town's older inhabitants like to remember those far-off days of hayrack rides, nation-proud parades and Sunday-school picnics. Schoolboys – Carthage prided itself on offering the best education in the state at the schoolhouse, affectionately known as 'Old Main' – were keen attendants of the tiny movie-house that had overthrown the nickelodeon's short reign on Carthage Square. Forbidden such decadent male pleasures, Virginia and her schoolfriends spent their after-class hours at Fred Reyer's roller-skating rink. Here, in alluring proximity to Carthage's first dance-hall, the little girls, pitching their voices high, to carry taunts and challenges above the roar of steel wheels, linked arms and promenaded themselves into a state of exhaustion.

The biggest treat of the Carthage year was the summer week during which the Circus arrived, blooming into life in a cluster of striped canvas tents and wooden stands that crowded together beside the railroad track, out on the town boundary. This was where, aged eight or nine, Virginia and her friends came to watch the clowns, goggle at acrobatic dancing ladies in pink tights, gasp at the tricks of aerial cyclists, and gaze up a column of shimmering sequins to the burnished copper face of Miss Ella Ewing, the Missouri giantess, as she exhibited to view an enormous broad-brimmed hat in which – snug as a caterpillar within the straw crown – lay curled Miss Ella's tiny fellow-performer, Great Peter the Small. These details are recovered from local press items and historical records: Virginia was there, we can be sure, but the old lady's memories of those far-off days are erratic and vague.

'I played an Irish fairy in a Carthage school play when I was seven years old,' she volunteers, wanting to help out in whatever way she can. 'I wore a white dress.'

Teresa, unable to make much of this information, changes direction: what, she asks, about the farmhouse at Durham, where Virginia and her mother still spent long periods of time? What was life like out there on the prairie? Didn't it get to feel, after a while, pretty dull? Virginia doesn't agree; she says that she always loved that prairie landscape, laid out so large and quiet under a sky vast as an ocean.

'Why do you suppose I went back there so often in my life? Carthage was where I had my schooling, but the farm was my home. That's where I belonged. All those years I lived in Europe, I always found myself looking for echoes, for the sight of a field or a sunset that could take me back there, just for a minute, you know. I never missed an anniversary at the farm.'

In 1918, Virginia's uncle Ted Wilcox got married, straight out of Old Main, the Carthage school where he was educated (and at which he was chiefly remembered for his prank of dragging a cow up to the belfry of the local church). Sometimes, so Teresa tells me, Virginia used to describe her uncle as a bully and a crook; just as often, the old lady would acknowledge the charm that allowed Ted Wilcox to get away with a lifetime of misbehaviour. Ted's wife, Ruth, adored her husband. A smart, pretty girl, she soon learned to look the other way. Ted's marriage, together with that of her own parents, helped to shape the early notions of what love was all about for the young, and watchful, Virginia.

'You put up, and you shut up. Men did as they wanted, and their wives were expected to go along with that. It wasn't fair, but it's what happened. It's how it was, back where I grew up.'

Ted Wilcox's first child was not long in coming. The young father soon made it clear that he didn't want his seventeen-year-old wife hanging about the house, or to connect her to the stench of diapers and sour milk. Afraid to object, Ruth looked for a solution; she found one close to hand. At the age of eleven, Virginia was drafted into the role that Blanche had played before her, of an unpaid nurse and surrogate mother.

'It didn't bother me, at first,' she tells Teresa. 'I'd put the baby into a wooden tub with a bit of warm water, and I'd set afloat a bar of Ivory soap with a flag stuck in the side, like a ship. I'd sing – any silly thing that came into my head – and the baby used to wave her little hands in the air. But another kid came along, and then I had to take care of the two little things almost all the time. I wasn't even twelve years old.'

The outlook for Virginia's future was not bright at this point; fortunately, a chance for escape was at hand. Blanche, since their return from Chicago, had acquired some basic secretarial skills, sufficient for her to obtain part-time work for a local politician who agreed to offer her his support.

In the summer of 1920, when Virginia had just turned twelve, her mother led her into the parlour at Grange Farm, sat the child down among the high-backed New England chairs and closed the door. All aglow, Blanche disclosed her triumph. Her political friend had written a letter of recommendation to the principal of one of the finest convent schools he knew. Kemper Hall, having noted the senator's endorsement, had agreed to accept Virginia Cherrill as a pupil. Kemper Hall was in Wisconsin, and a long way from home, Blanche went on, but she must act like a brave girl, and feel glad of her opportunity. Mother and daughter wouldn't be parting, not a bit of it. Blanche would be there, right beside her darling treasure, working as a matron to help defray the fees. The two would see each other every day.

Blanche produced a picture of a tall white house standing at the side of a lake. To Virginia's eyes, it resembled a palace; she felt frightened. How was she ever going to keep from getting separated from her mother in such a huge place? And when would she get back to the farm she so loved? Every holiday, Blanche reassured her. Nothing would change. Out here, on the prairie, everything would remain the same, just waiting for her daughter's safe return.

'And that's how it always felt,' Virginia says. 'Even when I went back decades later. Nothing ever changed. The minute I set my feet on Durham soil, I was twelve again, easy as opening a door. I didn't even have to blink my eyes.'

★

Blanche and Virginia left Durham for Kemper Hall in the autumn of 1920. For the next four years, while regularly travelling back to Illinois for the holidays, they lived out upon the eastern shore of Lake Michigan, two hours north of Chicago, in Kenosha, Wisconsin. In winter, the wind swept in like a scythe across the expanse of steel-grey water.

'My mother was in the news during one term for putting out a blazing fire, but it's the cold that I remember.' Virginia shudders. 'The chill went right through you, and the nuns didn't believe in making us comfortable. The baths were cold as ice; the windows were always kept open; I don't remember us having any kind of heating at all. I ate to stay warm. I ate so *much*!'

Sounding horrified by her famished gluttony, the old lady starts to describe the inevitable result.

'My face looked like an apple; my wrists hurt when I buttoned my cuffs. And Blanche always wanted me to look so elegant! "It isn't good for you to eat like you'd never been fed properly," she'd say, but food made me feel warmer. I didn't care about getting fat. I just loved to eat.'

Residual guilt about her unappeasable appetite seems to have driven all other memories of the Kemper Hall years out of the old lady's mind. Pressed for further information, Virginia makes it clear that she was simply doing as her mother wished, not as she herself might have chosen. Blanche was, she repeatedly explains, obsessed with getting her daughter a proper schooling.

'She was willing to slave away as matron for four years, just to see that I was properly taught and that I got to meet nice Episcopalian girls. She wasn't too pleased, though, when I made friends with Sue Carol. Sue was called Evelyn Lederer, back in those Kemper Hall days; she changed her name for the movies.'

Evelyn Lederer, the indulged daughter of a pair of Jewish immigrants, was a pretty, dark-haired girl with a pert grin and a clear sense of where she was headed. While most girls from

Virginia on a winter day by the lake at Kemper Hall.

Kemper Hall were lining up to attend the Giddings Seminary, a top-flight school in Chicago, Evelyn had set her heart on becoming a film-star.

'Sue Carol!' Virginia insists. (It's apparent that the name means nothing to her friend Teresa, the interviewer.) 'You know: "the college boys' sweetheart". That's what they called her, back then, before she married Alan Ladd. She went out to the Coast while I was still at Kemper Hall, and I used to hear all about it. That was when I first started to think I might like to travel out there myself. I did ask my mother about a visit to LA. Blanche wasn't pleased.'

Blanche's lack of enthusiasm isn't hard to understand. Evelyn Lederer arrived in Hollywood – and changed her name – in 1922, a year when the burgeoning movie capital was mired in scandal: William Desmond Taylor, a celebrated film director, had been murdered, possibly by the mother of his under-aged girlfriend, Mary Miles Minter; Roscoe ('Fatty') Arbuckle was rumoured to have raped a party-going girl to death. Blanche had not sacrificed four years of her life in order to take her child to raffish Hollywood. Words were exchanged between mother and daughter.

Hollywood having been duly swept off the agenda, Blanche reverted to her chief concern: the need to restore an overweight schoolgirl to perfect shape. Nice clothes weren't made for fatties, Blanche warned. Fat girls didn't find husbands, she scolded.

Evelyn Lederer (Sue Carol), and later, Mrs Alan Ladd

'Mamma always blamed her own misfortunes upon her size,' Virginia explains. 'And she wanted everything to turn out just perfect for me. She couldn't understand that a man like Jim Cherrill would have behaved just as badly if his wife had been as slender as a dancing-girl. It was never about Blanche's weight; it was about the kind of man her husband was. But that was my mother's view, and when Blanche had got her mind made up, there was no budging her. So I just stopped eating, that's all, until I weighed under a hundred pounds, and we were about to set off for my new school in Chicago. Meanwhile, my friend Evelyn kept on writing me about the good times she was having, out in Hollywood. I couldn't wait to get through school and off into the world.'

3

CHICAGO

(1924–1927)

'It's who I am. When a romantic situation becomes untender, I get the hell out. I always have. Story of my life.'

Nineteen twenty-four was the year in which sixteen-year-old Virginia and her mother moved back to Chicago, where Blanche rented a small apartment. Secretarial work and the last of her savings just covered the cost of sending her daughter to one of the most prestigious day-schools in the city. Questioned, Virginia recalls only that most of her classmates were Jewish girls from rich families and that one, identified as 'Marian', was the niece of Adolf Zukor. (Zukor, the founder and subsequent joint controller of Paramount Films, also oversaw the creation of America's most palatial movie-theatres during the Twenties.) Asked whether her mother was counting on the fact that such a friendship might be useful, Virginia sighs. Hasn't she *yet* succeeded in making her mother's attitude clear? Blanche's own lack of a decent education caused her to value a good school, with disciplined training, as the key to a cultured, privileged life she herself had never known. She wanted to be certain that her daughter could make her way in the world, but not – Virginia declares that the thought never crossed her mother's mind – not *ever* as a movie actress.

'I told you. All my mother cared about was getting me through school. She was an education snob, but only where I was concerned. She did everything for my sake.' ·

It is becoming clear that Virginia will not tolerate anything that approaches criticism of her mother: searching questions invariably produce a defensive response. To this writer, however, Blanche Cherrill's persistent concern about her daughter's weight, her clothes and her virtue is disconcerting. 'I always had to be home for supper,' Virginia states to Teresa; a little later, she makes the point again: 'I wasn't supposed to go anywhere without my mother's permission.' This suggests a protective mother who wanted more for her only child – the object of all her attention, the focus of all her hopes – than the mere possession of a well-stocked mind.

A studio shot of Virginia in her mid-teens, eyes glancing up, a garland of tight-clustered flowers encircling her head, and with – possibly for the last time in her life – a row of fake pearls around her neck, suggests a docile bride-in-waiting [plate 2]. Wasn't this what the process of preparation was all about? Hadn't Blanche sacrificed her own life to see her pretty daughter richly married and well maintained – and, perhaps, willing to take good care of a deserving mother?

Meanwhile, back in 1924, Virginia was bringing a little money home from holiday work at the whisperingly genteel glove department of Marshall Field's massive store on State Street, Chicago. The largest department store of the Midwest, this emporium – so the marketing boast went – was where everything on earth was made available, from an elephant's embroidered howdah to a mere papyrus roll.

Everything needed to be available in a city that luxuriated in conspicuous display and the lavish enjoyment of wealth. Chicago, back in the mid-Twenties, even from the perspective of a sheltered schoolgirl, was an astonishing place in which to live. With Al Capone as its uncrowned king, and liquor flowing faster than in the old days of legalised alcohol, Chicago was 'the toddling town', the city that boasted the finest ballrooms, the most flamboyant movie-theatres, the most expensive hotels, the showiest clothes and – as the black population flooded up from the South in search of better pay – the hottest jazz and wildest dancing of anywhere in America.

Chicago had changed out of all recognition since Virginia's birth in 1908.

'And I didn't even know it!' she exclaims.

As a small girl, Virginia Cherrill's consciousness of the city's old, pre-war way of life (beer-gardens, sleepy Sundays, concert halls and Schubert societies) had been as faint as of the square mile of stockyard pens in which her father worked. In 1924, the meat trade still thrived; Chicago's gentle Germanic past had vanished, a victim of wartime patriotism. The Bismarck and the Kaiserhof were forgotten; Virginia and her school-friends knew these big and bustling hotels only by their significantly altered names: the Randolph and the Atlantic.

The Chicago of Virginia's teenage years was a new-born, high-walled town brimming with energy, a modern metropolis of avenues gleaming with plate-glass windows, of elegant theatres and cavernous speakeasies and palatial hotels, of massive, ornate buildings and a shoreline overshadowed by the high and jagged towers of Michigan Avenue. But hers was also the Chicago that Nelson Algren would later look back on with uneasy melancholy. Algren's high-flown tribute – *Chicago: City on the Make*, published in 1951 – evoked a darker city, blaring with the noise of taxi-horns, trumpets and gunshots, resounding with the thud of heavy feet trudging through it, unobserved, out to the thirty sprawling miles of industrialised heartland, from the tenemented warrens of the South Side.

Chicago: a street scene at lunch break, 1926.

You could love Chicago, Algren wrote, but Chicago would never love you back.

The city's appetite for glamour made it a natural shrine for cinema. Celluloid celebrities were happy to show up and be worshipped at the latest gilded shrine to their art.

('Not that I ever saw the inside of a movie-theatre,' Virginia sighs. 'My mother didn't approve of cinema or the stage.')

The exuberant Tivoli was designed to resemble a high baroque chapel; at its rival, the Paradise, moviegoers nestled between banked terraces of flower-decked balconies, overhung by a celestial dome of twinkling electrical stars. Charlie Chaplin, Douglas Fairbanks and Mary Pickford attracted massive crowds for their Chicago premières; the biggest thrill of all came when Rudolph Valentino consented to publicise the new circular ballroom at the Trianon Hotel by giving a performance of his famous tango. The crowds around the Trianon's entrance, reporters announced, had almost crushed the handsome star to death when he stepped out of his limousine.

'And I wasn't there to see him!' Virginia laments. 'I was home, doing schoolwork.'

Rudolf Valentino's tango was one of the pieces of second-hand Chicago news with which Virginia sought to impress her former school-friend. Evelyn Lederer, having gone straight from Wisconsin to the West Coast, was also living a vicarious life. Virginia studied Evelyn's magazine clipping about the 4,000 electrical bulbs that had begun to flash the name of HOLLYWOODLAND above the studio lots; she registered the excitement with which her friend had found herself sitting next to William S. Hart, the silver screen's best-known cowboy star, when she lunched at one of the studio commissaries. It excited Virginia more to hear about an evening at the star-studded Cocoanut Grove nightclub, about a prize her friend had won for dancing the Breakaway, and about Evelyn's visit to a house in Beverly Hills that looked (she claimed) like a picture-book castle, with a canopied throne, and blue and gold ceilings. Such sights, to a dutiful schoolgirl who spent long evenings doing homework or – at best – playing cards with her mother, offered a glimpse of paradise.

A couple of L. Frank Baum's storybooks were still lodged upon Virginia's crowded bookshelves when she died. As an early fan of Dorothy's adventures in the Emerald City, she must have noticed that Oz had shifted location since Baum had first begun describing it in 1900. Back then, Chicago had been his Mecca; in later years, Baum transported the wizard's citadel to the West Coast, a shift of location that reflected the author's own move to Ozcot, a handsome little property just off Hollywood Boulevard. As always, Baum's own dreams mirrored the desires of his readers.

Baum's fantasy spoke not only to Virginia, but to the thousands of Midwesterners who had already travelled their own yellow brick road, in their real lives, to Los Angeles.

Anything, out there, in California, seemed possible, the military author Bruce Bliven wrote in 1927 for the *New Republic*: 'the future is yours, and the past? There isn't any.'

The City of Angels, back then, was where an average filmland contract player could earn more in a week than most American families could bring home in a year; where over a million new arrivals had turned Los Angeles into the fifth-biggest city in the country; where fortunes were to be made overnight and – if you believed the newspapers – the fun never stopped. Twenty years had elapsed since Sunset Boulevard's long studio strip had been sneered at as Poverty Row. Bruce Bliven's estimation was correct: history, out in Hollywood, was evanescent. Observed from afar, coloured by the glamour of celebrity, the West Coast shimmered and winked its promise of riches for all, just as it has continued to do, so seductively, to this day.

Virginia's school held a Friday night Hallowe'en dance the year she turned seventeen. Partnerless, and strikingly pretty, she caught the attention of a young man who was escorting one of her schoolmates. His name was Irving Adler, and he belonged to one of the richest families in the city.

'And he was so handsome!' Virginia exclaims. 'Dark, well built, curly hair, nice smile – like Walter Pidgeon before he started to play fathers. He hadn't been in the room ten minutes before he came up and asked me – he was very polite – if I'd care to dance. I said I would.'

Irving was a good dancer, she continues, and the two of them got along pretty well, sufficiently so for the young man to send her a big bouquet of flowers the following day, together with an invitation to attend a première at the Blackstone Theater.

'I was thrilled! I'd never been to a play before. My mother said I could go to the theatre, so long as I came straight home afterwards. No going out to supper.'

This visit to the fashionable Blackstone Theater on Michigan Avenue gave Virginia her first taste of elegant living, and she found that she loved it. The play to which Irving Adler escorted her was *The Dove*; the star, playing a fiery cabaret dancer, was tiny Judith Anderson, an actress best remembered now for her performance as an icy Mrs Danvers in Hitchcock's classic 1940 film *Rebecca*.

Virginia retained a clear memory of both the theatre, and the name of the play. However, when Dame Judith Anderson and she sat swapping life-stories across a Santa Barbara dinner-table some forty years later, the celebrated Australian was enraged to find that her own role had been entirely forgotten.

'I remembered some other pretty actress, the second lead, but the terrible thing was that I didn't remember *her* at all,' Virginia states. 'And Judith was so angry. She kept saying: "Who *else* was in it?" And I said: "Maybe Claudette Colbert? I don't know. Well, I can't remember anybody else." And she went wild. "You bloody bitch, *I* was the leading lady! It was my first big part in America!" She never forgave me. You know I told you how Judith always liked to drink? Every time she had a bit too much, she'd yell: "You bloody bitch, you didn't even remember me in *The Dove*!"'

From that night on – the Chicago première of *The Dove* – it seems that Irving Adler behaved as if he owned Virginia. His first proposal of marriage, she informs Teresa, was popped just one day after their visit to the theatre.

'I thought he was nuts,' Virginia states, but her suitor proved persistent.

'And it worked?'

Virginia laughs. 'The man never gave up!'

Virginia Cherrill was the prettiest and most charming girl that this ambitious and well-educated young Jewish lawyer – Irving Adler was twenty-six years old in 1925 – had yet encountered. The discovery that she was penniless did not trouble him; neither did her Christian upbringing.

'It wasn't even as though I had to become Orthodox,' Virginia remarks. 'Irving's own parents were divorced and his mother had married the son of the canon of Edinburgh cathedral, so religion didn't bother them one bit. His family were sweet to me,' Virginia adds with a sigh. 'And yet, they can't have been too pleased.'

The Adlers, it becomes clear, belonged to a different social league from anybody that Virginia or her mother had hitherto known. Irving's aunt had married a rubber-king. His uncle was the most successful surgeon in Chicago. His father was the lawyer who advised Sears Roebuck and the Illinois Central Railway. The Adler family must, as Virginia observes, have entertained high expectations about young Irving's choice of a bride.

'He was,' the old lady murmurs, 'quite a catch.'

Why then, Teresa wonders, did Virginia keep turning her suitor down? Was she in love with somebody else?

'I hadn't had time! I wasn't in love with anybody! And being a lawyer's wife sounded so respectable and middle-aged. I hadn't had any fun! You know what I mean, don't you? I had to stay in every night to play cards with my mother – and I was still only seventeen, see?'

Her voice, strangely light and girlish for a woman in her eighties, solicits sympathy; like Teresa, her interviewer, I find myself responding to it.

'And I did try,' Virginia pleads. 'I never *explicitly* went against my mother's wishes. But ten o'clock! Blanche didn't seem to understand that we weren't living out on the prairie any more. Nobody in Chicago went home at that hour – nobody, except me and my mother. That's how it felt. I just wasn't ready to settle down.'

Fate offered to lend a hand in the week leading up to Christmas 1925, when the parents of one of Virginia's band of school-mates took tickets for the Artists' Ball, a highlight in the city's social calendar. Virginia was invited to join their party. A girlfriend loaned her a sky-blue chiffon dress with matching stole.

The Artists' Ball was held on 18 December in one of Chicago's most gorgeous settings, the Gold Room of the Congress Hotel (connected by an underground passage of marble and mirrors, known as 'Peacock Alley', to the architect Louis Sullivan's masterpiece, the Auditorium Hall). Over 500 guests gathered that night in the Gold Room. Cameras flashed their lights; the next day's papers carried reports that the Golden Apple, a prize awarded to 'the most beautiful girl of the evening', had been won by Virginia Cherrill, 'a former Carthage girl'.

It was inevitable that a hitherto unknown beauty, crowned 'queen' at one of the city's most prominent social events, would arouse further interest. On 21 January 1926, the Chicago press announced that Miss Cherrill was to join the celebrated Follies of Florenz Ziegfeld. As a Chicago-born man, Ziegfeld might even have been present himself that night at the Congress Hotel, when a golden-haired girl with blue eyes and a porcelain skin stepped up to receive her prize.

Flo Ziegfeld had been presenting beautiful girls to the public since the Follies first opened in a rundown New York roof-garden theatre in the blistering summer of 1907, a year before Virginia's birth. Deficient in any of the usual theatrical skills of composing, writing or directing, Ziegfeld combined a discerning eye for female flesh with a shrewd sense of showmanship. (He also had wit: his 1908 revue presented the long-legged dancers as mosquitoes flying up the newly constructed Holland Tunnel into New York City from out in the marshlands of New Jersey). Sexuality was kept just short of porn: Ziegfeld's short-lived cabaret show, *The Frolics*, featured a glass walkway that allowed male spectators to peer up the inner thighs of the dancers. (Until, that is, the unrepentant impresario was confronted by the furious mother of a young actress who combined an endearingly unprotesting stammer with shapely legs – one Marion Davies.) Pretty, semi-nude girls, sly gimmickry and a genius for attracting publicity: these elements helped to keep Ziegfeld's Follies ahead of competition for over twenty years.

The chief attraction of the revues, however, lay in the leading performers: who but Ziegfeld could have assembled Sophie Tucker, Fanny Brice and dancer Marilyn Miller alongside such comic and vocal talents as Eddie Cantor, W. C. Fields and Will Rogers? Today, dancing in a revue may strike some readers as the equivalent in glamour to belly-rolling in a Turkish restaurant. Back then, Flo Ziegfeld was able to offer his young performers a true shot at stardom.

Virginia turned him down.

Since Virginia never speaks to Teresa about either the beauty prize or Ziegfeld's offer (my information derives from old newspaper cuttings, preserved by Virginia's Illinois relations), guesswork has to supply the reasons for her refusal. Some reasons are obvious. Blanche would have been horrified to contemplate the transformation of her carefully educated daughter into a scantily dressed performer at the Follies. Irving Adler, too, must have made his feelings clear. Such an eligible and ambitious young bachelor – his only connection to the stage being a maternal uncle who lived in Hollywood (and of whom his nephew disapproved) – would never have risked marriage to a mere chorus girl.

It is also possible that Virginia was receiving good career advice from her friends. She lived in a city that buzzed with show-gossip and in which, recently, it had begun to be rumoured that Ziegfeld had lost his edge. *No Foolin'* (lawsuits precluded the use of the word 'Follies' in the title of the 1926 show) offered spectators an opulent but overlong evening of fine costumes, ponderous sets and mediocre music. Well below the standard of his best, this latest Ziegfeld spectacular was not the ideal vehicle in which to launch the career of a girl whose gifts for singing and dancing were admittedly slight. For whatever reason, Virginia made a wise decision when she turned down the offer from Ziegfeld.

'So Irving asked me to marry him. And then he asked me again! I think he proposed every single day during those seven months after that first visit of ours to the Blackstone,' Virginia tells Teresa. She sounds plaintive. 'He just wouldn't give up. And I felt bad, turning him down when he was so good to me.'

This justification is the only rationale the old lady is prepared to offer for the fact that, on the day after her graduation in June 1926, she married Irving Adler at City Hall. Following the ceremony, the couple undertook to inform their parents.

'My mother had a fit,' Virginia sighs. 'Poor Blanche! I'm sure she'd wished for something more traditional than a registry office. And I never did get to wear – never in my entire life – a proper white dress for a wedding ceremony. Isn't that strange!'

Teresa ventures no reply. Possibly, she is thinking, as am I, that Mrs Cherrill must have cared less about the formalities of the marriage rite itself than the unimagined triumph of seeing her daughter suddenly allied to one of Chicago's most prominent and successful families. Possibly, Teresa is wondering how to phrase her next question, a delicate one, prompted by female curiosity, about Virginia's wedding night at the Drake Hotel.

The night was not, it soon becomes clear, a success, even though Virginia describes the Drake as having been a place of wonderful glamour.

Virginia in Chicago, shortly before she married Irving Adler.

'We had to show our wedding papers at the desk, because I looked too young. After that was sorted out, the hotel people apologised by ushering us up to a suite that looked as if it was part of a palace. We were given the best table in the house for dinner, champagne, all of it: hotels really knew how to treat their guests in those days. And then, later – Irving came into the bedroom and lay down next to me. I just started to shake. I was terrified. I didn't even know where the man was supposed to put it!'

'Put it?' The tape records a pause, a long one, during which I can detect a quiet gasp. 'You were eighteen years old, and you didn't *know* . . . ?'

'My mother didn't talk about things like that,' Virginia retorts, and her tone rebuffs further enquiry. 'I hadn't liked to ask anybody else. And then, when it happened, I didn't like it at all! So there I was – newly married to a dear man, a husband ready to give me everything a wife could wish for – and me, crying my eyes out, there in the best hotel on Michigan Avenue. It must have been hell for Irving. It certainly was for me. And, sadly, that's the way it stayed.'

I register another pause; her friend seems to be finding all of this hard to credit – and, perhaps, difficult to reconcile with the personality of the woman she feels that she knows so well. 'You're telling me that it went on that way *after* the honeymoon?'

'It most certainly did. The minute Irving climbed into bed, I went rigid, not a thing he or I could do about it. Sometimes I'd try drinking a cocktail or two, to help me relax, but the minute we reached home . . . !' She sighs. 'And Irving never said a word. Never. He was such a gentleman.'

Virginia did not, at any point in her life, have difficulty in making friends, but it would be reasonable to assume that the Adler family must have harboured severe reservations about Irving's schoolgirl bride, her undistinguished background, and the (premature) newspaper announcements of her future as a dancer in a Ziegfeld show. It is possible that an enraptured Irving employed his lawyerly skills to persuade his parents that Virginia had given up the chance of a promising theatrical career for the sake of love; it may have been his lovely young wife's unaffected manner that succeeded in charming the Adlers into submission. What is not in doubt is the fact that the bride received a swift and heartfelt welcome into her husband's family.

'I've never known such generosity,' Virginia exclaims. 'It was overwhelming! You want details? A big apartment on North Shore for the two of us, and a place near by for Blanche; jewels; a private maid; a Cadillac and – this was a personal wedding-gift to me from Irving's father – $20,000 worth of stock. The whole family behaved as though their brilliant boy had brought home a princess instead of a penniless girl from the sticks.'

Two troubling issues stood in the way of this marriage's chances of survival. One, already indicated, was that the couple were sexually incompatible. A second was that Irving's legal work often required him to be out of town for weeks at a time. His young bride grew lonely. Virginia's closest friends in the city were still off at school and, warm though Irving's family were, she didn't relish spending days on end in their company.

This period became, by default, a time of self-education. Friends who knew Virginia Cherrill in later years were often struck by the breadth of her interests and by, in particular, her love of history, art and archaeology. Those passions, she explains, dated back to the days she spent both at the Chicago Art Institute – where she acquired a lasting enthusiasm for French Impressionist paintings – and at the Field Museum.

'I loved the Field! I damn near lived there!'

The Field Museum of Natural History, endowed by Marshall Field and modelled after a classical Greek temple, stood in Grant

The Field Museum ('I damned near lived there!') in 1920.

Park, beneath the lofty towers ranged along Michigan Avenue. Affectionately known as 'the people's college', the Field, by bringing together under one roof the studies of zoology, botany, geology and anthropology, achieved for Chicago what Prince Albert's mighty row of Kensington museums did for London. Lecturers spoke at the Field every day; as a bright girl with a retentive mind, Virginia squirrelled away information upon an extraordinary variety of topics: the analysis of fossil shapes; the bone structure of a dinosaur (the skeleton of *tyrannosaurus rex* was one of the museum's prize exhibits); the monolithic statues of Easter Island; the significance, even, of Greece's Dodona oak. Here, Virginia tells Teresa, was the beginning of an enduring love affair – to which the bookshelves at her Santa Barbara home still attest – with the past, with art, and with the natural world. These days at the Chicago museums, she asserts, were the happiest of her marriage.

Daily lectures were not, however, a substitute for life, or for love. The marriage, increasingly, revealed itself as unsatisfactory.

'I wasn't happy,' Virginia states, 'and neither was Irving, poor man. We just weren't suited; it was nobody's fault.'

'We just weren't suited': Irving and Virginia in 1927.

In November 1927, one year and five months after he married Virginia, Irving Adler was called away upon a legal case, a trial in New York City. His departure was not, in itself, unusual. Virginia offers no explanation for why she chose that particular moment to leave him. She might have been tempted by the news that her friend Evelyn Lederer (now going about the film capital under her new name of Sue Carol), had just won a role in a movie, *Slaves of Beauty*. Virginia herself had already been extended an open invitation to visit Irving's most intriguing relation – 'the richest of them all!' – his bachelor Uncle Joe, an invalid, who lived in Hollywood. The Chicago Adlers did not get on with Uncle Joe; to them, Virginia said only that she planned to spend a fortnight with friends who lived on the West Coast. The family raised no objections.

On 25 November 1927, Virginia boarded a train heading out West. 'The Santa Fe line,' she sighs. 'Those wonderful Pullman coaches – and the food! My mother used to say that any memoir I ever wrote ought to be called 'View from the Dining-Car'. But where else would you want to be, on a train like that?'

And was she hoping to find herself a part in a film? Was that why she went?

'I certainly was not!' Virginia retorts. 'Come on, Teresa, you know what films are like! They're hard work. I just wanted to have fun. And once I was there, I knew I wasn't going back.'

Any particular reason?

'It isn't complicated,' she replies. 'There was nothing to stay for.'

'That's it?' Teresa sounds shaken by her friend's brusqueness. 'That's all?'

I'm craning forward, trying to catch the words.

'It's who I am. When a romantic situation becomes untender, I get the hell out. I always have. Story of my life.'

'So why didn't you ever leave *me*, Virginia?' These words, intervening abruptly, come from a new voice, foreign-sounding, guttural, a little anxious – almost as though the speaker feared this bed-bound old lady might still do just that.

'I got too tired.' The tape catches the crackle of laughter, before her voice softens. 'You're such an . . . I stayed – you *know* why I stayed.'

'Because she loves you . . .' Teresa murmurs.

The tape reels on, but at this point I can only pick up a sibilance – a sort of whispered silence – that might be the wind, or the ocean, or a sigh.

PART TWO

Hollywood

4

LIVING IT UP WITH UNCLE JOE

(1927–1928)

'I believe that if you want the golden fleece, it's more
sensible to go to the place where it exists than rush around
performing prodigies of valour in a country where the
fleeces all happen to be coalblack.'

MR PROPTER IN *AFTER MANY A SUMMER DIES THE SWAN*,
ALDOUS HUXLEY (1939)

Aldous Huxley's novel *After Many a Summer Dies the Swan* describes
a Hollywood magnate, 'Uncle Joe' Stoyte, whose dream it is – this
being Hollywood – to live for ever, and in fine fettle. Stoyte's wish
for vigorous immortality is fuelled by his passion for Miss Virginia
Maunciple, an appealing blonde upon whom the ageing magnate
lavishes gifts, while attempting to guard her – quite futilely –
against love affairs with younger men.

Huxley's sources seem obvious. Visiting California in the mid-
Thirties, he and his wife had spent a memorable weekend with
William Randolph Hearst and his girlfriend, Marion Davies,
staying at San Simeon, Hearst's kingdom on a hilltop, 200 miles
north of Los Angeles. It would appear, then, that Huxley's fictional
magnate and his saucy blonde mistress are mischievous portraits of

Hearst and Davies; however, given the fact that Huxley also met Charlie Chaplin during this period, the author could as easily have been drawing upon second-hand film-town gossip. Chaplin, Davies and Hearst were all familiar with the story of Virginia Cherrill's arrival in Hollywood, and of the rich 'Uncle Joe' who had taken her under his wing.

One crucial difference: Miss Maunciple was Mr Stoyte's mistress, although hardly a faithful one. Virginia is adamant in her insistence to Teresa that she never had a sexual relationship with Irving Adler's invalid uncle (whose home was a suite in Hollywood's most glamorous hotel, the 900-room Ambassador, on Wilshire Boulevard).

Marion Davies and Randolph Hearst, relaxing at Wyntoon, Hearst's second (50,000 acre) estate in North California, 1935.

'Uncle Joe just enjoyed showing me off to friends as his girl,' Virginia announces in her light, breathy voice. 'He never made a pass. I used to push his wheelchair when he went out to meals, and he'd have me sit beside him as his guest. Oh, he really was a darling, and so generous! All around the ground floor of the Ambassador, there were the most wonderful shops you ever saw, and the minute I so much as glanced at anything, Joe ordered it.'

Asked by Teresa to provide an example of Mr Adler's generosity, Virginia recalls an occasion when she stopped by a shop window to admire a dark sapphire brooch set in diamonds.

'Uncle Joe asked if I liked it and I said, yes, I did. Later, when we reached our lunch table, there it was, sitting in a box upon a plate. He did things like that all the time. And I suppose it was partly that he enjoyed having a little slap at Irving. He certainly never encouraged me to go back to my marriage. And I didn't want to!'

Never? She didn't feel any guilt, despite the generosity of Irving Adler's immediate family? Her answer is always the same: she felt no guilt at all. Irving, she goes on to point out, found greater happiness in his second – and enduring – marriage.

'I did the man a good turn!'

Try as she will, Teresa is never granted a precise account of what went on during Virginia's first year in Hollywood. The old lady chatters to her with enthusiasm about the Ambassador ('the most elegant hotel I've ever seen, anywhere'). But it assuredly was not the partly paralysed Joe Adler that Virginia remembers tango-dancing with at the Cocoanut Grove nightclub in which, a few months before Virginia's arrival, Zelda Fitzgerald had captured the attention of the club's clientele with a hip-wriggling display of 'The Black Bottom'.

Uncle Joe was a sociable man with many connections within the film community, but it's impossible to ascertain how many of the wealthy, sports-loving friends whom Virginia soon acquired were linked to his circle. Did she live in Mr Adler's suite, or did she stay with Evelyn ('Sue Carol') Lederer (whose pertly pretty face was about to be credited with inspiring the popular song 'Sweet Sue, Just You')?

It is also conceivable that Virginia settled in with the family of her own real uncle, out at Palm Beach, where Ted Wilcox was running a car dealership. But this possibility, given Virginia's consistently hostile attitude to a man she described as 'flaky', seems remote.

'Sarah was my godmother,' Virginia has told Teresa, while reminiscing about her early life at Carthage. 'She lived in LA.' No further identification is provided, but a godmother's protective home would have helped deflect gossip about a lovely young woman who had run away from her husband, and who now kept company with that husband's uncle. Care was required where a girl's reputation was concerned in America's new film capital, as Miss Lederer must surely have warned Virginia well before she left Chicago: Hollywood, from its earliest years as a film colony, was both scandal-filled and fiercely censorious.

Virginia reached Los Angeles shortly after its emergence as the central magnet of the movie industry in America. Ten years earlier, Sunset Boulevard had been a two-track dirt road, with a roofed hay-barn acting as its solitary covered set. By 1928, the endless stretch of studios was beginning to be interspersed by nightspots, residential bungalow courts (such as the celebrated Garden of Allah), dress stores and even – a recent arrival – an Isotta Fraschini saleroom that offered some of the world's most ravishing and expensive cars to the studio princes and their stars.

Glimpses of the more pastoral past remained in evidence. The Paramount sets, hidden behind a pair of huge triumphal gates on Melrose Avenue, were still held apart by the glossy citrus groves of a former Spanish settlement. Charlie Chaplin relaxed between takes at his personal studio on the corner of La Brea Boulevard by strolling amongst the fragrant orange trees that had charmed a certain Mr and Mrs Harvey Wilcox (the couple bore no known relation to Virginia's family) into buying 160 acres of Californian ground for a temperance community that they decided, back in the 1880s, to call Hollywood.

Old Los Angelinos, many of them settlers from the rural Midwest, cursed the coming of the Harvey Wilcoxes to California almost as vehemently as the day in 1911 when a pioneering film-maker discovered that Hollywood offered free lighting (the sun), cheap labour, and easy access to deserts, mountains and rolling valleys (the staple backgrounds of the first silent films to be shot on location). The film-makers flocked in; the old-fashioned farming gentry shrank back. Safe behind the protective gates of such sedate communities as Hancock Park, these settled residents rose early, attended church on Sunday, kept neatly annotated records of their family histories – and professed a sublime indifference to both the art and industry of this upstart: cinema.

Outside the gates of Hancock Park, the film world did not feel the sting of such disdain. Sports cars sprayed the verges with red dust as their drivers roared up the coast to Santa Barbara, off for a day of beach-lolling and cocktails at the Biltmore Hotel. Newcomers slowed down along Beach Palisades Road, striving for a view of the dazzling neo-Georgian columns of Marion Davies's Ocean House and the large, Spanish-style villas of Will Rogers and Harold Lloyd. No such luck: these homes kept their backs turned to the road, protecting their owners from the vulgar curiosity of their fans.

Strange stories did, occasionally, seep out. When Virginia arrived in California, she had already heard Evelyn Lederer's account of one of the biggest scandals in recent years. Towards the end of 1924, Evelyn told Virginia, a murder had taken place that had shaken Hollywood. The gun – it was rumoured to have been aimed by W. R. Hearst at Charlie Chaplin, whom the newspaper magnate suspected of conducting an affair with Marion Davies – had killed the wrong man, a producer named Thomas Ince. The incident had taken place aboard Hearst's yacht on 19 November; the following day, Chaplin's manservant, Toraichi Kono, witnessed Ince's body being carried ashore at San Diego. Bloodstains on the back of Ince's head led Kono to conclude that foul play had taken place on board the *Oneida*.

Hearst was a man of formidable influence. The *Oneida*'s crew, together with its owner's guests, were either sworn or bribed into collusion. Louella Parsons, a rising star in the Hearst newspaper empire, was suddenly granted a year's paid leave, followed by a considerable increase in both her powers and her salary. Marion Davies needed no bribing to declare that Mr Hearst (although his habit of firing a pistol at low-flying seagulls was well-known to his yachting cronies) had never allowed weapons on his boat. Thomas Ince's wife, eager to conceal the fact that her husband had been holidaying upon the *Oneida* in the company of his mistress, swore that her husband had never set foot upon the yacht; Chaplin went further still and fabricated an alibi, a meeting between himself and Ince that had taken place a full week after he attended the producer's private funeral.

The scandal – officially, Ince died in his home of a stomach ailment – was kept out of the newspapers (most of which were owned by Hearst). Privately, many people in Hollywood judged Charlie Chaplin to have had a lucky escape and to have acted wisely in falsifying the date of Thomas Ince's death. A few months after the incident, the friendship between Hearst, Davies and Chaplin was resumed. There were, however, no further rumours of sexual intrigue.

Loyal until the end, Marion Davies made no mention of the ill-starred trip of the *Oneida* when she dictated her memoirs in 1974 (they were published the following year). The yacht's voyage had never taken place. She remembered nothing about Thomas Ince's death. The sea had washed all trace away.

It was probably through Evelyn Lederer's links to Marion Davies (she was connected by the marriage of a Lederer to Miss Davies's sister) that Virginia gained her first invitations to Ocean House and San Simeon; these were venues where a pretty face, a love of fun, and the absolute lack of an ambitious agenda made Miss Cherrill an unthreatening and popular guest. But her preference in those days, so she tells Teresa, was for dining and dancing at one of Joe Adler's favourite haunts: the hangar-sized Cocoanut Grove, situated at the foot of the Ambassador Hotel.

Shrewdly managed by Johnny Manos, and decorated with palm trees from the set of Valentino's desert seduction scenes in *The Sheikh* (1921), the Ambassador's cavernous restaurant epitomised the combination of tawdriness and glamour that were becoming the trademark of Hollywood. As at San Simeon, where Hearst indicated the end of a guest's visit by shunting him to the far end of the dining-room table, away from the action, placing was crucial at the Grove. The securing of a prominent table from which to saunter on to the dance-floor mattered more here than elegant dress; Hollywood society spent too much time in costume to worry about the knot of a tie or the hang of a jacket.

Musically unadventurous (Paul Whiteman's Band and, a little later, Bing Crosby and his Rhythm Boys, offered the hits of the moment in a seamless medley), the Grove took more risks with its live acts and stunts. Diners cheered on the evening that a willowy nude girl was wheeled into the room, imprisoned and exposed to view within a block of clear ice. Johnny Manos also knew how to amuse his clientele: on Tuesday nights, adventurous diners shinned up the trunks of the Grove's fake palms in order to retrieve small, artfully positioned trophies. Reminiscing to Teresa, Virginia wryly boasts that she acquired a sufficient menagerie of velveteen monkeys from these Tuesday night dinners to have set up her own toyshop.

Virginia's favourite nightspot: the Cocoanut Grove, complete with fake palms.

Antics at the Grove provided succulent fodder for a new and avid breed of journalist, the gossip columnist. Elsewhere, good stories were surprisingly hard to find. Behind the scenes, despite the occasional shocking frisson – the Arbuckle rape case, the mysterious death of Thomas Ince – daily life in the film community was dull enough to make old-fashioned Carthage seem, by comparison, riotous. Devourers of Louella Parsons' glamorised accounts of life in the fabled household of Fairbanks and Pickford never learned that America's Sweetheart resorted to a diet of boiled spinach and milk whenever she was filming (it stopped her belching at the camera). Readers did not hear that Pickfair dinner-parties ended at nine, or that Doug and Mary offered for nightcaps, not whisky, but hearty mugs of Ovaltine.

Sleepy evenings were succeeded by somnolent days. Work at the studios, back in the era of silent film, was often so quiet that secondary actors fell asleep on set. Musical bands were brought in to keep the performers alert, while the director seized his chance to prep a yawning actress on her expression: ('You've just heard that your son is lost at sea. You're devastated: how can your beloved boy possibly be no more?') Virginia mentions that one old-school film-star met all such instructions with just two looks: one for joy and another for despair.

Subtlety was equally disdained in the film community's social life. A hot-dog stand advertised its wares by displaying a twenty-foot orange frankfurter; the Brown Derby on Wilshire Boulevard urged prospective diners to come and 'Eat in the Hat', where the waitresses wore skirts starched to mimic a Derby's rounded crown. Food at this celebrated haunt was as heavy as the humour of its sales pitch: corned beef hash was followed by the Derby's celebrated sponge cake, smothered in cream cheese and decorated with chunky slices of grapefruit.

The Brown Derby stood just across the way from the Ambassador; this was where, during Virginia's first months in Hollywood, she dined almost nightly with Joe Adler. Acting as his nurse-companion, she sat beside the crippled man at a circular table crowded with writers and producers: these were Joe's friends.

'And they were so much fun! It was like being at the Algonquin Round Table, hearing them all being so witty. I could never think of a thing to say, but I did love to listen.'

Teresa wants to know — and so, at an even greater distance in time, do I — just who came along to these lively evening gatherings. The year in question — 1928 — was the year, after all, when the talkies had just begun. Pressed by the need for sharp-witted screenplays, the big studios competed to recruit some of the world's best-known writers. Did Virginia meet Scott Fitzgerald during one of her visits to the Brown Derby . . . or Ben Hecht, or Anita Loos . . . ? Anxious to oblige, the old lady puts forward the names of Dorothy Parker and Robert Benchley. The dates don't quite compute; it's clear, from the moment of awkward silence, that Virginia knows it.

Changing tack, Teresa asks her friend what Uncle Joe's pals liked to talk about. Did one of them first give Virginia the idea of going into films?

The response takes me by surprise; she was, after all, an exceptionally pretty girl, living at the epicentre of the film industry. But Virginia is adamant. She had no plans to go into films; nobody suggested that she should do so.

'Joe's friends knew I was having too much fun. But they'd kid me about it, tell me how to behave if some producer offered me a private screen test at his home. "You don't just walk away," they said. "You run!"'

And now, at last, Virginia begins to tell the story that her patient friend, Teresa, wants to put on record. She starts to talk about the Friday night in October 1928 when Joe Adler took her along, in the company of his male nurse, to watch a boxing match at the Hollywood Legion Stadium.

'Everybody went to the Friday night fights, back then,' Virginia explains. 'It was a way to wind down, and very social. And maybe

Uncle Joe did set it all up in advance, knowing who'd be there. That's a possibility, but he certainly never told me.'

I imagine the elderly lady leaning forward here from her piled pillows, gesturing as she explains that Mr Adler's wheelchair entitled them to enjoy special seats, close to the ring.

'They put Joe beside the aisle, and he wanted the nurse beside him. So I was sitting over on the far side of the nurse, next to a wiry little man with white hair and a tan. I remember he was wearing tennis shorts; I thought he must have driven up from some place like Charlie Farrell's Racquet Club in Palm Springs. And honest to God, I had no idea who he was.'

'But you must have known!' Teresa breaks in.

'Not a clue,' Virginia says. 'Well! You know how bad my sight is. I'd left my glasses behind, so I had my eyes scrunched up, to watch what was going on in the ring. Of course, Charlie was on the hunt for somebody to play the blind flower-seller in *City Lights*. He told me later that he'd seen a blind girl in a London park years ago; it made a big impression on him. That's the face he kept searching for. It was hard for him to find an actress who could look blind and yet not ugly. And then he saw me squinting at the boxers, and it seems that I didn't look too plain, so he just kept staring.'

The story of what followed has passed into film legend.

Still unaware of the wiry little sportsman's identity, Virginia imagined that he was trying to pick her up when, suddenly, he leaned towards her and offered her a part in his film. Virginia knew from her friends at the Brown Derby what an overture of this kind meant. Turning to Joe Adler's male nurse, she asked him to change seats with her.

Later, when the prizefight was over, Joe Adler told her who the 'sportsman' really was.

'I didn't believe him. I mean: Charlie *Chaplin*? To me, Charlie was a skinny little guy with black hair and a moustache; I'd never

65

seen him except up on the screen. Uncle Joe told me off for being so rude to him, and I did feel foolish. I hadn't made any plans to be in films, but to be invited by Charlie Chaplin – well, I can't think of a girl in Hollywood who would have refused an offer like that. He didn't even want a screen test.'

The following day, Joe Adler told Virginia that she had been granted a second chance; Chaplin had invited the two of them up to his beach house for lunch and a talk.

'And then, Joe threw in that Charlie's chef was supposed to be the best cook on the West Coast. Joe knew how I loved to eat. So I said: "Sure." '

I'm entranced; it's clear that Virginia herself is finding the story wearisomely familiar. Describing the journey to Santa Monica, she digresses into one of her visits to the beachside palace of Marion Davies. 'Fifty ensuite bedrooms, and a bridge copied from the Rialto across the swimming-pool!'

It's almost with a sigh that Virginia, submitting to Teresa's prodding, returns to her Chaplin story. She's recalling now how she and the nurse had started to lift Uncle Joe out of his car when a man with a charming ugly face ('like a smiling horse') walked out of the Chaplin house. He stared at her hard for a moment, after which he called to someone inside to come and take a look.

'So then Charlie strolls out the door – not a word to me or to Uncle Joe – just a nod. He could be so *rude*! He starts boasting to his friend about how he's found the blind girl. Then, the horse-faced man – that was Harry d'Arrast, who married my beautiful lifelong friend Eleanor Boardman, after she was through with King Vidor – he says that he'd already spotted me when I was fooling about on the beach, just a day before the prizefight. So then they're arguing about which of them discovered me first, and nobody's even bothered to ask if I want to be an actress!'

'But of course . . .' Teresa says. 'Don't tell me you thought of refusing.'

'Well, I did,' Virginia states. 'For a start, the pay he offered was terrible: $75 a week! Norma Shearer was earning five thousand. But Uncle Joe wouldn't let me argue. Charlie gave me a date to sign the contract and meet the publicist. And then we all had lunch.'

It was, although she makes light of it, an extraordinary moment of life transformation.

Aged twenty, with no prior experience of acting and without (this was almost unheard of) taking even a rudimentary screen test, Virginia Cherrill had been chosen to play the leading female role in a film opposite the world's most famous actor-director. A lively unpretentious girl who had come to Hollywood in search of fun and a few laughs while escaping from an unsatisfactory marriage, was launched, without effort or endeavour, upon a pell-mell road to celebrity.

Gathering for their family celebrations in Carthage that December, the Cherrills and the Wilcoxes pored over a half-page clipping from the *Los Angeles Times*. A glowing Virginia stared up at them, with an outsized and overdressed china doll perched upon her knee. Miss Cherrill, the reporter noted, seen here distributing gifts to needy girls (in the company of Hollywood's own Kris Kringle), had just been selected as Charlie Chaplin's next leading lady; this pretty socialite from Chicago (no mention here of Carthage or Grange Farm) was already being hailed as 'a distinct find'.

It's possible that Virginia's mother had clipped the press item from the newspaper and dispatched it through the mail from her new home in Hollywood. The ink on the agreement was scarcely dry before Blanche Cherrill had been summoned from Chicago to Los Angeles and established (the studios must have helped with funding the rent) at an apartment in the highly respectable area of Hancock Park.

Previously, Virginia had been free to spend her time with Joe Adler and his friends at the Brown Derby; now, under the terms of her new agreement, she was required to appear decorous. The address where Virginia would be seen to reside henceforth was to be the home of her mother.

Blanche Cherrill, during her daughter's six hectic years of life as a movie-star, would never be far from Virginia's side. This arrangement, while it gave a loving mother genuine pleasure, was equally good for business, as Blanche herself was shrewd enough to understand. Chaplin, who had faced some difficult mothers in his time, notably those connected to the young girls with whom he had frequent affairs, produced plenty of complaints about Virginia, but never one about her loyal mamma.

Blanche Cherrill, to the surprise of all who had imagined that they knew her, took to the City of Angels like a perfect native. Hollywood, for the next twenty years, would be Blanche's chosen home.

Charlie Chaplin was just short of forty and emerging from a singularly difficult period of his life when he decided to cast a girl with no previous film experience as the romantic lead in *City Lights* [plate 3]. Born in England, Chaplin had spent almost the full span of Virginia's life in America. A graceful and brilliantly inventive master of mime, he had first won international acclaim with his creation of the shabby, playful character of the Tramp, a romantic dreamer with a powerful instinct for survival. By 1916, when he was still only twenty-seven years old, Chaplin had become – until Mary Pickford decided to up her own salary – the highest-paid artist in the world.

Immense wealth provided Chaplin with the freedom to purchase his own studio, to work at his own speed, and to indulge what sometimes struck his assistants and fellow-actors as an

*Blanche Cherrill, as she looked during the first years
of her life in Hollywood.*

obsessive desire for absolute perfection. Hard upon himself – he
required 700 takes for that brilliant scene in *The Circus* (the film
directly preceding *City Lights*) during which the Tramp is clawed
by mischievous monkeys while walking a tightrope – he was
equally demanding of his co-stars. Pressure never diverted him
from his singular goal: to produce a flawless masterpiece.

The Circus tried Chaplin to the limits of his endurance. A major
fire at his studio on La Brea Boulevard was the least of his problems;
the blaze came at a time when, having evaded public scandal over
his fling with Marion Davies and the mysterious death of Thomas
Ince, Chaplin was being described by his second wife, Lita Grey, as
an adulterer and sexual deviant. Meanwhile, the Internal Revenue
Service, suing him for $1.6 million in unpaid back taxes, placed his

entire fortune into receivership. Chaplin's hair turned white – almost literally – overnight. In January 1927, he suffered a nervous breakdown and, to escape the scandalmongers prowling the film capital, fled to New York City.

The fact that, during this turbulent period, Chaplin still managed to complete one of his finest works, testifies both to his dedication and his courage. One extraordinary scene from *The Circus*, filmed in a lion's cage, required 200 takes. What had not been faked, Chaplin later admitted, was the expression of absolute terror upon his own face.

Chaplin had another reason to look worried. In 1927, Warner Brothers had caused a sensation. Using their new Vitaphone equipment, they had introduced rapturous film-goers not to the mere spectacle, but the actual sound, of Al Jolson, the highest-paid live entertainer of the time (and, incidentally, the first who made no secret of being Jewish). *The Jazz Singer* presented Jolson in blackface make-up (a theatrical convention of that time), breaking out of the usual silent sequences into song and even – briefly – into speech. 'Mammy' became the movie's best-known live song, but the moments that thrilled the audiences were when Jolson ad-libbed asides, the best-known being: 'Wait a minute, you ain't heard nothing yet.' Audiences had indeed heard nothing like it; they wanted more. Jolson's first all-talking role followed in 1928. *The Singing Fool*, from which the signature tune of 'Sonny Boy' sold one million copies, held the box-office record for attendance until it was capped by *Gone with the Wind* in 1939.

Talkies were not good news for Chaplin. His fame depended upon physical contortions and facial expressions; his voice lacked the strength and range needed to succeed with early sound equipment. His response was to start plans for a new silent film, one that would use blindness as a metaphor through which to assert the transcendent power of human expression above that of speech. Blindness was key to the film. This was the only thing in *City Lights* of which, even before work began, Chaplin felt certain.

Initially, the actor-director had considered playing a clown whose loss of sight would need to be hidden from his sickly little daughter; this sentimental idea was soon abandoned. Talking to Virginia, in the early stages of developing his new plot for *City Lights*, Chaplin often mentioned the blind girl he had glimpsed in a city park during his early years in London.

'It made a great impact on him,' Virginia says. 'Charlie always thought highly of the character I played.'

The fact that Chaplin was prepared to talk to Virginia about this significant memory suggests a friendliness and ease between the director and his young star. This impression is confirmed by Chaplin's use of Virginia's own name in the notes he made about her part during the slow process of filming *City Lights*. Was the director's vision of the blind heroine influenced by the sweet personality of the girl with whom, caught together in one unguarded studio shot, we see him laughing, complicitly, at the camera?

This photograph might suggest shared sympathy, except, that is, for the overwhelming counter-evidence on offer elsewhere. Well liked by almost everybody she would meet throughout her life, Virginia nevertheless aroused a feeling in Chaplin that might almost be called loathing, a feeling she herself returned. Neither the director nor his pretty co-star offered explanations, back then or at any later stage, for this strong and mutual hostility.

'I didn't like Charlie,' Virginia states, cryptically. 'And Charlie didn't like me.'

Pressed by Teresa to offer reasons, after a gap of over sixty years, for this reciprocal aversion, Virginia resolutely declines.

The story of *City Lights*, a film that took almost two years to complete, appears deceptively simple. Wandering around a city, turning a street corner (almost every scene was shot in Chaplin's studios, on a T-shaped set) the Tramp spots a pretty young woman selling flowers. Her movements, as she searches the pavement for a dropped bloom, reveal her blindness. The Tramp, touched, proffers a coin. Afterwards, hearing the heavy slam of the door to an expensive automobile close by, the girl deduces that her benefactor must be a man of wealth.

The Tramp's riches are only of the spirit. Befriended by the luxurious car's real owner, he eventually begs a loan to cover the cost of an operation to cure the Flower-girl's blindness. The capricious millionaire, while inebriated, hands over the money, but then, after sobering up, discovers that he has been robbed and sets the police to arrest his friend.

The Tramp, having made his gift to the Flower-girl, is resigned to his fate: a lengthy imprisonment for his 'crime'. Later released and once again penniless, the Tramp discovers that the Flower-girl now runs a small florist's shop. The girl, watching two urchins through her window as they persecute the shabby, bashful Tramp, leaves her shop to comfort him with a flower and a coin. Only when she touches the Tramp's hand and then his arm – the movement offers an echo of their first encounter – does the girl begin to identify her benefactor. The Tramp asks if she can now see. Still touching him, she nods mute acknowledgement. Virginia Cherrill's astonished, tender gaze reminds us that the girl is now beholding the Tramp for the first time. Chaplin's eyes glow; they fill the screen; we, too, seem never to have seen him before. Some truth, beyond the scene, is being conveyed here, something about the nature of human vision, and perhaps of cinema itself.

This most complex and emotionally powerful of all Chaplin's films was preceded by the death of Hannah, the actor-director's mentally unstable mother. Guilt ran deep: Chaplin had been just fourteen when he first helped to arrange for one of his mother's stays in an asylum; later, while paying for her to be supervised in a private home in Hollywood, Chaplin nevertheless kept his distance until the final weeks of Hannah's life. Possibly, the redemptive behaviour of the Tramp offered him some relief from guilt; certainly, the death of his mother in August 1928, at a time when his new film was already in pre-production, contributed to Chaplin's tense emotional state throughout the filming of *City Lights.*

Virginia as the movie press first promoted.

5

CITY LIGHTS

(1928–1930)

'Charlie was awfully keen on Napoleon, you know.'

The contract was signed in late November 1928; Virginia's initiation into studio life began two months later.

In the early hours of 29 January 1929, Chaplin's twenty-year-old recruit walked past the line of fake Tudor houses that fronted the La Brea Studio, and lifted the latch on an old-fashioned oak door. Ahead of her, beyond a narrow row of single-room offices, the *City Lights* set had been prepared for a street scene. Chaplin was standing out there, already dressed in the threadbare, jaunty uniform of the Tramp. The scene due to be rehearsed involved only the Flower-girl and the Tramp, but a cluster of actors were loitering about beside the wooden stage. Chaplin, as Virginia had yet to discover, liked his full cast to show up and pay strict attention throughout the filming process. (Jean Harlow, appearing only as an extra in a *City Lights* party scene, escaped this particular form of tyranny.)

Standing on the set with Chaplin were his two assistant directors. Harry Crocker, a handsome young journalist from a rich San Francisco family, had been involved with Chaplin's films since acting as unit publicist on *The Gold Rush*. Henry Bergman had been working alongside Chaplin – as an actor, adviser and ubiquitous sounding-board – since his first years of performing with the Mack Sennett company. The cameramen were busy on another corner of the set, checking out their equipment with another familiar figure, Chaplin's regular director of photography, Rollie Totheroh.

Standing in a glazed office at the side of the set, the publicist, Carlyle Robinson, was on the telephone, discussing a possible interview for Mr Chaplin's new leading lady. Miss Cherrill came from a distinguished Chicago family, he reported; this was her first film, but everyone shared the belief that she would go far. Watching Virginia through the window as she smiled back at Harry Crocker, Robinson doubtless wondered how long to give her before the trouble started. It was a while since Chaplin's relationship with Merna Kennedy (the athletic young female lead in *The Circus*) had been broken off; this untrained new girl looked both pretty and lively, just Chaplin's type.

On set, at least, there was no hint of flirtation. It puzzled Virginia that Chaplin neither turned to look at her nor even offered her a welcome greeting; instead, he directed his comments to the smiling young man, Harry Crocker. It was Crocker, not Chaplin, who instructed Virginia to hurry up and get her costume on so that they could all get to work.

Straightaway? This came as a shock.

'I never imagined that I'd be going in front of the camera to perform on my first day at the studio. But that's how Charlie wanted it. I hadn't even had a screen test, remember. I wasn't thrilled.'

The dressing-room, small and sparsely furnished, seemed a disappointment; so were the clothes Virginia had been told to wear. The loose, full-skirted skirt hung like a sack; the black woollen stockings made her skin itch; the scuffed pair of black flats featured thin straps that bit into her ankles. Schoolgirl shoes, she thought, and then realised their function; it wouldn't do for the Flower-girl to tower over her diminutive saviour.

'And the make-up was terrible, so thick and heavy. I could feel it running down my neck, and that was before I was anywhere near the lights. But they did leave my hair alone. I'd just had it marcelled.'

Turning towards her as she walked back to the set, Chaplin smiled. He had clearly made the right choice; his co-star was peering at him with the gentle intensity that had led him to suppose, back at their first encounter, that she actually was blind. The girl looked pale, innocent and tentative: all was as he wished. His sense of relief communicated itself to the cast; perhaps, after all, this was going to prove an easy day.

It wasn't.

Unprepared for Chaplin's unusual methods, Virginia was initially mortified to see him set out to perform, not only his part, but her own. Perching himself in front of a faked line of park railings, he offered her a coy smile. He then stood up, mimed the little dipping curtsey of homage that he always choreographed for his female star, and held out an imaginary bouquet. Leaning forward to address an invisible customer, he seemed to drop a flower. He sank to his knees, patted the ground around him with searching, delicate little movements, and then looked up at his puzzled leading lady.

Had she got that clear? Should he go through it again?

'It felt so strange,' Virginia tells the various interviewers who, years later, want to know every detail about her work on the film. 'Charlie acted out every single part, you see, every glance, every movement, just as he wanted it played. You found yourself thinking that he was you, and that he was also that person he wanted you to be. It wasn't easy.'

She did her best. But why, Virginia wondered, as she returned for a fourth day of filming the same tiny scene of her first meeting with the Tramp, *why* should it matter how she mouthed the question 'Flower, sir?' when nobody, in the end, was going to hear her speak? Had Charlie forgotten that he was making a silent film?

This question infuriated Chaplin. There was no other form of film, or none that counted, he told her; the sooner Virginia understood it, the better. All he asked – this was said loudly and slowly, as if he were addressing someone hard of hearing – was that she should do as he asked. Was it really so difficult?

It was, and the fault was not wholly hers. Reflecting upon the making of *City Lights* decades later, during the year that he published his autobiography, Chaplin admitted that he had worked himself up into a neurotic frenzy, a craving for faultless perfection. When he spoke to an interviewer, Richard Meryman, in 1968, the neurosis appeared still to be at work. Virginia Cherrill was dismissed as useless, an amateur, a socialite who had cared for nothing but party-going. Her mind was always somewhere else, the director claimed, and it showed.

'I'd know in a minute if she wasn't there,' Chaplin told Meryman, 'when she'd be searching, or looking up or just too much or just too soon. Or if she waited a second. I'd know in a minute.'

Reading that strange description, I begin to wonder if Chaplin had not become obsessed by the young girl he had plucked, untried, from the audience at a sporting event. The level of watchfulness that he describes seems not simply directorial – it's manic.

Rehearsals of the same pavement scene continued for over a fortnight; after a break of five days, they were resumed. On 25 February 1929, Chaplin fell sick from a stomach bug, followed by flu; throughout March, the crew and cast were kept on hold. On 1 April, Chaplin returned to the studio and announced that they would film the initial scene once again.

The scene that Chaplin shot 342 times: a record that has not been passed.

'I thought he was playing for time,' Virginia muses. 'I don't believe he knew what he was going to do next, so he'd go on shooting the same scene over and over again until an idea came. And none did. We did that scene 342 times. It's a record!'

Virginia may have been right; Chaplin was struggling to work out how to convey the simple error by which the Flower-Girl would imagine the Tramp to be a rich man, and so embark upon a fantasy romance. Chaplin knew how he wanted her to envision him – bizarre scenes that showed the Tramp posing as the Flower-Girl's dream lover in a lavishly braided white uniform were later dropped from the film – but he couldn't figure out how to contrive her innocent mistake.

On 11 April, Chaplin announced that they would try something else, without the Flower-Girl; instead, he would film the Tramp's first meeting with the party-loving millionaire who befriends him. A request by Virginia to take a few days off, since she was not needed, earned her no favours: with steely calm, Chaplin reminded her that she was under contract.

The actor-director's nervousness had by this time been noticed by everybody at the studio. The reasons were clear; this was a film that could not afford to fail. The audiences of the Depression were enthralled by the almost lifelike experience offered to them by the new 'talkies'; what, now, would cause them to flock to a seemingly dated silent film and the familiar spectacle of the Tramp up to his

Take 342: The Tramp's hands touch hers – and allow her to identify him when they meet after she is cured.

old tricks? The romantic attraction with the Flower-Girl was – for a Chaplin film – a novelty; the comic boxing scenes would surely help to sell it; nevertheless, the acting performances needed to be flawless. For one of these leads, Chaplin had picked a perfect novice with whom – it had become increasingly apparent – his relationship was problematic.

Improvising as he went along, Chaplin was haunted by the possibility of failure. His tension, evident in the obsessive rehearsals of Virginia's scenes, surfaced in other ways. In June, six months into filming, Chaplin sacked one of his major performers, Henry Clive. Playing the role of the millionaire, Clive had been rehearsed for a scene that required him to attempt to drown himself (the unheated studio pool was standing in for a lonely stretch of the Embankment-flanked Thames), and then to dive in again and rescue the Tramp, who had been accidentally yanked into the water. Filming was due to start early in the day; Chaplin arrived to be told that Clive, suffering from a cold, had pleaded for a break until the pool warmed up. Dismissed on the spot, Clive was replaced on Chaplin's orders by Henry Myers, a vaudeville pro. Two months later, with no reasons given, assistant director Harry Crocker was ordered off the set and told not to return. Crocker was both charming and attractive, a type of man who might easily appeal to Virginia. Could jealousy have had something to do with his dismissal? Chaplin never discussed any rationale for his arbitrary whims.

Virginia does not discuss either of these brusque dismissals with Teresa, but it seems fair to guess that she might have welcomed the same treatment. Obliged by contract to spend her days loitering about at the studio, she remained baffled by Chaplin's behaviour. For weeks at a time – so she later claimed – Charlie himself abandoned the studios, to watch tennis matches in Palm Springs. Returning abruptly, he would issue impulsive orders that bore no apparent relation to the film.

'We had to follow whatever fad he'd taken up,' Virginia recalls. 'Charlie even took control of what we ate. One time, we couldn't have anything but vegetables; another week, he wanted us living on cheese and fruit. Charlie was awfully keen on Napoleon, you know.'

It was unlucky for Virginia that she sprained her ankle in September and was confined to bed during one of the brighter moments of filming, when Winston Churchill, memorably, called in to watch. The fact that Virginia's small mishap was reported in the press as a significant item of news, however, shows that the Chaplin film was already bringing her some benefits; Louella Parsons, freshly established upon her throne as queen of Hollywood gossip, urged readers to watch out for Virginia Cherrill, loveliest of all the new stars.

LOS ANGELES, Sept. 30.—Miss Virginia Cherrill, leading woman for Charlie Chaplin, is confined to her home suffering a sprained ankle and injuries to her hand.

Miss Cherrill turned her ankle and fell recently, driving bits of gravel into the palm of her right hand. Physicians administered serum to prevent lockjaw.

The actress will be able to return to "the set" in a few days, it was said at her home.

Miss Cherrill, a society girl and recognized as a Chicago beauty, went to Hollywood a year or so ago, saying she was not intending to enter the movies. Some weeks after it was announced she had agreed to become Chaplin's leading lady.

VIRGINIA CHERRILL, Who sprained her ankle.

Virginia accepts no responsibility for what happened next at the La Brea Studio. The incident for which she was sacked from the film in mid-November was, she claims, absurd.

'There was no commissary at the studio. I had to "brown bag" it every day. None of us were allowed to leave for lunch. Usually, I just curled up in my dressing-room and read a book. But one day, I did go to lunch, and I came back five minutes late. I'd kept Charlie waiting; that wasn't allowed. We got into a screaming row. And he fired me.'

Memory here is letting Virginia down; the firing was done by a reluctant Carlyle Robinson, who warned Chaplin that he was acting against his own best interests. Virginia also asserts that the entire cast took her side. That contention is possible; Chaplin's reaction to one slip in punctuality must have appeared unduly harsh. Until that November, when she had been recalled to face the cameras, his leading lady had been living in limbo. For the previous six months, while dutifully showing up at the La Brea Studio each working day, she had been kept off the set. Abruptly restored to an active role, with neither explanation nor apology, Virginia's next assignment had been a week of relatively easy scenes, lulling her into a sense of false security. It's probable that she supposed a slightly extended lunch-break would cause no huge problems; it is conceivable – Chaplin had announced his plan to begin shooting the difficult final scene – that Virginia actively courted dismissal. Her pay for a major role was, by Hollywood standards, meagre; the awful possibility of being subjected to yet another 300 retakes could not be ruled out.

Ordered to leave, Virginia made her departure with genuine (or perhaps just well-assumed) insouciance, while Chaplin announced his plans for her replacement. Georgia Hale, who had starred in *The Gold Rush* (playing the dance-hostess with a soft spot for the Tramp), would bring a more professional talent to the role of the Flower-Girl.

Georgia Hale's tests for the part have survived; they show her being tried out in the crucial final scene. Competent and charming, she performs to an invisible Chaplin as if the vampish dance-hostess had suddenly blundered into this later, more subtly nuanced film. Her acting appears knowing and coquettish; leaning forward to coax the Tramp into taking the flower that she proffers, Hale widens her eyes and pouts. Chaplin expressed complete satisfaction. The actress was taken out to supper and informed that the part was hers.

Carlyle Robinson, Chaplin's hard-working publicist, deserves credit at this juncture in the story for rescuing *City Lights* from potential disaster. Courageously, he advised his employer that Hale simply wouldn't do; cunningly, he went further and warned Chaplin that Hale, having been assured the part, was likely to sue if she did not now get what she had been promised.

It's an indication of Chaplin's overwrought state that he accepted Robinson's warning as given fact. Hale (she did not sue) was immediately banished, never to be employed by Chaplin again; instead, to the publicist's dismay, his employer produced yet another candidate. Her name was Marilyn Morgan and she was sixteen years old.

Miss Morgan's age caused as much alarm at the La Brea Studio as her lack of experience. The scandal of Chaplin's divorce from young Lita Grey was still fresh in public memory; nobody wanted the risk of a second scandal over some pregnant teenager. Robinson and one of his colleagues spoke their minds. Marilyn Morgan possessed none of Virginia Cherrill's near-transcendent beauty. Thousands of feet of film had already been shot; whatever Chaplin himself might think, Cherrill looked perfect. There was no reason to replace her; the only concern now was whether or not they could persuade Virginia to come back.

They located her, finally, at San Simeon, enjoying herself with Marion Davies up at Randolph Hearst's private estate.

Virginia's introduction to the giggly, delightful and astute Marion Davies may originally have come through their mutual friend, Evelyn Lederer. By 1929, Virginia herself had become a popular member of the coterie of girlfriends surrounding Miss Davies, of whom it was required only that each should not flirt with Mr Hearst and that none should betray to him Marion's fondness for a drink. (Hearst knew of his mistress's weakness, but wanted to believe that a bad old habit had been brought under control.)

Marion, hearing about the *City Lights* débâcle and wishing, perhaps, to give experienced advice, had swept Virginia off to her lover's hilltop Xanadu, a treasure-house of European loot that also offered an athletic, country-bred girl the chance to go riding, walking and wildlife-watching. (For Virginia, a passionate lover of animals, the nature-loving Hearst's decision to use his vast estate as a safari park was one of the chief attractions of San Simeon.)

Hearst, lacking Marion's sociable nature, had retreated to the couple's private rooms on the fateful day when a frantic call came through from the La Brea Studios. Marion had set off with Virginia on a hunt for one of her secret liquor stashes. The two women had tracked down the missing whisky bottle to a certain laundry-basket when, distantly, they heard Hearst's shrill call: Chaplin was on the line, and demanding to speak to Miss Cherrill. Virginia claims now that she picked up the telephone extension while Marion stood beside her, bottle in hand, laughing and swigging, as she listened in.

'I said to him: "Charlie, you've forgotten. I don't work for you any more." And Charlie said: "You get back down here at once." And then I said: "You go to hell!" And he said: "Listen, I want you here in the morning." And I said: "If you think I'm coming back now . . ."'

At this point, acting as prompter, Marion whispered that her friend should tell Chaplin that her terms had changed. Heeding instructions, Virginia announced that she wasn't prepared to work for $75 a week any more and that, since she had now turned twenty-one, her film contract was no longer valid.

'"It won't do," I told him. So then he rang off. And when he called back, he just said: "OK, what do you want?" And Marian said: "Tell him to double it." So I did. "And besides," I told him. "I can't come back just yet because Queen Marie of Romania is on her way here for a visit, and I've promised to stay." Charlie was wild, but he couldn't do a thing!'

On 21 November, the cast and crew watched Virginia saunter back through the La Brea studio door. Fresh from her encounter with the spirited and publicity-loving Queen Marie, she looked both pretty and determined. For an hour, the Great Director and his Leading Lady conferred with each other in private, in Chaplin's office; when they emerged, both were smiling. Back in her shabby skirt and scuffed flat shoes again, Virginia resumed her familiar post by the studio railings, ready for yet another series of takes of the Flower-girl's first meeting with the Tramp.

'Still doing that damned first scene, and we had a whole year of filming to go,' Virginia sighs. 'It took two years to make *City Lights*, imagine that. It was all the improvising. Everything had to be changed, all the time. Charlie was such a perfectionist. He couldn't let it alone until it was just *exactly* what he wanted.'

And would she have turned the initial offer to be in *City Lights* down, had she known what she was letting herself in for beforehand?

The hypothetical question is too vague, perhaps, to hold Virginia's attention. She gives no answer; instead, the old lady shifts tack. She begins by describing a scene in which Marlene Dietrich, dressed in tight, transparent pink chiffon and high-heeled shoes, dyed to match, paid a visit to the set one dusty summer afternoon. From that, she drifts on, without a pause, to one of her few happy recollections of life at the studio. Strangely, the scene Virginia evokes is the filming of a prizefight, the setting for her own first encounter with Chaplin.

'Everyone in Hollywood loved boxing back then, and Charlie was so funny when he was dancing around in the ring. Oh, that scene from the film was such a joy, it was wonderful to watch! There were about a hundred extras and Charlie asked all his friends to come along. It was like a party; we had such fun. And Charlie, well, he loved every minute of it.'

I have listened to the taped interviews many times. This is the only moment at which Virginia Cherrill speaks about Chaplin with something that approaches tenderness.

The filming of *City Lights* officially ended on 5 October 1930. Chaplin remained anxious and dissatisfied. Towards the end of the month, Virginia was summoned back to the studio for one last afternoon session before Rollie Totheroh's camera. Once more, Charlie needed to film that extraordinary culminating scene: the final moment of recognition. This time, however, Chaplin's enormous demands were all focused upon his own performance; for once, he made no complaints about Virginia.

The result, after seventeen takes, was sublime; Chaplin never again communicated emotion with such enigmatic power and poignant sensitivity as in the closing seconds of *City Lights*. His shining eyes seem to fill the screen. The viewer is left with a sense of overpowering joy, reconciliation, and grief. For, although, in this classic scene of silent cinema, nothing can ever be explicitly said, it's clear that the moment of recognition is also the moment of finality. The Flower-Girl may be moved almost to tears by the discovery of her benefactor, and devastated by the evidence of the hardship he has endured, but no future for them together is ever promised, or even intimated. The Tramp, we know, must walk away; the Girl, albeit with newly opened eyes, must go back to her everyday life. All this, miraculously, is communicated in Chaplin's tender, tragic gaze. Understandably, Chaplin considered it to be the finest single scene of his career.

Audiences seem to have agreed. On 30 January 1931, a crowd of 25,000 assembled outside the palatial new Los Angeles Theatre to watch Charlie Chaplin arrive, together with his special guests, Mr and Mrs Albert Einstein, for the première of *City Lights*. Still celebrated as one of the ten greatest romantic films of all time (*Casablanca* usually rates top prize), *City Lights* became an immediate, and international, hit. In New York, it set new records for attendance over a twelve-week run. Arriving for the London opening, a fortnight later, Chaplin, mobbed by fans, was proclaimed by an admiring George Bernard Shaw to be the film world's only true genius.

Chaplin, who spent most of 1931 touring the globe and promoting his work, ended the year with a worldwide profit of five million dollars and a thicker waistline. Virginia Cherrill, who had not even been invited to the Los Angeles première, and who had managed to earn just over $5,000 for two years of work, suddenly found herself praised across the globe, and in demand throughout the film industry.

Whatever Virginia's view of Chaplin, his act of plucking an unknown girl from her seat at a Friday-night boxing match had shaped for life how others would perceive her. From that moment on, Virginia Cherrill would forever be identified with her performance as the Flower-Girl whose serene face forms a luminous contrast to the undertones of criminality, vice and financial havoc that ripple through this most emotional, and sorrowful, of Chaplin's works.

'I watched you in *City Lights*,' a glamorous young Indian admirer (Bhaiya, Maharaja of Cooch Behar) would write to Virginia several years later, his memory of her performance as vivid then as upon first viewing. 'Oh, and darling Virginia, how much I cried!'

6

THE BEAUTY AND THE TOAD

(1930–1932)

'Underneath all the phoney tinsel on the outside . . .'

City Lights was the only major Hollywood film of the Twenties on which Chaplin worked without going to bed with his female lead. While no suggestion has ever been made of a sexual relationship between Chaplin and the twenty-year-old Cherrill, it is difficult to believe that such a practised womaniser never tried to lay a finger on such a ravishing young woman. It would have been out of character for him not to have done so. If he did indeed make advances and if she in turn rejected him, the atmosphere upon the set of *City Lights* must have become almost electric with rage, and the blame can be laid at the director's door.

There's no doubt that the relationship on set between director and star was fraught: was the fault Virginia's own? Comments were made, over the course of years, about Virginia Cherrill's lack of commitment to a role she was considered fortunate to win. Chaplin, a fiercely professional workaholic who had reached a crisis point both in his career and his private life, needed to draw an unforgettable performance out of a young girl who does not – as an old lady – dispute that she had looked upon each day spent on the La Brea set as a personal martyrdom.

Rumours circulated, back at the time, that Virginia behaved, throughout the filming of *City Lights*, like a privileged minx, turning up at the studio exhausted by late nights out on the town. Such behaviour – when we remember the austere regime that even such a celebrated actress as Mary Pickford imposed upon herself when working – would have infuriated Chaplin. But were the rumours true? One member of the studio team later alleged that a thick coat of cosmetics was needed to mask the evidence of Virginia's off-screen activities.

'We all had to wear a ton of stuff on our faces,' the old lady protests. 'Including Charlie!'

The possession of a beautiful face, in combination with top billing in a Chaplin film, must have caused envy; recollections of Virginia's behaviour were assuredly tinged with malice. Nevertheless, a glance at Miss Cherrill's private life during her last year of working, on and off, on *City Lights* suggests that her mind was often occupied elsewhere.

There was, for example, the case of her engagement, broken off in 1930, to the actor James 'Buster' West. A gangling, good-looking and – at the time – celebrated comedian, Buster West had made his name as a brilliant exponent of the sole-slapping form of tap dance that he best demonstrated – clad in a pair of oversized shoes – in his cameo performance in the 1924 film *Broadway After Dark* (a young newcomer, beautiful Norma Shearer, took the lead opposite Adolphe Menjou). Seven years older than Virginia, West was working, at the time of their brief romance, on a series of comic short films in which he appeared alongside his actor father.

West's star soon faded, and Virginia, in later years, seldom spoke of him, perhaps because the relationship had lacked significance. The brief news item reporting an end to their engagement states only that 'work' had separated the young couple, and that 'Virginia prefers her career'. The accompanying photograph of a cheery Virginia flourishing the page of a screenplay suggests that the Chaplin studio had seized upon an excuse to promote her forthcoming role in *City Lights*.

Buster West merits a mention here mostly because of the nature of his career. He was a comedian. If one quality continued to attract Virginia in both men and women until the end of her life,

(DAILY TIMES Photo)

CAREER BEFORE LOVE.—Virginia Cherill, Chicago girl appearing in pictures as leading woman for Charlie Chaplin, has broken her engagement to Buster West, stage comedian. Their work separated them, and Virginia prefers her career.

Virginia announces a broken engagement — and looks radiant.

it was their ability to make her laugh. It was for this gift that she adored Marion Davies, Carole Lombard, Humphrey Bogart, David Niven and, above all, Cary Grant. Wit came to this group of performers as easily as breathing. 'Hearst Come, Hearst Served' was Marion's lewdly comic way of apologising when her lover snatched her away from a group of friends; Virginia, recalling how Carole Lombard presented Clark Gable (upon their first date) with a shoulder of ham emblazoned with his portrait, thought Carole crasser than Marion, but even funnier ('pure filth, though, worse than a truck driver'). Yet none of them, not even the stylishly comic Cary Grant, sharp as a rapier with his wordplay and double entendres, could match the wit of the musician and composer with whom Virginia began a relationship shortly after ending her engagement to Buster West. This brilliant depressive was the man with whom she maintained an erratic affair that lasted, sporadically, over the next two years, even surviving her lover's first brief stab at married life.

'Oscar Levant!' Virginia says suddenly, retrieving his name. 'Darling Oscar! Oh dear God, you have no idea what a slob that man was.'

'Underneath this flabby exterior,' Oscar liked to say of himself, 'lies an enormous lack of character.'

The memory of this former flame puts a girlish brightness into Virginia's voice. When Oscar Levant stayed at the Beverly Wilshire, she tells Teresa, he wouldn't let the maid in. Every chair in the suite was full of music manuscripts, papers and coffee cups with cigarettes put out in them. It was filthy, and so – as Virginia is quick to stress – was its chaotic and talented young resident.

'There's a fine line between genius and insanity,' Oscar was sometimes at pains to point out to friends. 'I have erased that line.'

'I can't remember a time when he wasn't covered with cigarette ash and food, and he looked like a toad. And he was an absolute darling. I *loved* Oscar.'

The old lady sounds fond and elated, and it's a little sad because, while Teresa can be heard exclaiming at her friend's connection to such an intriguing character, it is plain that she herself isn't sure who Oscar Levant might actually be. I, too, knew nothing of Oscar – a virtuoso pianist with a mordant wit and a genius for insults that even his witty Irish namesake could scarcely have matched – until I began researching Virginia Cherrill's life.

'I'm a concert pianist,' Oscar would occasionally lament. 'That's a pretentious way of saying I'm unemployed.'

Oscar Levant arrived in Los Angeles on the tidal wave of musical and theatrical talent that swept into town with the coming of the talkies. Actors who owned splendid voices were being eagerly sought; so were composers who were prepared to work to tight deadlines. Oscar was exaggerating when he wrote that every songwriter who could play a chord was hired by Hollywood – but not by much. Imported in 1929, to recreate the performance he had recently delivered on Broadway in the musical *Burlesque*, the talented Oscar stayed on to compose film scores for RKO, while enjoying a brief fling with *Burlesque*'s pretty star, Nancy Carroll.

An additional incentive to remain on the West Coast was the arrival in Los Angeles of the one man of whom young Oscar Levant (he was just twenty-three) felt in awe. George Gershwin, already famous for musical scores that included the celebrated *Rhapsody in Blue* (1924), had been commissioned to produce the music for *Delicious*. (This was the disappointingly mediocre film in which Virginia played her first role following the success of *City Lights*.) Gershwin arrived in Hollywood in November 1930, together with Ira, his songwriting older brother. Oscar, starved of congenial company, welcomed the musical siblings with open arms, as his worthy peers.

'What the world needs is more geniuses with humility,' Oscar once wistfully opined. 'There are so few of us left.'

Oscar Levant: 'I loved Oscar'.

Levant had already made friends with the Gershwins back in New York where, entranced by George's music, and always eager for home comforts without the responsibility of home care, he had settled into a near-familial role in the cosy ménage presided over by George's sister-in-law, Lenore. His lack of domestic graces was forgiven for the passion with which young Oscar took on the role of medium and interpreter, playing Gershwin's music (with the surprising concurrence of the composer) more sympathetically than anybody else the Gershwins knew.

'I play Gershwin,' Oscar would assert, 'even better than *George* does.'

(Significantly, when George Gershwin took up the baton for a concert of his own new music at New York's Lewisohn Stadium in 1932, Oscar was there along with him, straddling the piano stool and taking applause with the ferocious grin that his friend Harpo Marx compared to sunlight in Moscow – delightful, and rare.)

At some point in the autumn of 1930, Virginia sat down at a Hollywood dinner-party and heard herself being addressed, out of a cloud of smoke, by a sallow, broad-shouldered youth with slicked-down curls and heavy-lidded eyes.

'I'm sorry,' Oscar said in a rasp that Harpo later described as sounding like an oboe being played under a blanket. 'They shouldn't have sat me next to *you*! I mean – hell, that's not what I mean. They should have sat *you* next to somebody *else*!'

And that, they both confirmed, was how it all began, with Virginia growing offended and then, as the considerable force of Oscar's charm became apparent, feeling herself ready to melt. By dessert, they had made a date.

Oscar Levant was an unlikely beau for the girl who was currently being described as the prettiest in Hollywood. Physically unprepossessing, he was untidy, surly, selfish and opinionated. On the other hand, he was the most entertaining man she had ever met.

'I only make jokes,' Oscar (who made jokes incessantly) would warn Virginia, 'when I'm feeling insecure . . .'

For herself, Virginia loved walking, dancing, looking at nature, strolling on beaches and listening to stories. Oscar didn't like listening to anybody else for more than a minute.

'I have given up reading,' Oscar would confess to Virginia. 'I find it takes my mind off myself.'

Oscar loathed exercise, never danced, fretted about his health and thought looking at nature was a waste of his eyes. Intolerant of fools, he liked the company of people as sharp-witted as himself. But he also had a weak spot for beautiful women – so long as they were bright; not all of them were.

'Every time I look at you,' Oscar would growl at a simple-minded starlet, 'I get a fierce desire to be lonesome.'

Virginia was a witty woman, but she could never have matched her eccentric lover's line in jokes. What bewitched him – besides her undeniable beauty – was her quick intelligence, her lack of pretension, her affectionate nature and her delight in anything that made her laugh.

And she?

The response, this time, is crisp. 'Oscar was sexy, clever, and the funniest man I'd ever met. Good enough? It was, for me.'

It was Oscar, rather than Chaplin or Buster West, who gave Virginia the entrée into Hollywood society, a world he knew to his fingertips, as the most coveted and dreaded of guests, the man who could reduce a spoilt beauty to tears before enthralling the room with the eloquence of his piano technique. Oscar knew everybody.

'I knew Doris Day,' Oscar once famously bragged, 'before she became a virgin.'

Listening to Virginia's tales of those times, it isn't always easy to be sure how many of her stories are based upon firsthand experience. Did Lenore and Ira Gershwin really want Miss Cherrill to marry their cherished George? Apparently, so.

Virginia at home in Hollywood.

'I used to sit next to him on the piano stool when he played at parties,' Virginia informs Teresa. 'At least, whenever Oscar didn't get there first! Lenore was sure that George and I would suit, and we did like each other, but we never actually did a thing. We didn't even kiss. George was crazy about that dancer Marilyn Miller – you know, the pretty one who was in the show he wrote the music for: *Rosalie*. I don't think she felt the same way about him, and that was a shame because George was sweet.'

Virginia and her mother were living together, by then, in North Havenhurst, just around the corner from the famous Schwab's Drug Store – where all the young stars went to be noticed – and close to the Garden of Allah. That august establishment, according to Virginia, was where everybody interesting stayed when they first arrived from New York. The food, she says, was terrible. She thinks that there's a photo of her battling to finish some undercooked horror at the Garden – somewhere.

'It's in one of the scrapbooks. Who else was there, back then? Sheilah Graham and Scott Fitzgerald. Erroll Flynn – or was that later, when he was sharing with David Niven and waiting to be discovered? And Tallulah! Oh yes, Tallulah . . .'

Voted one of the ten most remarkable women in England in 1927, after making her stage début there in 1923, the Alabama-born Tallulah Bankhead had been lured to Hollywood in 1931, as Paramount's challenge to the supremacy of Marlene Dietrich and Greta Garbo. On screen, Tallulah proved wooden; in private, she combined sexual voracity with a witty tongue of which she herself was the most frequent target. ('I'm as pure as the driven slush,' combined self-mockery with a dig at a lady of questionable morals whose maiden name had been Sledge.)

'Tallulah . . .!' Virginia once again sighs. 'She had a maid then, very proper, called Evie. One morning Tallulah looked up at Evie bringing in her breakfast and announced that she'd just had the best lay of her life. "Anyone we know this time, madame?" Evie asked. Tallulah was *so* bad! When she was in England, she'd drive down to Eton for a day and screw the little boys. I expect they loved it. Bea Lillie used to tell such stories about her. You'd never believe them. Bea had been in England herself, you know, when she was first married to Robert Peel, that man who was so mean to her.'

Beatrice Lillie, whose reputation for being the funniest woman in the world kept her employed in revues and musicals for over fifty years, made her début in England in 1914 and was already a popular celebrity when she married Sir Robert Peel in 1920. Sir Robert, showing scant respect for his wife's reputation, promptly took a mistress and introduced her to British friends as his preferred spouse.

'He lost a lot of friends that way, and Bea came out to Hollywood. She never divorced him; she was always Lady Peel, but not one bit grand about it.'

Teresa, like me, needs to be reminded that Bea Lillie was once classed with Bert Lahr and Gertrude Lawrence, and that her best-known sketch was as a flummoxed matron attempting to make an order for one double dozen double damask table napkins, and that Cole Porter wrote songs for her.

'Bea was wonderful. She was a friend through all my life, although she must have been going on twenty years older than me, I'd guess. She never told me her age. Bea wasn't a film actress, any more than Tallulah. The stage was where she belonged. She could sing, she could dance, and she never cared what she looked like. And she was *so* funny. Even Oscar didn't make me laugh so much as Bea . . .'

The memory of Oscar has stirred up forgotten scenes in the old lady's mind. Now, as Teresa sits listening, Virginia starts to describe the time when Oscar Levant and Irving Berlin occupied adjoining suites at the Wilshire and discovered that neither of them could compose unless they had room to pace. The suites, it emerged, shared a single balcony that both men coveted.

'So they fixed this schedule: Oscar from two to four, Irving from four to six, and so on. And Irving wanted Oscar's help in transposing – everything had to be shifted to his key – but he couldn't bear to go into Oscar's room, or to ask him into his. Irving was a most fastidious man and Oscar – well, I told you about Oscar's habits. They were the original Odd Couple, those two.'

Bea Lillie, revue and musical star, hailed in her day as the funniest woman in the world. She became one of Virginia's closest friends.

Prompted by Teresa's suggestion that Harpo Marx, like so many others, might have been staying at the Garden of Allah back then, while working for Paramount, Virginia recalls that Harpo was one of Oscar Levant's closest friends – one who had even, some time later, endured him as a daily house-guest for a year.

'And Oscar was *not* a good guest,' she adds. 'But Harpo himself wasn't the easiest of men.'

Making her case, Virginia describes a time when Harpo was indeed staying at the Garden of Allah and Rachmaninov moved into the adjoining room. The eminent composer promptly installed a piano, upon which he liked to practise, loudly, and over long periods of time. Harpo – an incessant reader – grew irritated.

'Harpo couldn't stand any form of background noise,' Virginia explains.

So, during an entire afternoon, as Virginia tells it, a baleful Harpo sat twanging out the first four bars of the Maestro's celebrated Prelude, a popular chestnut that Rachmaninov had penned at nineteen, and that – after a thousand encores – he had come to detest. The composer soon got Harpo's message.

'Harpo stayed; Rachmaninov left,' Virginia finishes. 'End of a friendship that never was . . .'

But Teresa seems eager for her friend to offer a more detailed portrait of party-going life back in those days of old Hollywood. On the tape, I hear her enquire whether Virginia remembers much about going to Ocean House, Marion Davies's enormous seaside mansion at Santa Monica? Did Virginia attend the birthday-dinner at which twenty-one waiters paraded monumental slabs of ice-cream around the dining-table, each festooned with an initial from the name of Marion's lover . . . ?

'Marion could eat more ice-cream than anybody I knew, except for Clark Gable.' Virginia laughs. 'They'd compete. But I don't remember the birthday party for WR . . .'

That Ocean House bash, she speculates, must have taken place around the time when Leslie Howard, one of a group of Broadway actors – Tracy, Bogart and Gable were among them – came out to try their luck in Hollywood.

'Leslie had his first break in a film with Marion. She was crazy about him. WR never knew what was going on, but Mrs Howard certainly did. They were the strangest combination. Ruth Howard was built like a bus and Leslie was delicate as a deer – and so clever! He used to write parodies for *The New Yorker*. Leslie was sharp as a whip.'

Listening to Virginia's recollections – and too absorbed here, for a while, to make notes – I begin to wonder how the energy and charisma of all these fabulous personalities could possibly have been contained within a single room. It's unimaginable, and yet I can hear her starting to describe yet another such gathering, where all the stars showed up swathed in baby clothes, and how Oscar and his friend Gershwin were there – although more formally attired than the other guests – fighting over which one of them could first sit on the piano stool.

And what about Chaplin, Teresa asks: did he often go along to such events?

'Never,' Virginia answers. 'Charlie didn't like parties. Marion said that Charlie would rather walk the streets all night than stand around drinking and swapping gossip. But Oscar – Oscar never went to bed. He made that joke, the famous one about Hollywood tinsel – "Underneath all the phoney tinsel on the outside . . ."'

'"... Lies the *real* tinsel!"' Teresa completes. 'That was him? I never knew who first said it.'

'Oscar had all the best put-downs. Although being cynical didn't stop him from having a good time – he should never have married that girl!' Virginia suddenly announces. 'She didn't approve of his going to parties – and that's what Oscar enjoyed best. He liked to be there, right at the centre of things, but playing the piano, so he was cut off from the crowd. That's when he looked happy.'

Virginia herself never contemplated marrying Oscar Levant. She withdrew gracefully when, early in 1932, her lover announced his betrothal to a former showgirl from the Follies. Perhaps she knew him well enough, by then, to guess that a wife who didn't approve of his jokes or his domestic habits was unlikely to last long (the Levant marriage was over within a few months). Perhaps – having found another admirer – Virginia was relieved to see the back of witty, moody, exhausting Oscar Levant.

In March 1932, several papers printed reports that Miss Virginia Cherrill, the celebrated Chaplin star, was about to marry one of America's wealthiest men, a philanthropist from the upper reaches of New York society. Their marriage, it was announced, would take place in Tahiti, aboard the *Nourmahal*, the recently built luxury yacht belonging to Vincent Astor, head of his American clan. In none of the newspaper reports was it indicated that Virginia Cherrill had only just secured her divorce from one Irving Adler.

Vincent Astor, twenty years old when his unappealingly acquisitive father drowned on the *Titanic*, displayed a more conscientious attitude towards his great fortune. While John Jacob Astor had accumulated enormous swathes of New York property with no care for the welfare of his tenants, Vincent dedicated himself to social reform. The worst of the family's city slum housing was sold; the money was reinvested in charitable enterprises; Vincent's first wife, a handsome and forceful lesbian, endorsed and supported this attitude as zealously as did his third, Brooke Russell, who outlived him.

Vincent, while honourable, lacked both charm and good looks; his closest friend and favourite yachting companion, William Rhinelander Stewart, was more Virginia's type, a handsome playboy who kept company with the likes of Cole Porter and Elsa Maxwell and who never rose from bed before midday.

'Mr Stewart,' he instructed his valet to inform over-eager morning callers, 'has gone out for a run around the reservoir.'

William Rhinelander Stewart was a regular attendant of the Hollywood parties that Virginia has been describing to Teresa. The two met at a dinner given by Beatrice Lillie; a few weeks later, the handsome and eligible Stewart invited Virginia to come along with him on Vincent Astor's annual yacht-trip to the South Seas, or to join them there. As the party prepared to depart, reports were published of the couple's plans for marriage.

Those stories were, according to Virginia's recorded memories, no more than fantasies, cooked up by the press. She speaks with equal affection both of 'Will' Rhinelander Stewart and of the beautiful and unpretentious woman he later married. Making her point, she shows off a picture of the three of them dining together at Ciro's, in New York City, in 1939.

'There's the proof,' she states. 'Nothing to it. Never was.'

Much later, Teresa unearths, in the cause of my research, a large glossy photograph sent to Virginia from a smart nightclub in Cuba. Virginia herself, in old age, has written a note on the back, confirming that the two men in the photograph are Astor and Stewart. Stewart sits alone across the table, facing camera; Astor, typically, has his back to the photographer. The sender, Bea Lillie, tells her that Rhinelander Stewart ('Will') is 'all alone and pining for you', hopes that she, too, is behaving herself ('being as good a girl as Will is – I mean – you know what I mean') and finishes by telling Virginia to 'hurry up and come to Tahiti – but don't tell our plans.' A further note by Virginia confirms that she did sail out to Tahiti – she travelled on a New Zealand-bound freighter from San Francisco – to join Bea Lillie and Rhinelander Stewart aboard the *Nourmahal*.

Discretion emerges from her taped interviews and press-cuttings as one of the chief virtues possessed by Virginia. Her surviving friends praise a woman who was vivacious and witty, but never

Virginia's latest fiancé, William Rhinelander Stewart, alone across the table. Back to camera: Vincent Astor. The card is written to Virginia by Bea Lillie.

knowingly unkind. Amidst all the frivolous chat about Hollywood life, there never escapes from her lips a single word of personal betrayal or real malice. Chaplin's predilection for young girls, for example, is never mentioned by Virginia, and she herself never speculates upon the mysterious death of Thomas Ince, or alludes, beyond a passing reference, to the drinking habits of Marion Davies. Harm is not consciously inflicted.

Given that context of uncommon reticence, it is intriguing that Virginia says little about her friendship with Astor and Stewart, and that she makes no mention of her expedition with them in the South Seas. It's possible that she and her fellow passengers – they included Irving and Ellen Berlin, Bea Lillie and Princess Marie Bonaparte – were unaware that they were travelling upon a spy ship. It is more likely, however, that they did possess such knowledge and shrugged it all off: in an era when many an elegant yacht was quietly transporting an unofficial cargo of liquor, drugs or even guns, a little patriotic espionage was surely not to be regarded as high crime?

Astor, the yacht's owner, stood at the centre of a gentlemanly spy ring, operating for the benefit of the country. The focus point of the ring was a private room on East 62nd Street in New York City. Here, since 1927, Astor had been holding monthly meetings with a group of powerful friends: Nelson Doubleday (the publisher, and – with his wife – a lifelong friend to Virginia), Marshall Field (the store-owner's heir), Winthrop Aldrich (one of the directors of the Chase National Bank) and David Bruce (a career diplomat). Voyaging each year in the Pacific aboard the *Nourmahal*, Vincent Astor gathered and brought back to the club information that he had gleaned from private meetings with politicians and public figures. Pooling their information at their monthly reunion, the influential friends arranged to pass on their distilled knowledge to the appropriate government authorities. Long before the establishment of the CIA in 1947, Astor's espionage ring formed one of America's most pragmatic ways of gathering information crucial to its foreign policy. The network's existence, never publicly discussed, would remain hidden for close to half a century. Virginia, at the time that she was being interviewed by Teresa, believed that the group's activities were still unknown. This, perhaps, explains her reluctance to discuss anything to do with the *Nourmahal*.

A life that embraced both Oscar Levant's Hollywood and the elegant social world of men like Rhinelander Stewart is likely to have been both demanding and privileged. Perhaps it was as well that Virginia still had a career to maintain; little though she enjoyed working as a screen actress, employment provided a degree of ballast. Evenings spent in the company of George Gershwin or lounging in a steamer chair aboard the *Nourmahal* helped keep at bay the hard realities of the worst economic crisis America had yet experienced. In the film world, however, as we know from Scott Fitgerald's bitter stories about Pat Hobby, and Nathaniel West's savage tale of Hollywood's outsiders, *The Day of the Locust*, the spectre of depression was difficult to escape. Here, however blessed her own life might seem, Virginia could not fail to note the misfortunes of a thousand hopeful starlets who were almost as beautiful as herself – and certainly, in professional terms, more experienced and hardworking. She had, as she readily acknowledges to Teresa, been extraordinarily blessed; the lives of these young women could so easily have been hers. What if Uncle Joe had not taken her under his wing when she came to Hollywood? What if she had chosen not to attend the Friday night boxing match? What if Chaplin's publicist had not opposed his employer's dismissal of an unknown and, on occasion, unpunctual young female lead? Fortune had smiled; one of Virginia's most likeable qualities – a large part of her endearing lack of pretentiousness – was that she always acknowledged the fact. She was lucky, and she knew it.

In March 1931, following the enormous success of *City Lights*, Fox Films placed her under contract. A few days later, Virginia was called in for the traditional publicity photograph. Two pretty blondes pose inside an imposing studio limousine. '*Miss Marion Lessing: Miss Virginia Cherrill: Fox Film Stars*' reads the sign propped beneath them upon the convertible's running-board. Flowers bedeck the limo's hood, as if for a wedding, but the chauffeur looks as if he's been embalmed, and the girls have the frozen stare of a pair of lovely does transfixed by headlights, unsure of whether they are being escorted to a tranquil deer park or the slaughterhouse. Miss Lessing disappeared, quite rapidly, from view; Virginia's newfound celebrity ensured that she was called upon to consolidate that early success [plate 5].

'*Up the River?*' Virginia ventures despairingly, when Teresa prompts her. 'I can't remember. I think that was the first I did for Fox. With Bogey, yes, that's it. I was playing the romantic lead, with George O'Brien and Spencer Tracy.'

This recollection sounds promising: I'm eager to check it out. Humphrey Bogart did indeed have his first success in *Up the River*, along with that other newcomer to the screen, Spencer Tracy. But there's a problem: the film was released in 1930, when Virginia was still under contract to Chaplin. On tape, she describes the movie as a western, and claims, inaccurately, that George O'Brien was among the cast. Could she be thinking of *The Holy Terror*, from 1931, a western in which both Bogart and O'Brien played, but *not* Tracy – and certainly not Virginia Cherrill?

Was that the answer? I'm beginning to realise the difficulty with being literal-minded about these informally taped interviews: Virginia's just chatting to her trusted friend; she doesn't feel under pressure to be accurate. The titles and dates of old films interest her less, now, than the memories they serve to trigger within her of lost times and cherished friends.

'Spence and Bogey had made a terrific lot of money as actors in New York, you see, but out in Hollywood, nobody had ever heard of them. Busy film directors didn't often find themselves back in New York City.'

Bogart and she used to sit about, around lunchtime, in a place called the Thomas Club, Virginia remembers, while her friend waited for somebody to notice him and display an interest.

'All the producers went there. We could see them, but nobody ever looked over at Bogey. He and I used to spend every minute together, back then, fooling around and cracking jokes. We weren't lovers, but we really were like soulmates. And later, we never lost touch. I think they cast me in that western film simply with the idea of keeping him off the bottle. I was good at that. He even started to claim he liked the taste of milk! We had such fun: I remember how we'd catch each other's eye and just start laughing. Nothing ever seemed to get done.'

One of this merry couple was an ambitious professional actor; the other was a pretty young woman who liked to enjoy herself. Bogart stopped laughing long enough to turn in a creditable performance in *The Holy Terror*. Virginia, never disguising that she preferred time off the set to the tedious hours during which she had to toil before the cameras, was replaced by a more dedicated actress.

Virginia Cherrill did succeed, however, in making three films for Fox in 1931. *Delicious* starred the popular combination of tall, handsome Charlie Farrell, an athletic New Englander, playing a millionaire, with tiny, pretty Janet Gaynor as a poor Scots girl travelling to America. Virginia, appearing as Gaynor's ousted rival, turned in a good performance and was well liked by her co-actors. But not even the pair of co-stars who had, four years earlier, launched the internationally successful *Seventh Heaven* – nor even, for that matter, a glorious Gershwin score (including the whole of his Second Rhapsody) – could rescue *Delicious* from the doldrums. Charlie Farrell's handsome face carried less appeal for the audience now that they could hear the flat, impassive vowels of his New England voice. Virginia, while witty in person, also suffered from having a lightness of tone which – captured by the primitive machinery of early sound recordings – sounded thin. I find it hard to connect Virginia's brittle film accents to the humorous warmth and liveliness of tone I have become familiar with on Teresa's tapes. Nevertheless, she was allowed to feed a few weak jokes to her co-stars:

> DIANA VAN BERGH (Virginia Cherrill): 'Bet you fifty dollars you don't even know the words to "The Star-Spangled Banner".'
>
> LARRY BEAUMONT (Charlie Farrell): 'I don't even remember what show it was in.'

Delicious flopped. Next came *Girls Demand Excitement*, in which Virginia's finishing-school English earned her another part as a pretty socialite, the love interest for a hard-working young college student with dark eyes, floppy hair and a pronounced jut to his chin. John Wayne, liberated at last from drudgery as a prop man, laboured hard to make an impact; a weak plot and unconvincing dialogue failed to attract substantial audiences. Wayne's friendship with Virginia managed to survive what he would later dismiss as the worst film of his career [plate 6].

Finally, there came *The Brat*. This project, based like *Delicious* upon a Broadway production, appeared more promising. The seasoned director was John Ford; the star, a tiny, saucer-eyed girl with eloquent legs and a vivacious screen personality, was a certain Sally O'Neil. Virginia, here, was shackled with the thankless role of the snobbish sister to a smart young novelist (the stalwart Alan Dinehart), who brings home a lively gamine (O'Neil) to provide inspiration for his work.

Back in Carthage, proud posters announced the presentation of their very own home-grown movie-star in a 'girl-fight' film; the artist's poster depicted blonde and delicate Virginia squaring off with a truculent Miss O'Neil. Director Ford himself later described the film as a complete dud; even the most loyal Carthaginians had to give a thumbs-down to *The Brat*.

Virginia, thanks to the fact that her own roles had been slight, survived this trio of disasters without much damage; critics, remembering the performance of the exquisite Flower-Girl of *City Lights*, continued to describe her as a star. Fox Films, not displeased by her friendships with the Gershwins and Vincent Astor – and delighted by rumours of her engagement to William Rhinelander Stewart, one of the richest men in the country – decided that Miss Cherrill's publicity value outweighed the lack of progress in her cinematic career.

The Fox producers' faith was rewarded in the autumn of 1932 when, following a brief return to the embrace of Oscar Levant (Oscar's marriage to a New York showgirl had collapsed almost as soon as it was formalised), beautiful Virginia Cherrill's name became linked to that of one of the most promising newcomers in all of Hollywood.

His name was Cary Grant.

7

CARY

(1932–1934)

'Cary and Florek. Truly, they are the only men I ever was in love with.'

They laughed and they squabbled, Virginia remembers, almost every day of the three years that they spent together.

They couldn't even agree about the occasion on which they first met. Was it, as Cary told one biographer, during one of those beach parties tossed by Marion Davies, out at Ocean House? Or did Virginia come along, as Grant told another, to a party thrown by handsome Randolph Scott in the house the two actors had agreed to share (after they'd got talking one day, in the commissary, at Adolph Zukor's Paramount Studios)?

Definitely, the meeting took place in the autumn of 1932, shortly after the newly separated (and, yes, greatly relieved) Oscar Levant had sauntered back into Virginia's life. But Oscar, on this particular occasion, wasn't present. As Cary remembered it, he glanced just once over the bevy of pretty girls Randolph Scott had summoned to their home on West Live Oak Drive; immediately, his eyes fastened upon a slightly built blonde with an appealing laugh and the most enchanting face that he had ever encountered (recognisable, only after a while, as belonging to the exquisite Flower-Girl of Chaplin's most recent film).

'I fell in love with her the moment I saw her.'

That statement, throughout the course of Cary Grant's entire life, never varied. Cary's first meeting with Virginia had been, for him, a *coup de foudre*. He had found the girl with whom he wanted to spend the rest of his life.

'She was the most beautiful woman I'd ever seen.'

Such praise was an uncommon tribute, especially as it came from the actor millions of women across the globe would, one day, declare the most handsome *man* they had ever seen.

It isn't clear whether the two of them had the chance to exchange more than a few words before Virginia left the party (probably intending to spend the rest of that evening with Oscar). Cary only remembered that he himself spent the remainder of that night placing phone-calls to the home in North Havenhurst that the young actress shared with her mother. Blanche Cherrill, who would always afterwards harbour doubts about Cary Grant as a suitable consort for her daughter, was made uneasy by such persistence. Virginia, however – arriving home two hours later – laughed off her mother's fears and took the next call herself. An agreement was made for dinner the following evening. One stipulation was imposed on the eager young man: his date (in his recollection) announced that she would be bringing her mother along.

Virginia offers her friend Teresa a different version of how the romance commenced. Her story starts at an angle, as she thinks back to the fun she was having during the summer of 1932 with the man she calls 'my first real beau', a breezy, sporting type called Tommy Mullins, a yachtsman from a wealthy San Francisco family, with whom she used to enjoy dancing the tango (when Sabio Cougar took to the bandstand for 'Latin Hour' at the Cocoanut Grove).

'Tommy Lee was the best dancer in California,' she declares – and sighs when Teresa queries this dashing boyfriend's sudden change of name. Never *mind* about his name, Virginia responds. The point – the link to meeting Cary – is that Tommy had a lawyer-friend who used to crew for him. And now she simply has to say something about Silver!

Silver?

I expect the interviewer to grow impatient with these butterfly-flights of digression from a voluble old lady, but long friendship (Teresa tells me that she has known Virginia Cherrill for over fifty years) enables her to be relaxed and amused.

Silver, as Virginia is eager to explain, belonged to Milton Burns, a former lawyer who became a film agent. Milton crewed for Tommy's yacht, and Silver was always with him.

'Silver was one of the gang, a German shepherd, and a wonderful dog. He held the rope in his mouth whenever we docked, stood there for as long as it took, gentle as anything. Oh, I did so love Silver!' Virginia cries out.

I'm already conscious of how often the old lady breaks off her monologues to ask Teresa about the whereabouts of her own dog, or whether her husband has yet taken the animal for a walk. Her flights from Irving to Buster, to Oscar, to Bill Rhinelander Stewart and now a new beau, Tommy, suggest that Virginia inherited or replicated her own father's restlessness; this need not preclude a longing for fidelity of the undemanding kind that a friendly German shepherd could supply.

'So did Milton Burns introduce you to Cary?' Teresa prompts, but first she has to hear about Milton's marriage to an actress called Marion von Nielberg.

'You'll see,' Virginia insists, as her friend audibly sighs. 'It all connects. Marion was still in love with someone else, after she married Milton. She made me act as her beard – you know, the cover. We'd do foursome dates with her beau. And that's what we were doing, one September night, when Milton took us along to a preview of *Blonde Venus*. They were showing it downtown, at the Paramount Theatre. Marlene was doing her siren act, with Cary for her leading man. Not that they gave him much to do, except to look excited when Marlene stepped out of her gorilla-suit.'

I'd forgotten that film, but now, as Virginia summons it back for Teresa, I recall the bizarre scene, filmed by a doting Joseph von Sternberg, in which Dietrich performs a monkey-dance, complete with armpit-scratches, in a Paris nightclub to which playboy Cary has come for a drink.

'You know how men sit with their knees like this?'

(Virginia's voice sounds excited: is the sound I now detect on the cassette the rustle of bedclothes, brushed aside for a demonstration of Grant's posture?)

'Cary's at his table, watching Marlene slip out of her costume, ready to start vamping. He's sitting there and Marlene walks right up between his thighs. You can see the nipples standing out like bottle-tops under her dress. "Boing" – like this. So crude.'

Pen poised, I await a revelation. Biographers of Cary Grant and Marlene Dietrich have always dismissed the idea of an off-screen romance. Could this moment of displayed desire have implied to Virginia some deeper significance?

'They never got along,' Virginia says; and then she starts to relate how Milton Burns took his wife and their two friends for dinner, after the preview, at the Brown Derby. Across Wilshire Boulevard, as they walked to the parking lot after the meal, Milton took note of two tall men, chatting to their female companions, over on the far side of the road. He hustled his little group through the traffic, plainly anxious to effect immediate introductions.

'Girls,' Milton announced, 'meet Randy Scott. And – what a coincidence! – this is Cary Grant, the guy you just saw in the movie.'

'We both knew who Randy Scott was already. He was famous from those early cowboy films. I don't remember who Cary's date was, but the girl with Randy was obviously Doris Duke! She was plumb crazy about Randy. All the girls were, back then, only Doris was a lot richer than the others. We didn't know anything about Cary, although I told him I'd enjoyed the film. But then, Cary, he lit a cigarette for me and he murmured something – I don't remember exactly what – some remark that made me laugh out loud. Cary could always make me laugh. So we got talking. Next day, he phoned up Milton Burns to get my number and ask me out. And that, as they say in the films, was the beginning of our beautiful friendship.'

Here, Virginia starts to chuckle at her own choice of words.

'. . . if you can call it that. God, how we argued! And of course, Cary was furious when he found out about Oscar.'

'You didn't give Oscar up . . . ?'

'Why ever would I, when we'd only just got together again?' Virginia responds.

A pause follows, but Teresa doesn't pass judgement. Wisely, she just sits quiet and waits for the story to continue.

'I didn't plan to stop seeing Oscar,' Virginia says. 'Not until Cary got violent. That scared me. I've always hated violence in men. Oscar had a sharp tongue, but he wouldn't have hurt a fly. So Oscar and I were settled in one night, tucked up in bed and fast asleep, when, suddenly, there were headlights flashing on the walls and shouts out in the street. I peeked out and there was Cary, ramming his Packard into Oscar's old Ford, hammering it as if he meant to kill somebody. We kept the drapes drawn and stayed quiet. After a while, Cary drove off home. The Ford was a wreck. Oscar got the message. We said our goodbyes for a while.'

I'm astonished. Could the suavely elegant Cary Grant ever have behaved in such a thuggish manner? Teresa, more familiar with the story, tells me that the man Virginia Cherrill met on Wilshire Boulevard had not yet created the laid-back screen persona that would one day help to win him a massive and devoted following. Cary Grant, in 1932, was still extremely insecure: both obsessive and fearful. Aged twenty-eight, he was known chiefly as the handsome – and always well-dressed – English actor who had recently moved into a house with Randolph Scott and who, through Scott, had become friendly with the maverick millionaire film-maker Howard Hughes.

The biographies confirm Teresa's account. Back in 1932, Cary Grant was still honing his image, courting fame. He had taken to heart his impecunious English father's view that one good suit is worth seven cheap ones. After watching Douglas Fairbanks Sr's diligent cultivation of his tan during a transatlantic crossing (Cary, fresh out of England, was travelling to New York below decks), he had concluded that a bronzed skin symbolised wealth and exuded success. Languid ease was also carefully noted in other, more successful actors, and replicated by ambitious, watchful Cary. Hints of emotional turmoil, the struggles beneath, surfaced elsewhere: in the three packs of cigarettes he smoked every day; in his compulsive whistling in times of stress; in the care with which he sidestepped any attempts to delve into his past.

Cary Grant's real name was Archie Leach. He was born in 1904, in a small terrace house in the port of Bristol, England. His parents had previously lost an infant son; Elsie, his mother – somewhat like Blanche Cherrill – would never entirely recover from this early bereavement. Hungering for a gentility beyond the modest circumstances of her husband (Elias Leach worked as a clothes-presser), Elsie focused on her second child as the means by which to achieve her social ascent. On the rare occasions in later life when Grant consented to discuss his childhood, he remembered the need to please his mother more strongly than the sense that Elsie Leach's habits – she hoarded food obsessively, locked all the doors in their home, scrubbed her hands until they bled – rendered her strange, or different, from the mothers of his friends. Informed one afternoon by his father, when Archie was only ten years old, that Mother had left them, never to return, the little boy (it is unclear whether he voiced this feeling) blamed himself. The fault, he did not doubt, was in him; this guilt, the root of a lifetime of well-masked insecurity, helps to explain the cultivation of that urbane, well-dressed perfect gentleman of the screen: matchless Cary was the son that Elsie Leach had wanted, his apology for having let her down.

Elias Leach's lie may have been intended to spare the boy distress; the truth was that he had signed the papers for his wife's confinement in a Bristol asylum. Over twenty years were to pass before mother and son would see one another again.

'Cary never talked about his background more than he could help,' Virginia tells Teresa. 'Back then, he never mentioned his mother. I thought that she'd gone off with some other man. It wasn't a topic that Cary wanted to discuss.'

Rebellious and unhappy at his school (one to which, aged eleven, he had won a scholarship), Archie Leach's moment of epiphany came two years later. He was thirteen years old when, led backstage by a teacher who had helped to install an electrical switchboard for one of Bristol's two music-halls, he caught his first glimpse of the transforming power of the stage. Watching the shabby performers as they ran out from the dusty wings into a circle of light, young Archie beheld an image of escape. From then on, all his holiday-time and evenings were spent volunteering as an unpaid stagehand at the music-hall. Such a life, the boy felt, was the nearest he could get to happiness. When Bob Pender, the genial manager of a youthful vaudeville troupe, offered him actual work, Archie jumped at the chance. A week's employment as a runaway performer, armed only with a forged letter of approval from his father, began his education in the skills of juggling and tumbling. When a worried Mr Leach tracked his son down, and returned him to the confines of school, Archie promptly succeeded in getting himself expelled for delinquency.

In 1918, as the Armistice was signed, ending the Great War, fourteen-year-old Archie had already established himself as a junior vaudeville performer, travelling around Britain's provincial theatres with the Pender Troupe. Elias, having settled into unregistered domesticity with a more stable consort than his incarcerated wife, offered scant opposition when Bob Pender, a bluffly respectable man, invited Archie to join his newest venture: the Pender Troupe was taking its act to America. Mr Pender had already reassured Mr Leach with the revelation that he, like Elias himself, was a Freemason, a sure sign of his respectability. Permission was granted. Archie was liberated, ready to commence a new life.

'I'm not sure Cary planned to go home again, even then,' Virginia states. 'He wanted to start over.'

Aged sixteen, sleeping below decks with Mr and Mrs Pender and their gang of eight teenage boys – and with Douglas Fairbanks sunning himself on the liner's boardwalk above their heads – Archie Leach travelled to America. An unnerving début at the enormous New York Hippodrome – the Pender Troupe performed there twice each day, for six days a week – was followed by a whistlestop national tour. When Bob and Margaret Pender returned to England in 1922 – shrewd Bob had foreseen the imminent defeat by cinema of old-fashioned music-hall entertainment – Archie stayed on, working as a slapstick double-act with the Penders' youngest son.

Interviewed in 1932, at the time of his first encounter with Virginia, Cary Grant brushed aside the hard times he endured before venturing to try his luck out in Hollywood. Briefly, he acknowledged that, during his first four years on the East Coast, he had been employed as a stilt-walker at Coney Island fairs, as a tie-vendor on Sixth Avenue, and even as a mind-reader's stooge. (Nothing more was ever admitted; if a muscular and attractive boy had also been driven to use personal collateral in order to survive his years on the 'mean streets', the information was withheld.)

In 1927, however, Archie Leach's luck changed. A friend introduced him to the Hammerstein family, and Arthur Hammerstein offered the young man a couple of juvenile roles in Broadway shows. A series of short-term contracts soon brought in a substantial $450 a week. Fiercely prudent, Archie squirrelled his earnings away; when he at last granted himself a couple of luxuries, they were picked out with care. One was a raccoon coat; the other, a gleaming Packard Phaeton. These trophies, as Archie might have gathered from his work in the theatre (or perhaps from studying photos in the daily press), were the essential trappings of the stardom that he craved. In November 1931, as the Depression bit deep into the American way of life, Archie Leach set off for Hollywood, one of the few places that could still offer the chance of prosperity to a talented and handsome young man.

'And ambitious! Cary was driven!' Virginia exclaims. 'Randy Scott always worked hard and took care to keep himself in good shape, but he wasn't set upon becoming a star. Cary never lost sight of his goal.'

The car, the coat and a well-selected hotel created the intended aura of glamour, and it won instant rewards. Presenting himself and his Broadway credentials to an agent, Archie was invited to attend a private dinner at the home of B. P. Schulberg, the powerful co-head of Paramount. Once again, Archie made a good impression. A female guest was due to take a screen test the following day. Schulberg invited the young English actor to come along and feed her lines.

Here was a chance of the kind that might never again arise. Despite a sleepless night – the intense nervousness of this most debonair of actors has been well documented – Archie Leach performed well. Following the test, he heard that he had won the offer of a five-year contract at Paramount. Gratified to learn that he would be in line for any parts that Gary Cooper didn't choose to play, and that he would continue to receive the equivalent of his Broadway salary ($450 per week), Archie scarcely blinked when told that he would have to change his name. This stipulation, for a man who was in search of a new identity, was no hardship. 'Grant' was one of several names put before him on a typed list; 'Cary' sat well with it. 'Cary Lockwood' was the name of the character he had last played as his goodbye to Broadway, in a short-lived musical called *Nikki*. It may have seemed an auspicious choice: Fay Wray, who had also played a part in *Nikki*, had just won the role in *King Kong* that would make her name (if only as a girl who knew how to scream).

Early in 1932, then, the newly created 'Cary Grant' was feeling optimistic. He had not yet fully grasped that he had signed away his freedom and, to a significant extent, any chance to control his immediate destiny. Paramount's contract gave the studio complete power over him; as a new actor, Cary had no say at all.

'And he did have a run of bad luck,' Virginia observes. 'I can't remember the names of those first films Cary was in, but he told me that the press notices were awful.'

Friendless and dispirited, the obscure young actor was preparing to break his contract and return to whatever stage work he could find in the East, when 34-year-old Randolph Scott crossed his path. A friendship was struck up while the two men worked on *Hot Saturday*, a lightly engaging Paramount film. Within days, Randy Scott and Cary Grant had agreed to save on costs by living together. This mutual decision showed either great arrogance or considerable naïvety: handsome film actors did not share homes while living in Hollywood; still less, did they flaunt the fact by giving parties together and allowing their house to be nicknamed 'Bachelors' Hall'.

To certain biographers, the situation has seemed self-evident: Grant and Scott were bisexuals. Why else would two men share a home? (The third inhabitant was a Sealyham terrier upon whom Cary Grant intriguingly bestowed his own old name: Archie Leach.) Why else would two male actors, rumoured to be fond of fooling around at Hollywood costume parties, have occasionally dressed in women's clothes? Didn't all of this point to one, inescapable conclusion?

Other interpretations can be placed upon Cary Grant's decision to share a home with Scott. Cary aspired to the smart social world in which his new friend seemed to be at home. He liked the fact that Scott, the son of an accountant, shared Grant's own careful attitude to money. Both actors needed to work on their voices. (Cary Grant had not yet masked his Bristol vowels; Randy Scott, brought up in North Carolina, was under orders to lose his Southern accent.) More importantly, Randolph Scott's sunny and easygoing personality offered welcome respite to an insecure young man who was struggling to overcome feelings of despair and inadequacy and who – as his ramming of Levant's car indicates –

was capable of angry acts of violence. The least complicated explanation may come nearest to the truth. Randy was good company. With Randolph Scott around, Cary Grant could keep his fears at bay.

Virginia's own attitude is revealing. Talking to Teresa in the summer of 1994, she dismisses all the biographies of Cary Grant that she has yet read as works of fiction. Why is it, she asks, that these muckrakers waited until Cary was dead before they began to slander the man? Perhaps, she suggests, they were frightened; they remembered that Cary Grant, at the height of his fame, had sued Chevy Chase for saying on television that he was gay: under threat of financial ruin, Chase publicly retracted his words.

'Douglas Fairbanks once told me that Cary said I was the best lover he'd ever had,' Virginia announces. 'Well, it was mutual.'

Teresa, at this point, reminds Virginia that Betsy Drake, the third Mrs Grant, remarked that she never had time to check out whether or not her husband was a homosexual because they'd been too busy fucking. I can hear, on the tape, a peal of laughter.

'Well, of course! Cary was crazy about women. He didn't like me to wear make-up and he hated it when other men started eyeing me up – that's pretty normal, isn't it? But he was great in bed – and so funny. We'd sometimes roll out on to the floor, we were laughing so much. And Randy – Randy was a darling. We used to double-date, back in those early days, when he was seeing Doris Duke. Randolph Scott was no more gay than Cary was. And he was *so* handsome, he had women falling all over him.'

A photograph of Virginia, standing between Grant and Scott, seems to confirm her words; certainly, it's hard to interpret the photo of this glamorous trio other than as a tableau of uncomplicated friendship: three beautiful, active young people immensely enjoying one another's company.

Gossip, even back then, had been fanned by the resolute and – to journalists – infuriating way in which Virginia, along with

Scott and Grant, refused to be drawn into discussing their private lives.

'There was once a triangle without a rift: Cary, his wife Virginia Cherrill, and Randy Scott', ran an article in *The Sketch*, for 1936; the writer had interviewed Scott about his friendship with Grant, and had come away dissatisfied. 'Locked up in his own past, present and future, Cary Grant is . . . an enigma,' the thwarted reporter wrote: 'no one can get over the outside barriers into what he thinks.'

Cary, Virginia and Randolph ('Randy') Scott: an inseparable trio, at the Melody Ball, March, 1934.

Over twenty years later, the playwright Clifford Odets reached the same conclusion. '[Cary's] simplicity covers up one of the most complex men I've ever met,' Odets remarked in 1958. 'After sixteen years, I sometimes feel that I really don't know him at all.'

Virginia pasted the comment from Odets into her cuttings-book. Possibly, she'd identified with what the celebrated playwright and screenwriter had confessed. Who *did* know what Cary Grant was like? 'Everyone wants to be Cary Grant,' the actor, late in his life wistfully joked. 'Even *I* want to be Cary Grant.' That was the voice Virginia knew. The nonchalant, elegant icon of the screen, beloved by millions, was as much of a mystery to her as to the man who created him: the witty, chain-smoking, impetuous and hot-headed actor with whom, back in 1932, she had embarked upon a passionate affair.

Virginia, at the time she first met Cary Grant, was treating her filmwork as a frolic. For Cary, her light-hearted attitude offered a welcome antidote to the grimness of his first months at the Paramount Studios. In October, 1932, however, his good looks attracted the attention of a formidable professional; tiny, ribald Mae West wanted Cary Grant for her co-star in *She Done Him Wrong*, a film based on West's Broadway smash-hit, *Diamond Lil*.

Mae liked the performance Grant turned in as a diffident young policeman enough to recall the actor the following year. The new film was *I'm No Angel*. Prudently, Grant kept to himself the horror he felt at having once again to appear smitten with a woman whose teetering heels, powdered face and pouting scarlet lips made her nearer to a pantomime dame than an object of desire. Did Miss West awaken suppressed memories of ageing Manhattan dowagers on the prowl for youthful companions? Certainly, Cary Grant's reaction to tough, witty Miss West was not favourable.

Mae was, Grant recalled with uncharacteristic bluntness, 'an absolute fake'.

Miss West, who could give as good as she got, penned a script that hinted, none too subtly, that her bashful screen suitor had a secret life to hide.

'I always did like a man in uniform,' purrs Mae, displaying her customary gift for self-mockery. 'That one fits you grand.' And then, sure of herself, she drawls out the notorious line: 'Why don't you come up sometime 'n s-e-e me? I'm home every evening.'

'Yeah,' responds Cary, begging off. 'But I'm busy every evening.'

'Busy?' retorts, contemptuously, the ever-elegant Miss West. 'So what are you tryin' to do, insult me?'

'Why no, no, not at all,' Cary nervously assures the film's prima donna. 'I'm just busy, that's all.'

'You ain't kidding me any,' shoots back Mae, her scorn replete with her complete lack of nuance. 'You know – I met your kind before.' And then, taunting him now: 'Why don't you come up sometime, huh?'

'Well, I . . .'Cary stammers, hard put.

'Don't be afraid,' Mae mocks. 'I won't tell.' She presses on, emphasising the sense of vulgar double entendre. 'Come up, I'll tell your fortune . . .' And then, with a roll of the eyes and a dismissive sneer: 'Aw, *you* c'n be *had* . . .'

For all his distaste, Cary learned to hone his professional skills of precise comic timing from playing opposite this consummate veteran.

'Cary was a comedian. His timing was just perfect,' Virginia sighs. 'He was the best storyteller *ever*.'

Inadvertently, Mae West also did Virginia a favour; by comparison to the toughness of this bawdy and cosmetically enhanced old pro, the young actress seemed all the more enchantingly free of artifice. Increasingly, Cary Grant became convinced that the woman he wanted to marry was Virginia Cherrill.

'And, being an obsessive man, he wouldn't let the idea go. But I'd been married and divorced already. I didn't want to get involved in something that was going to be a bust. Besides, I wasn't feeling ready to settle down. Cary himself was having hard fights with the studios. But – between times – the two of us were having so much fun!'

Teresa asks her friend to tell more about these early years. Virginia seems eager to comply. I'm struck by how happy and

Cary and Virginia at San Simeon, 1933.

excited the old lady sounds during this section of the tapes; she seems almost to become a girl again as she drifts back to those carefree days.

'Lots of times, we'd drive up to San Simeon to stay with Marion and WR: you've seen the picture of Cary and me there in our tennis clothes. There were always a pack of people around – journalists, actors, politicians, girlfriends of Marion's, pals of WR's sons. Marion never had any children of her own. She did say once that WR paid for her abortions, so as not to embarrass his wife. I'm not sure that was true. Marion didn't always think too clearly about what she was saying when she'd had a glass or two. WR treated her well. He thought the world of Marion . . .'

Asked to name some of the people she met at Hearst's home, Virginia says: 'Everybody!' She produces only one name, however: Edwina Mountbatten. Edwina, who had spent part of her honeymoon at Pickfair, the Fairbanks' house, had returned there with one of her lovers. She brought him up for a few days at San Simeon. Edwina was always sweet to her, Virginia remembers; she thinks it was Lady Mountbatten (followed by the great collector and actor Edward G. Robinson) who first steered her interest in Impressionist paintings towards the idea of acquiring some herself.

'I'd seen lots of them back in Chicago, of course, at the Art Institute, where I first fell in love with Renoir and Monet, but I'd never thought of actually buying them. And anyway, I didn't have that kind of money.'

(Later, Virginia continues, when she travelled to England, it had been Edwina's generous introductions, especially to Lord Mountbatten's own family, that had helped a lonely young American to gain acceptance from a notoriously clannish world.)

'But I was telling you about the fun I had with Cary. We got thrown out of San Simeon once. Cary and one of WR's sons were fooling about. They took up a little plane and started bombing the house with sacks of flour. WR didn't like it one bit: he was always

Cary and Virginia out on the town, 1933.

a stickler for proper behaviour. Cary and I were never able to share a room when we visited, even though everybody knew we were a couple. The day after the flour-throwing, Cary found his bags packed and sitting outside his bedroom door.'

This misdemeanour put an end, for a time, to visits to Hearst's hilltop kingdom. The snub was not, according to Virginia, one that caused much heartache, however, to a lively young couple who were much in demand.

'One night, we were invited to some big ball at either the Ambassador or the Biltmore. It was tremendously smart. Cary was in white tie and tails – so were all the men. Right in the middle of the evening, one of the guests tapped Cary on the shoulder, told him that he remembered seeing him as a kid in vaudeville on the East Coast. I'm not sure how pleased Cary was about that; he didn't like talking about those early years. This man swore that Cary had been one of the best acrobats he'd ever seen outside a circus. The guy asked Cary if he was still up to performing one of his old stunts.'

'Give me $50 and I'll do any stunt you like,' Cary told him.

'So the guy laughed and told him he was on. I saw him grinning. I think he reckoned Cary would make a fool of himself. Cary just walked up to the bandleader and asked him for a roll on the drums. He stripped off his jacket and tie and waited there for the roll – 500 people staring at him – and then he flipped over backwards with a twist and turn in the middle and he landed back – just like that – perched flat upon his feet again. I never saw anything so quick. It was wonderful. Everybody in the place started to applaud. And then Cary walked over to the guy's table and simply stretched out his palm for the fifty. He got it.'

Afterwards, the man, who seems to have been bent upon goading Grant, told Virginia that only a fellow with Arabic blood could do a twist and a jump like that. She didn't – and she still doesn't in her conversation with Teresa – register an insult in the sneer. Her escort did; Virginia remembers that Cary Grant retaliated with a quip, some sharp phrase that silenced the man like a shot.

'Cary could do that. He was so quick with words! I always loved wordplay, but I could never match him. *Coup de grâce* for a lawnmower; *tête-à-tête* for a tight brassiere; *mal de mer* for a seasick mother, oh, and silly heaps of others. He wasn't serious, like up on screen; that was all a pose. I never knew a man who could laugh so much, just giggling until the tears ran down his face, and then he'd set me off with stories he'd tell, in every kind of dialect. And soon, we'd both be laughing so much we couldn't speak.'

Mildly, Teresa reminds Virginia that she hasn't always looked back with such affection. What about the man's nearly manic bouts of jealousy? What about her stories of his terrifying rages? What was that story about their quarrel somewhere at a garage?

'That was when we were driving down to get married in Mexico. It was Cary's idea, of course; he was always going on about marriage – and I was always putting him off. We had a quarrel along the way, near San Clemente. He started to shout; he was threatening me. I didn't say a word. I just waited until he pulled into a filling station. I walked across the road and climbed on to the bus back to LA, left him flat, to work it out. There were a few other occasions like that. I'd get so angry that I couldn't bear to stay around.'

And what about when she was away, off somewhere filming? Didn't those prolonged absences upset him?

'That's true. The studio stuff didn't bother him so much, but he didn't like it when I left the country. He'd get so jealous. He was always jealous. And that's when he tended to get violent. It used to scare me.'

Did Randolph Scott help her to calm him down at all?

'Randy was good with Cary, when he was around,' Virginia states. 'But he wasn't always there. It's not like you read in the books. They lived in the same house, and they got on well, but they didn't necessarily lead the same lives. They had different friends. Randy became tremendously friendly with Fred Astaire, you know, but that was later, after they did *Roberta* together . . .'

Despite an exuberant off-screen life, Virginia appeared in four feature films during 1933, and Cary in five, of which only the two made with Mae West won him significant attention. Cary worked hard for his plaudits; Virginia put no conspicuous effort into the minor roles she played in some (rightly) forgotten films: *The Nuisance, Ladies Must Love* and – a miserable postscript to the eminent careers of both director Tod Browning and that former giant among silent screen actors, John Gilbert – *Fast Workers*. (Browning's film charted the lives of two womanising navvies.)

Offered a cameo role in *Charlie Chan's Greatest Case*, towards the end of the summer of 1933, Virginia only took it – she now claims – because she wanted a vacation in the South Seas. The successful series of detective films was always shot on location around Honolulu, the fictional headquarters of the Chan family; Virginia, fondly remembering her cruise aboard Vincent Astor's yacht, welcomed a chance to visit Hawaii.

For the cynical theory that saw Virginia embarked upon a long-term strategy for Cary's hand in marriage, the Hawaii film offers fuel. The island had a reputation as a holiday spot for lovers engaged in secret trysts; surely, Virginia Cherrill chose to go there as a way of nudging Cary Grant into a proposal, spurred by jealousy? Listening to Virginia's own recollection of the relationship, it's difficult to maintain that view. A 25-year-old beauty, she still remained (despite appearing in some atrocious movies) one of the most sought-after young women in Hollywood. Virginia may have adored Cary Grant and laughed until she cried at his jokes, but she felt no haste to acquire him as a husband. Grant was not, back in 1933, perceived as a phenomenal 'catch'. The man we now view as an icon of the screen did not yet exist.

Virginia Cherrill's sojourn in Hawaii did not please Cary Grant. Visions of his pretty girlfriend frolicking through the sultry nights amidst her fellow-actors were heightened by both jealousy and ignorance. (Cary seemed to forget that Virginia's favourite among her fellow-performers, Robert Warwick, was a man in his seventies.) The best thing, Cary decided, was to proclaim his own love by giving Virginia, upon her return, a romantic surprise.

A less frugal suitor might have chartered a yacht on which to sail out to meet his beloved as the *Monterrey* liner steamed back towards the California coast; Cary, to the delight of the gossip columnists, saved on costs by hiring instead a small tugboat, into which an embarrassed Virginia was obliged to descend by ladder, in full view of the press. It isn't entirely surprising that no engagement announcement followed this penny-pinching stunt. Nevertheless, as Cary travelled to Arizona – he had been recruited to replace Bing Crosby as the Mock Turtle in Paramount's Christmas season all-star version of *Alice in Wonderland* – Virginia came along.

It was towards the end of that film, and shortly before Cary's next commitment, that the pressure towards a marriage began to build. Snatching, at a nearby hotel, a two-week break from Cary's filming, the lovers found that they were being stalked by a mysteriously alerted press. What did this celebrated pair of beautiful young people have to say for themselves? Was there perhaps an announcement in the air . . . ?

Whatever the mundane truth of Cary Grant's domestic life at Griffith Park, the studio had never relished the image of two handsome and athletic men sharing a home. Randolph Scott found himself being subjected to some searching enquiries about his close friendship with Doris Duke at the same time that reporters tracked Cary Grant down in Phoenix, Arizona. Cary, like Scott, was given a grilling, as the journalists called his attention to the presence of

Miss Virginia Cherrill, who just happened to be staying at the same hotel as Mr Grant.

Adolph Zukor and B. P. Schulberg, the controlling powers of Paramount, lurked behind these interrogations. Pressure was being exerted and strings were being pulled; two of their most attractive stars-in-waiting were being nudged to show off their chosen brides, the sooner the better. Virginia, unfortunately for the plans of the studio heads, had other ideas.

'You have to remember how jealous Cary was. He kept asking me to marry him, but I knew, deep down, that I could never be happy with a man who made me feel so trapped. And yet, I couldn't bear to think of living without him. Around that time, I was offered the chance of some work in England; I had friends there already: Edwina Mountbatten, and a couple of others I'd met at San Simeon. They told me to look them up if ever I came over.'

Virginia doesn't specify just what drama or quarrel caused her to feel that the time had finally come to make the break; she states only that she had to get away.

'I just suddenly felt I couldn't cope any more. Cary went wild. First off, he said that I'd be miserable in England. Then, he told me that he was not going to *allow* me to go. That did it. I said: "Watch me." He was at the station when I left, yelling at me to come back, but the train was already pulling out. It took four nights and three days to get to New York City.'

But, had a harassed young woman really wanted to escape from an oppressive suitor, wouldn't she have travelled straight on to England without leaving behind a forwarding address? Virginia doesn't explain what caused her to delay her departure from Manhattan. Neither does she disclose how it was that Cary Grant knew precisely where to find her.

For anybody who wanted to look, however, the detective's job was a simple one. Cary must surely have known that Virginia, during her pleasurable month of filming in Hawaii, had made friends with Laurence Olivier and his wife. (The couple were solacing themselves there with a holiday at Waikiki Beach, following Olivier's brusque dismissal from the role of Greta Garbo's Spanish lover in *Queen Christina*.) The Oliviers told Virginia that they were about to return to New York for rehearsals of a play, *The Green Bay Tree*; couldn't she, they urged, find time to come and visit?

'I ended by staying with them, up in their suite at the Algonquin. They weren't getting on well with their director, but we still managed to have fun. You remember Jill Esmond – Larry's first wife? Jill was a darling. We were having a cosy tea together by the fire, early one evening, before they set off for the theatre. Somebody knocked at the door of the suite: we thought it was a telegram. Larry went to get it. He opened the door – and in fell Cary. He'd had a drink or two by then. It seems that he'd walked off the set of a film he was making, drunk a bottle of Scotch, jumped aboard a mail train, and come journeying all the way across the country to New York, just to beg me not to leave. I told him I'd made plans.'

According to Virginia's recollection, she left the next day for Britain, where she was met at Southampton, and taken to their home by two of her recently acquired British friends.

'Simon and Miriam Marks. I met them through Bea Lillie, and they remained friends of mine all through their lives. Simon was the Marks of Marks and Spencer, you know – did I ever tell you about the wonderful party they gave for their daughter, Hannah . . . ?'

I can hear Teresa's voice, prompting the old lady back to her story. So, she travelled to England – and Cary stayed in New York?

'I remember him sending me a pleading cable. I asked Miriam and Simon what I ought to do, because I really was crazy with love and at the same time I was so scared of the way Cary behaved sometimes. I was afraid what might happen if I did go back to him.'

'Virginia,' Simon Marks warned her, 'if you run now, you're going to be running for the rest of your life. Stay here. We'll take care of you.'

Helped by these friends in London, Virginia found somewhere to stay.

Crossing the Atlantic in style: a Cunard liner's lounge in the Thirties.

'It was a little attic flat, just a couple of rooms, way up under the roof, at 20 Grosvenor Square. My bedroom was tiny. The work I was going to do had fallen through, and I didn't want to keep plaguing the Markses, and I was a long way from home. Everything felt so complicated, so hard. I spent a lot of time in that little bedroom, crying, simply crying and wishing Cary could just walk back in and take me into his arms. I started to wish I'd never run away. One night, I remember standing by the window, throwing razor blades from the medicine cabinet down into the gutter, where I couldn't reach them. I didn't mean to be so melodramatic. It just frightened me, to know what I might do, when I thought I might never see Cary again.' [Plate 7].

She's out of breath. I can hear the sound of wheezing. Or might it be weeping? Still, after all those years?

'Just Cary and Florek,' she whispers. 'Truly, they are the only men I ever was in love with. Just them. Nobody else.'

8

HIS FAVOURITE WIFE

(1934–1935)

'Cary is my favourite actor. He was not my favourite husband.'

Cary Grant had the perfect cover-story for his pursuit of the woman with whom he had become obsessively in love. He had not seen his father for over fourteen years; if his plans to marry Virginia were foiled, he could still save face by claiming to have returned to England for the purpose of a family reunion.

The order of events seems clear. On reaching England, Cary made his way first to Bristol, where the chauffeur-driven car underwritten by Paramount caused almost as much excitement as the appearance of the city's own Hollywood star, gloriously tanned, speaking with an impressive drawl, and enveloped in a magnificent camel coat.

Sitting awkwardly down to an early supper with Elias Leach, his father's long-term companion, Mabel Bass, and their young son, Cary was at last enlightened about the mother who, he believed, had chosen to abandon her husband and ten-year-old son. In actual fact, as Elias revealed, finally, in 1934, Elsie Leach was still living behind the walls of the Bristol asylum to which her husband had committed her back in 1914. Her condition had stabilised; the possibility of an imminent release had been mooted.

Cary could have visited his mother at this point. He did not do so: time was needed to digest the extraordinary news that he had been given, and his thoughts were concentrated elsewhere. He travelled directly from Bristol to London, where – with their eyes upon the good publicity which they expected to result from a possible forthcoming Grant marriage – the Paramount executives had booked their runaway actor into the film world's favourite hotel, the Savoy, with a view across the Thames. Cary, less interested in the splendour of his suite than in locating Virginia, promptly raised a search; a resourceful concierge traced Miss Cherrill to a rented flat in Grosvenor Square. The couple agreed to meet, and to talk things through over dinner.

'His father was a nice old man, a working type, very friendly.' That remark, made to Teresa, is the only comment upon Cary's family background that Virginia vouchsafed. It is hard, however, to believe that Cary did not share his feelings of shock, betrayal, and, perhaps, anguish about his mother, with the woman he loved and longed to marry.

Virginia's friends testify to the strength of her loyalty in times of crisis. Whatever her doubts may have been about once again becoming a wife, she now gave Cary the answer he wanted. Following a brief visit to her fiancé's home city, arrangements were made for a small wedding reception to be held at Bristol's old-fashioned Grand Hotel.

These plans were made in late November; two months later, the *Chicago Daily News* informed its readers that Virginia Cherrill had postponed her wedding. Stories that Cary Grant had been taken to hospital began to leak out. Had he suffered a nervous breakdown, or was he – this was a favourite theory among the less-elegant commentators – undergoing some discreet nose reconstruction?

HAS LICENSE, BUT WON'T WED YET

Pretty Virginia Cherrill, who won't be marrying Cary Grant for a while, even though she applied for a license early in the month to wed the handsome actor while both are visitors in London. "The engagement is still on," she said in announcing the postponement, perhaps until after the two are back in Hollywood. Rumors say, however, that the wedding is indefinitely postponed.

The Chicago Daily News *reports on
Virginia's wedding postponement.*

The Cherrill archive confirms only that Grant spent time in hospital, and that there had been anxiety about his health. Sending news to her family in Illinois, Virginia reported that Cary '(Thank Heavens!)' was quite recovered and hoped to meet them all soon, although film work summoned him to Hollywood in the near future. Speaking for herself, she felt 'terribly homesick'.

It seems reasonable, in the absence of any further evidence, to hazard that the words 'terribly homesick' acknowledge Virginia's unhappiness, at a time when Cary had been undergoing some form of breakdown. 'Thank Heavens!' is an expression that seems less appropriate to her fiancé's recovery from minor cosmetic surgery than to his survival of a mental crisis.

On 8 February, the date of Elsie Leach's birthday, Cary returned to Bristol alone, and visited his mother at the asylum. Returning to London that evening, he announced to the press that an urgent summons – for film work – back to Hollywood had forced a change of plan. He and Miss Cherrill would plight their troth the following day.

At eleven o'clock on the morning of 9 February 1934, a modest crowd of onlookers gathered outside the steps of Caxton Hall, London's best-known register office. The group included none of Virginia's growing band of English friends, and no members of the Leach family. Everything contributes to suggest that Cary's decision was an impulsive one, influenced by the meeting with his mother and undertaken without much prior consultation with Virginia.

Delivered by cab to the door of the Hall, Cary, clad in his new camel coat and muffler, greeted a scattering of photographers, and looked anxiously around for his bride. Virginia was nowhere to be seen. Shaking his head, the groom disappeared inside the building. The doors closed. Fifteen minutes later, a flustered bride-to-be arrived, her day-clothes hidden by a coat, her hair pushed hastily back under a winter hat. She smiled briefly – and hurried into the Hall. Emerging twenty minutes later as man and wife, Mr and Mrs Grant posed for a few shots.

Cary and Virginia pose after their marriage at Caxton Hall.

'We're so happy!' Cary called out; Virginia nodded.

The spectators thought the bride looked pretty but bewildered. Ushered by her husband into the first of two waiting taxis, she climbed in and was promptly swept away, disappearing from view along the narrow street, while the groom, aghast, remained stranded among his well-wishers upon the pavement. The older, more assured Cary Grant might have turned the débâcle to his advantage and played it as a comic scene; the younger man panicked. Unsmiling and no longer waving to the crowd, he scrambled into the second cab and sped away in pursuit of his bride. Unsure of whether an actual wedding or a tragicomic film-scene had been enacted, the crowd dispersed.

The Paramount publicity machine had missed the opportunity to make capital from the wedding ceremony; attention was now focused on the possibilities arising from a honeymoon at sea. Cunard was alerted to the importance of their newly married passengers. The Grants, to their delight, travelled home free of charge, and in considerable state.

'The liners loved having theatre people on board,' Virginia explains. 'It was good for business; all we had to do was to walk about and smile at people, although Cary would have preferred to work on his tan.' She laughs; she's evidently remembering good times. 'They gave us the biggest suite on the ship. We spent a lot of time in our rooms.'

Cunard reaped the reward of their generosity. Thirty years later, the charms of sailing on the *Queen Elizabeth 2* were advertised with a magnificent photograph of the honeymooning movie-stars, hand in hand, strolling along the deck and beaming as if they hadn't a care in the world. By that time, of course, Cary's name was big enough to launch a fleet of liners, whereas Virginia appeared only as an anonymous bride.

Fêted, well fed and relaxed by their ocean life, the newly-weds still radiate happiness in the pictures snapped as they disembarked at New York. Virginia, snug in her wedding-day fur coat and jauntily tilted hat, snuggles into Cary's side; her handsome husband looks as if his dreams have all come true. Endearing, gorgeous and elegant, the Grants made a magnificent couple. The studio chiefs at Paramount (Cary) and Fox (Virginia) could congratulate themselves upon the birth of a publicity-perfect match.

Making Paramount happy: Mr and Mrs Grant meet the Press in 1934.

Towards the middle of February 1934, Virginia and Cary settled into a house near to that of Randolph Scott, their closest mutual friend. Randy's name, at this point, was rising faster in Hollywood than Cary's; when one of Virginia's relations from Carthage arrived on a family visit, it was the famed hero of the cowboy films she was eager to meet. Recalling the experience for me some seventy years later, Virginia's cousin admitted that, back in 1934, as an excited little girl going to stay with her movie-star relative, she didn't have the faintest idea who Cary Grant might be.

Professional rivalry never damaged the close relationship between the two men; a photograph taken at the Melody Ball in March 1934 shows the pair of them cheerily posing on either side of Virginia. Such images helped fuel continuing whispers about Cary's friendship with his former housemate.

Virginia, discussing those early days with her friend Teresa, has already ridiculed the notion that Cary Grant and Randolph Scott were lovers. Had this been the case, however, some evidence of latent resentment would surely surface upon the tapes. On the contrary, she speaks warmly of Scott; she never suggests that the easygoing Southern actor hijacked her husband, or that she had been required to share her man.

Scott did have a role to play in the marriage of his friends, and it was one that Virginia valued. Randy was, from her point of view, a congenial buffer, a friendly intermediary, protecting a sometimes fearful young wife from the increasingly volatile moods of a husband she both loved and feared.

Cary Grant, in 1934, harboured the despairing sense that his career was going nowhere. Briefly, during his trip to Europe, Paramount had allowed him to imagine that they were ready, at long last, to let their hard-working contract actor demonstrate the versatility of his talents. The studio chiefs, in fact, entertained no such plans; Cary Grant's value to them was as a reliable performer in undemandingly mediocre productions. They had not, to do them justice, glimpsed any sign that the young British actor was capable of carrying off anything more ambitious.

Contract actors worked hard for their taskmasters; during 1933–4, Cary appeared in nine films. He had only been back in Hollywood (fresh from his whirlwind wedding trip) for a single day when he was kitted out in white tie and tails to play a newspaper publisher in *Thirty Day Princess*. Further, and equally anodyne, roles followed. On the one occasion, in 1934, when a real opportunity emerged – the brilliant young Irving Thalberg of MGM offered Grant a strong supporting role in *Mutiny on the Bounty,* with Clark Gable in the lead as Fletcher Christian – Adolph Zukor refused to loan his actor out from his contract at Paramount. Instead, poor Cary was assigned another feeble romantic lead, in *Enter Madame.* Released in 1935, the film kept his career in limbo.

Children are not a subject which Virginia often addresses in her interviews; all I know from Teresa is that her friend had longed to become a mother and that she suffered, during her life, a series of miscarriages. The first occurred during the spring of 1934; it caused Virginia considerable distress and increased the despondency of her increasingly unhappy husband. Cary had already started to rely on alcohol; shortly after her miscarriage, he developed a theory that Virginia was having affairs.

'Cary was so suspicious,' Virginia tells Teresa. 'Every man I spoke to instantly became his enemy. He didn't want me to go to work; he didn't even like to go out in the evenings. And when we were home, he liked to drink. And when he'd had a drink or two, and got angry, he used to kick and hit me.'

Three months after their marriage, Virginia rebelled. A woman director, Lois Weber, wanted her for one of the main female roles in a cross-cultural romance she planned to shoot on Kuai, one of the Hawaiian Islands. Virginia was invited to play the part of Lucille Cheney, a wealthy young socialite whose plantation-owning husband (Whitney de Rahm) prefers the company of a pretty native girl, to be played by the Argentine actress Mona Maris. A weak screenplay did not deter Virginia from accepting a chance to get away.

Virginia and Whitney de Rahm in White Heat (Cane Fire), *on Kuai, 1934.*

A sheaf of typical holiday snaps from Kuai suggests that Virginia enjoyed this third visit to Hawaii, even though the film itself turned out to be one of her worst. *White Heat* (also known as *Cane Fire*) was an ill-conceived romance in which overt racism helped to put an end to the directorial career of Lois Weber. (One of the posters showed a dark-skinned and near-naked islander glowering out of a palm tree at well-dressed and white-skinned strangers.) Virginia, although graceful and assured, looks embarrassed by the silliness of her lines; it's clear that she chose this film not because she had found a worthy role, but simply as a vehicle of escape from a marriage to which she returned with a heavy heart.

Randy Scott shared Virginia's view of the sullen husband to whom she came home; nothing, they both thought, could be worse for Cary than to sit brooding over a bottle. Dragged out against his will, Grant became increasingly resentful. Looking through Virginia's collection of invitations, cuttings and photographs, it's hard not to sympathise.

Virginia, throughout her life, loved to be with people. The late summer of 1934 brought in a flood of tempting suggestions. She and Cary were invited everywhere: to go up to San Simeon; to dine at Marion Davies's spectacular Ocean House; to catch up with visiting friends from England; to go to Carole Lombard's beach party; to help arrange a dinner being thrown for Edwina Mountbatten. As a lively, beautiful and socially accomplished young woman, Virginia was welcome everywhere; naturally, it was expected that Cary would also attend. The result is plain to see in one photograph that has survived, snapped during a fancy-dress ball at the Biltmore Hotel [plate 8]. Here, the Grants are coyly flanked by two smart young male friends. Virginia, impersonating Eliza Doolittle in an ankle-length skirt and slouch hat, radiates good cheer; her husband, magnificently attired as a highwayman in narrow white breeches, glossy boots and a feathery pantomime hat, looks about ready for a second breakdown. Cary's smile is taut; every line in his body registers discomfort. Side by side, the Grants stare forward, neither touching the other. A glance is all it needs to perceive that here is a marriage under stress.

The absence of adverse comment or speculation in the film colony's gossip columns during the summer of 1934 suggests that the Grants succeeded in hiding from view their domestic troubles. Behind closed doors, however, the tension built. The chief problem, exacerbated by Cary's continuing lack of professional success, was sexual insecurity.

'He was so jealous.' Virginia sighs. 'Even of my *mother* . . .!'

Later, wistfully, Cary Grant was ready to acknowledge that his own lack of confidence had been the major factor in destroying his marriage to a woman he adored. His behaviour, back at the time, spiralled out of control.

'My possessiveness and fear of losing her brought about the very condition I feared,' Grant lamented, too late. 'The loss of her.'

On 10 September 1934, just seven months after marrying Virginia at Caxton Hall, Cary Grant threatened to kill his wife. The cause for provocation remains unknown (the incident was not reported). Terrified – her husband was tall, athletic, and strongly built – Virginia threw some clothes into a case and fled to the home of her mother. Blanche, who had never warmed to Cary, recommended asking their lawyer, Milton Cohen, to initiate a divorce. Virginia refused to discuss such a possibility.

'I did still love him,' she tells Teresa. 'I always loved him. I knew he'd come after me. I didn't even bother to unpack my suitcase while I was sleeping at my mother's house. And after three days, Cary turned up at the door in his Packard. Blanche wanted me to stay with her. I just kissed her and walked out the door. I was certain everything was going to come right. That was when I suggested to Cary that we take a trip to Illinois, since I still hadn't yet introduced him to the family.'

The visit went well; Virginia's idea of getting her unhappy husband away from Hollywood for a while appeared to pay off. Cary, on his best behaviour, delighted the Wilcoxes with his relaxed manner and handsome looks; a photograph taken by Virginia shows him standing at his ease under the boughs of one of the Durham farmhouse's ancient elms. He looks, at first glance, like the Cary Grant of later years, a master of consummate grace and charm. The old Wilcoxes beam at the camera, bewitched by their delightful guest. Cary's wife, framing Grant for her snap, could have been excused for believing that all might yet work out for the best. Looking more closely at the photograph, however, it's hard to ignore the size, and strength, of the hand Grant clasps around his own pocket camera. Neither, looking still more closely, can an observer miss the expression of strain on Cary Grant's face.

Cary's good humour lasted all the way home to California. According to Virginia, Grant's little Sealyham terrier (the dog upon which his owner had conferred the name of 'Archie Leach') scampered off through the back door just as the couple came in at the front entrance. Virginia was never a superstitious woman, but she took that canine welcome for a sinister omen. It wasn't, as she points out, in character for the terrier to run away.

'I think there was a cause,' she says. 'I think that dog sensed something bad, because it never came back.'

A fortnight after returning to Los Angeles, the Grants were invited out to dine with friends at the Cocoanut Grove. Virginia was placed next to Sir Guy Standing, a British character actor who had joined Paramount after a long and respectable career in the theatre.

'There were about eight or ten of us there,' she tells Teresa. 'I was asking Sir Guy about his home in England. He was the sweetest old man, polite as anything. Honestly, he must have been seventy, if a day. But Cary couldn't stand for me to talk nicely with any man except himself or Randy Scott. Randy didn't count, in his mind, and neither did Howard Hughes.'

'And why was that?' her friend enquires, but Virginia seems not to hear her.

'They were about the only men, except my grandfathers, that he trusted not to try to go to bed with me. So the two of us were chatting away, and Cary started whistling under his breath – that was always a bad sign. He leaned across the table and told Sir Guy he'd better think twice about trying to make a pass at me. And then, of course, our friends started to prick up their ears. I tried to turn it off, make a joke so nobody'd notice. I think I said that if I had my glasses on nobody would flirt with me, and that if I didn't, I'd never know if they had. Cary wasn't amused. He broke up the party and took me home. He didn't say a word, but he kept up that damn whistling all the way back. I went to bed and switched off the light. I wasn't taking all these things too seriously. I thought he'd feel differently in the morning, when the drink had worn off. But then . . .'

The old lady's voice drops. 'Have you ever known . . . ?' she whispers.

'What?' Teresa asks. 'What's that, Virginia? I can't hear you.'

Virginia coughs, tries again. 'I woke up and the light was on and Cary was sitting forward on the bed. He was glaring down into my eyes and his fingers were squeezing my throat so *hard* – I was still bruised and croaking like a bullfrog a week later. "You hate me enough to want me dead?" I asked. That stopped him. I was trembling. But – you know what I mean – I couldn't help wondering what would have happened . . . what if I *hadn't* woken up?'

Teresa doesn't make an answer. I wonder if she's feeling as surprised as I am. Cary Grant, trying to strangle his wife, just because she smiled too much at an elderly actor?

'I didn't say anything more. I got dressed, packed up my clothes, went downstairs and got in the car. Cary didn't try to stop me. I think he was pretty scared himself.'

A few days later, on the morning of 29 September 1934, Virginia took a call at her mother's house from columnist Louella Parsons. Under pressure, Virginia admitted that the marriage had been going 'from bad to worse'. She told Parsons, nevertheless, that she was still in love with her husband, and that she hoped the two of them might yet manage to rescue their relationship.

Louella told her readers that the Grants' wedded life was over, finished.

Cary Grant was not about to accept Louella Parsons as an authority on the state of his marriage. Throughout the following week, Blanche's home was besieged by telephone calls from her frantic son-in-law, begging to speak with his wife. Mrs Cherrill dealt with these curtly: Virginia was said to be unavailable. When Cary became more menacing, Blanche called in detectives to investigate the possibility of a plan to kidnap her daughter. A couple of articles about the threatened abduction appeared in the papers, and were widely circulated.

For a while, the calls ceased.

On 4 October, Blanche went out to spend a night playing bridge – her favourite recreation – with a group of friends. When Cary called, a little after two in the morning, his wife picked up the receiver. Cary's voice sounded blurred and tearful; he begged Virginia to give their marriage another try; he promised that there would be no more threats, no more violence, if only she would not leave him.

'I don't know what I said to her,' Cary admitted later. 'Things got hazier and hazier.'

Eventually, Grant hung up.

Alarmed by the slowness of his speech and his lack of coherence, Virginia rang back; when the houseboy answered, she told him to go and check in the master bedroom. Her fears were well founded. Cary Grant lay unconscious, his limp hand stretched towards an empty bottle upon which the frightened houseboy glimpsed the word *Poison*.

At 3.28 a.m., an ambulance drew up at Hollywood Hospital; within a few hours, the word was out across town that Cary Grant had tried to kill himself.

Had he? The actor's stomach revealed no trace of poison. Perhaps Grant, as certain reporters were quick to suggest, had been the victim of some macabre kind of practical joke.

Nobody in Virginia's and Cary's circles believed this theory (a tale hastily concocted by the press team at Paramount). Later, Cary dismissed the episode, claiming that he had passed out after two days of heavy drinking. Was that the truth, or had Cary set up the scene to terrify his wife into returning? The fact that he was found with his hand pointing at the empty bottle marked 'Poison' does suggest more than a touch of stage-management.

The attempt to scare Virginia into submission – if that indeed was what the incident was – did not prove a success. A month later, on 11 December, in the presence of Judge William Valentine, Virginia entered the witness box to testify against her husband. She had not, she said in a low voice, been in a fit state to work, following their separation; Cary had produced a mere $125 for her maintenance; she had pawned her engagement ring and watch; a loan had even been taken out against her car. Asked what sum would meet her needs, Virginia requested a thousand dollars a month. Cary, taking the witness box in his turn, unsportingly remarked that a woman of Virginia's talents didn't need more than $150 a month. Why could she not support herself, as she had done before the marriage?

That comment, given that Grant's own salary at Paramount had just been raised to $1,250 a week, did not meet with Judge Valentine's approval. Unimpressed, he ordered a payment to be made to Virginia of $725 every month during the months leading up to the decree absolute; as a rider, he exempted Virginia from any of the legal costs, and froze her husband's assets until the final completed sale of the marital home.

The marriage had been short-lived. There were no children. Cary Grant was still far from commanding the salary of a major star. Judge Valentine's decision seems, in these circumstances, to have been reasonable. The case was not, however, a closed one. The following week, Virginia Cherrill's attorney lodged an amended claim. Startling new evidence was supplied (it would be interesting to learn how influential Blanche Cherrill, a fiercely loyal mother, had been in bringing this forward). The court now received a franker account of the causes for the marriage's breakdown; it was alleged by the attorney (Milton Cohen) that Cary Grant drank to excess, beat and kicked his wife, choked her and had threatened – the actual attempt on her life was withheld from view – to kill her.

These assertions, voiced in a period when Hollywood was struggling to conform to the Hays Code, threatened to end the career of one of Paramount's most useful young actors. If Virginia was prepared to go this far, what more might she disclose? Rumour had already connected Randolph Scott's name to his former housemate; would Grant's wife produce incriminating details? Knowing nothing, explicitly, for certain, the studio bosses became alarmed.

On Christmas Eve, less than ten months after the wedding ceremony, Virginia went to a meeting with Cary Grant's lawyers. An agreement was reached. In exchange for half the worth of the marital home – it was valued at $50,000 – she withdrew her allegations.

In the opening months of 1935, Cary Grant, ostensibly for the purpose of celebrating his mother's birthday, sailed for England.

Virginia, meanwhile, took up an offer of Hollywood film work. *What Price Crime*, a pedestrian thriller, offered her the role of a gangster's sister. Noel Madison played the villain with wooden-faced charm; Charles Starrett, a brawnily handsome New England actor, took the role of the undercover detective for whom Virginia falls. ('It's not just love; it's a cyclone!' she gasps to Madison.)

Cherrill's delicate beauty lights up the screen, each time she appears, in this mildly pleasant caper. She may never again, after *City Lights*, have been cast in a great film, but at least, watching her performance here, we can understand why Josef von Sternberg – the project foundered due to the great director's ill health – would later become eager to work with Virginia. While she lacks the extraordinary charisma of von Sternberg's beloved Marlene, Virginia possesses the indefinable quality that connects to a camera and attracts the viewer. Given her anguished state of mind at the time *What Price Crime* was shot, the mediocre film offers an impressive example of grace managing to thrive under emotional pressure.

Fortunately for Virginia, one of her fondest supporters had returned to Hollywood, just at the time when she most needed consolation: the rude, soft-hearted, venomously funny Oscar Levant had arrived to study music with composer Arnold Schoenberg. Levant's daily host, during much of this period, was his old friend Harpo Marx, who was then renting a vast and old-fashioned mansion in Beverly Hills.

'For one year and one month,' Harpo would later lament, 'he [Oscar] ate my food, played my piano, ran up my phone bills, burnt cigarette holes in my landlady's furniture, monopolised my record player and my coffee pot, gave his guests the run of the joint, insulted my guests, and never stopped complaining. He was an insomniac. He was an egomaniac. He was a leech and a lunatic – in short,' Harpo concluded, 'a licki nut.' (Whatever *that* was.) And then, with an unexpected turn, he softened the indictment of his eccentric friend: 'But I loved the guy.'

Oscar, offering his own account of this period of his life, defended himself by stating that 'the leech' had always returned home to his own bed at night. (Virginia, having abandoned a very different Leach, was often there to share it.)

Levant's excellent biographers make no reference, at this stage of his career, to Virginia; they do, however, cite an evening at Harpo Marx's Beverly Hills home that fits snugly as a missing jigsaw piece with her own memories. The occasion they describe was one on which Oscar brought along the celebrated Schoenberg to Harpo's house; the other guests were Fanny Brice and Beatrice Lillie. Virginia, who may have been present that night – she describes similar evenings to Teresa – recalls the additional presence of Alexander Woollcott, the man who helped put the Marx Brothers on the map.

'You know, he wrote for *The New Yorker*. They said he went to a dinner in the country once and stayed for eight weeks! Aleck Woolcott was even worse than Oscar! There was a famous play written about him later, called *The Man Who Came to Dinner*. He was a brilliant man, terribly funny and extremely selfish. And Dorothy Parker, Robert Benchley – they all came up to Harpo's house. They were all linked up through the Algonquin Round Table.'

Expanding on her memories, Virginia explains how it comforted her to be welcomed into that raucous, ebullient household. The scenes she conjures up are strikingly at odds with the usual Hollywood reports of showy parties and silly pranks. Harpo, Oscar and Virginia, it is worth remembering, all had one thing in common: none of them cared for alcohol. Their high spirits were the product of their own vivid personalities.

'So Oscar came in with a musician called Clark one night,' Virginia says. 'And I remember Clark talking with Professor Schoenberg, and a string quartet was playing, and Oscar smoking and pacing around the room, and Aleck Woollcott was talking away on the sofa, and there was a big fire blazing on the hearth. I curled up near the fire, listening away – you know how I love listening to people who make me laugh – and just for once, I forgot to be miserable. But that was just one night. I missed Cary all the time. You have no idea.'

Not even Oscar could console Virginia for the loss of the man who, as she remained painfully aware, continued to adore her and longed for her return. Meeting his ex-wife at a charity function in England, a full year after their separation, Cary left his own group of friends to spend the evening in her company; asked, much later, to compose an imaginary dinner-party of his favourite people, he immediately named one: Virginia Cherrill, 'my former wife'. Gossip journalists, tracking the course of an increasingly celebrated actor through a series of romances over the seven years that followed his divorce from Virginia (he married again in 1942), noted that Cary's girlfriends almost invariably bore a startling physical resemblance to Miss Cherrill.

On 26 March 1935, Virginia and her mother returned to the Los Angeles court, for the third, and last, time. (Cary had been advised not to appear.) Dressed in a navy-blue suit and wearing dark glasses, Virginia won a murmur of sympathy for her fragile appearance; after apologising to Judge Charles Haas for the fact that she had been unwell, she allowed her attorney, Milton Cohen, to interview her.

True to her word, Virginia offered the court a censored description of the failings of her husband. She affirmed that he was addicted to liquor, drinking 'steadily, and in large quantities' and that (responding to a question from Judge Haas) he had been 'quarrelsome and sullen'; she said nothing about violence or threats to her life. Blanche Cherrill, taking her own brief turn in the dock, supported Virginia's evidence; she also took the opportunity to state that she had seen Cary Grant insult her daughter in public. Since the settlement division of $50,000 had already been agreed (this being the estimated value of the home the couple had shared), and no alimony was sought, there were no remaining issues to be discussed. The divorce was finalised over a year later, on 28 July 1936. Neither member of the couple had made any attempt to hasten this slow unravelling of their life together. Neither felt any inclination to do so.

'If he cannot have [Virginia] – and obviously he cannot,' gossiped one Tinseltown commentator, writing a 1936 feature for *Movie Mirror*, entitled 'Why Cary Grant Can't Stay in Love', 'he must eternally seek women who resemble her.'

The item, preserved in Virginia's scrapbooks of memorabilia, is one among a considerable number of cuttings about Cary that she kept, possibly because they all testify to Cary Grant's restless search for another Virginia, a substitute for his first love, ever lost. One, written for *Film Pictorial* (August 1937) by Clarence Winchester, makes a more intriguing observation. Grant's acting changed after his marriage ended, Winchester notes. From 1935 onwards (he was thinking in particular of the actor's striking performance in the film *Sylvia Scarlett*) Grant played his characters with an edge of bitterness that made them more real, and more likeable, than his blander early performances.

And Virginia?

One of her favourite of Oscar Levant's witticisms was his definition of happiness as being 'not something you experience . . . it's something you remember'. This aphorism, as she embarked on a new life, became an apparent, and painful, statement of the precise truth.

'I was carrying a torch for Cary for years after we parted,' Virginia tells Teresa. She goes on, speaking low, almost as if to herself: 'I was *so* in love with him!'

Part Three

A New Life

9

SOCIETY GIRL

(1935–1936)

'Leaving him broke my heart . . . but I could never have gone back.'

'Jeez, Virginia, can't you tell him to turn it down?'

'It's not so loud that we can't talk,' Virginia responds.

From the darkened cell of her husband's den, the acid crackle of a television sputters into a series of pistol shots.

'Please?' Teresa coaxes. 'Go on. He won't mind, if you ask him.'

But Virginia comes to the old man's defence. 'You know how he loves cowboy films. Did I ever tell you that was what Florek wanted to be, when we first came out here. I mean, can you *imag*ine that man as a cowboy?'

'No, I can't.' For once, Teresa makes no secret of her impatience. 'Hey! Florek! Do us a favour, can't you? I'm trying to hold a conversation with your wife!'

'It's John Wayne,' murmurs Virginia. 'His favourite. He never cared much about meeting actors, but John was Florek's hero.'

'It's John Wayne!' a male voice calls, above another volley of shots.

'See?' she smiles. 'Isn't it strange, when you think of all those courageous things that Florek himself did? But he never talks about that – you know how he is.'

'I certainly do.' Teresa seems to be trying to keep her tone neutral.

'And yet he'll watch films like that all day long and never get bored!'

'Tell me, did you ever love a man quite so much as Florek?' Teresa asks, after a moment's pause. 'I mean, I know you were crazy about Cary for a while, but . . .' She lets her question hang there.

'Florek's always been a good husband,' Virginia answers. 'A truly reliable man. And that, you'd better believe me, isn't easy to find. Cary . . .' (I notice how gently she speaks his name) '. . . Cary made me laugh like nobody else ever did, and he was sexy as hell. But he shouldn't have married me. And I should never have said yes. On the other hand . . .'

'Do you regret it?'

The tape whirrs. Virginia seems to be thinking what answer to give. 'Remember when I told you how I kept throwing razor blades out of the window of that little London flat, so that I wouldn't harm myself?'

'Yes. You told me. That was when you'd decided you weren't going to marry Cary, right?'

'I got it wrong. I've been trying to get those days clear in my head this past week. I did that thing with the razor blades when I came to London later, after our divorce. I was so unhappy.'

'Un*happy*!' Teresa's normally low voice shoots up by half an octave. 'You've got to be kidding me. My God, Virginia, you've shown me the scrapbooks. You were going out with every eligible man in London; balls, parties on the Thames, weekends in Biarritz, racing at Ascot – you never stopped.'

'Well?' Virginia's voice has grown so faint that I can scarcely pick up her words. Perhaps, she doesn't want her husband to hear

her talking about how she felt after the divorce from Cary. Pressing
the little recording machine hard against my ear, I push the replay
button once more.

'You never stopped!'

'Isn't that what you do when you're unhappy? You go out. You
see people, do everything you can. It gets you through the days.'
Virginia pauses. 'And it's true that if you're crazy about a man, if
you don't have those feelings for anybody else, then others, the
ones you *don't* love, just seem to want you more.'

'Mmm,' returns the interviewer. 'And I suppose it might help
if you've been called the most beautiful woman in Hollywood,
and starred in a film by Chaplin? Come on, Virginia, you know
it's not that simple. So, tell me about when you arrived in
London.'

But there's a knock on the door.

'Father Virgil! He's here!' cries Virginia. 'Time to get out the
sherry!'

Relief shimmers through the old lady's voice. Teresa may want
to know about the glories of her friend's past, but Virginia herself
always sounds happiest when the two return to the present.
Recalling old times may be something of a duty, I begin to suspect,
a kindness to a friend in return for her welcome company.

These tapes are not some swan-song for past triumphs.

Who was responsible for Virginia's decision, after her short
marriage to Cary Grant, to move to England? One lady who was
later keen to take the credit was a middle-aged Hungarian beauty
who, following her lucrative career on stage as one of the
celebrated 'Dolly Sisters', had settled for marriage to Irving
Netscher, a Chicago attorney. A 1934 photograph in Virginia's
scrapbooks shows the former Mrs Grant on the beach at Santa
Monica, alongside Mr Netscher and his wife. Had Mrs Netscher,
Rosie, been passing along the story of her past triumphs in Europe,

of the fabulous wealth that she and her twin sister had managed to acquire from a chain of suitors? Was she boasting about Jenny Dolly's French château, or the hoard of jewellery bestowed upon the two girls by Harry Selfridge, the spendthrift department-store king? And would such stories have made Virginia eager to travel the same road?

'Virginia was never a gold-digger,' Teresa tells me. 'What she really liked to do was to give. And I never heard her talk about the Dolly Sisters.'

Hollywood, in the mid-thirties, was a regular port of call for aristocratic Brits who liked being photographed with film-stars and fawned over by producers. Once the word was out that Virginia Cherrill was divorcing Cary Grant, the young actress was besieged by invitations from a whole new circle of acquaintances. Mrs Netscher's voice became simply one among many.

'England will love you', Virginia's friend Simon Marks had once promised; true to his word, he told Virginia now that Miriam and he had come up with the perfect way to settle her into London life. Rosie Nicholl, one of four sisters, had also just come to the end of a short-lived marriage. Rosie (more familiar to modern readers as Lady D'Avigdor-Goldsmid, the name she took when she remarried in 1939) was a charming and warm-hearted young woman; the Markses had just helped settle her into a flat at 20 Grosvenor Square, the handsome corner building where Virginia herself had stayed, briefly, on her previous visit to England. Rosie needed company; the two young women were sure to get on. What could be more perfect?

Still, Virginia remained hesitant. The British were so proper; would she not, after all, be marked out through her history of two failed marriages? Divorce meant next to nothing nowadays, Simon Marks reassured her. All she needed to know was that the English had gone mad about America and the movies. Chaplin, ever since his triumphant return to London in 1931, for the opening of *City Lights*, had been hailed as a hero throughout his native country: could Virginia not get into her pretty head that she, as Chaplin's charming co-star, might also have garnered a following?

'I suppose there was something in that,' Virginia concedes. 'It always amazed me how many people in London wanted to hear how I came to play the Flower-Girl, and how well I knew Charlie. Of course, it was a while before he made another film – and *Modern Times* wasn't so romantic, even though Paulette Goddard was wonderful.'

Events conspired to prompt Virginia's decision to put an ocean between herself and the troubling, persistent presence of her handsome and unhappy former husband. The American director Albert Parker was travelling to England in 1935 to shoot a thriller. *Late Extra* was intended to showcase a young man, James Mason (formerly an archaeologist and sometime stage actor), who had been talent-spotted by Parker at a cocktail party. Most of the parts for Al Parker's film were already cast, but the role of Mason's girlfriend had yet to be filled. The lightness of Virginia's voice could allow her – almost – to pass as English. Eager to attract her interest, Parker described James Mason as an English version of Cary Grant.

'But Al Parker never got close enough to James to know how badly his breath stank. It was terrible!'

Teresa is more interested in learning how Virginia had dealt with the impending separation from her mother.

'Was Blanche willing to let you go? I remember your mother being a woman of pretty strong opinions.'

The separation from her mother, as Virginia is quick to acknowledge, proved difficult. Blanche, upon hearing of Virginia's decision to move to England – a country of cold houses, grey skies and wintry faces – wept. What would become of her fragile child (Virginia's weight had plummeted during the divorce hearing), without a mother to shield and protect her? When Virginia reminded Blanche that her daughter was, at twenty-seven, well able to care for herself, she was accused of ingratitude. Their parting was not happy. Virginia's crossing to England was blighted by feelings of guilt. Should she, perhaps, have stayed on, and returned to a quiet family life in Carthage or Durham?

'Your mother would never have let you go back to Illinois. I'm sure she wanted you to get on in the world.' Teresa is responding to a faint quaver in her old friend's voice. 'We all know how good you always were with Blanche. You didn't have any cause to feel guilty.'

But guilt, as Virginia came to realise, isn't necessarily eased by the absence of a rational cause. Nearing the docks at Southampton, and shuddering as the March wind whipped colour into her pale cheeks, she resolved to send for Blanche, just as soon as she had the means to take care of her mother. Compensation would be made, in full, for the sacrifices this loving daughter was never allowed to forget.

'My mother always said she had the best fun when Virginia and she shared a flat,' says Chloe Teacher, the tall, hospitable daughter of Rosie d'Avigdor-Goldsmid. 'They went everywhere together that first summer in London, and I believe there were some wonderful parties. My mother told me that Virginia was the only girl besides herself who always wore her glasses to go out, no matter what the occasion. I think they were both too pretty to trouble with being vain. They used to share a pair of spectacles with red frames.'

'Anything else you can remember hearing?' I ask.

'I can't always tell which of them it is that I'm looking at in the old albums. They could be sisters! Same fair curly hair, delicate features, blue eyes, wonderful milky skins. And they both had a kind of indifference – they never seem to have cared what they wore or how they dressed. Here: do you see what I mean?'

*Virginia's London flatmate and
lifelong friend, Rosie (Nicholl)
d'Avigdor-Goldsmid.*

*Rosie d'Avigdor-Goldsmid,
visiting Virginia in California.*

The photograph Chloe shows me of her mother displays the vigorous face of an old lady out swimming somewhere in the ocean, hair tucked up underneath a battered raffia sunhat, between her teeth a clenched cheroot. Her eyes are screwed up with mirth; it's a face that simply exudes vitality.

'People say my mother was a beauty,' her daughter comments. 'But she always told me that Virginia had an extra quality. It didn't come from trying to make an impression; it had to do with the kind of person she was. And something else: Virginia possessed a wonderful mouth. My mother said it always looked soft, as if she'd just that minute been kissed. She probably had. Irresistible: that was what people always said about Virginia. My mother adored her.'

She catches my glance.

'And they both loved *men*,' she says, laughing. 'So please don't misquote me.'

The description Virginia offers Teresa of James Mason, her new young co-star in *Late Extra*, is less flattering [plate 9]. While normally easygoing, she hasn't a word to say in the celebrated actor's favour. Bad breath, she states, was the least she had to complain about from a man whom she considered arrogant, bad-tempered and – an unpardonable sin in Virginia's eyes – short on jokes. Viewers, nevertheless, seemed to enjoy their pairing together in this hastily shot film (*Late Extra* is usually described as a 'quota quickie', filmed only to complete a contract). Virginia, playing a journalist, becomes a sleuth and the accomplice to an eager junior reporter (Mason) as he sets out to hunt down a bank robber. Donald Wolfit and a very juvenile Cyril Cusack are today almost unrecognisable; Alastair Sim's distinctive voice and domed head make him easier to spot. A follow-up, *Troubled Waters*, starring the same cast, was scheduled to begin production later in the year.

Virginia's professional career dwindled, at this point, almost to the point of invisibility. A third project for 1935, *The Village That Wanted a Murder*, was abandoned. Her announced role as Princess Beauty in *What a Witch!*, a seasonal theatre revue being developed by the ageing impresario André Charlot, failed to materialise. Announcements that Miss Cherrill would be co-starring in the London stage transfer of *Transatlantic Rhythm* (alongside the fiery Mexican beauty Lupe Vélez) were withdrawn when it was realised that Virginia could neither dance nor sing. A few weeks before rehearsals commenced, her role was given to the more versatile Ruth Etting.

The two James Mason films, together with a light-hearted theatre comedy, *Uneasily to Bed*, in which Virginia went on tour at the beginning of 1936, quietly rounded off an acting career that had never been vocational.

'It didn't bother me,' Virginia insists. 'The Fox Studios still helped to take care of the bills and I didn't need a lot of money to live on. Besides, with the way Rosie and I were running around, there wasn't much time left over. People were so welcoming. I'm always told that Americans are hospitable. All I can say is: you should have just seen how I was treated when I came to England. The Queen herself couldn't have asked for more!'

Arriving in London in the mid-Thirties, Virginia entered a world over which the Queen (Mary of Teck, wife of George V), a representative of the old world of rigid etiquette, discreet affairs and the observation of class boundaries across the limits of which only a favoured few might be permitted to leap, held less sway than David, her forty-year-old playboy son. The most photographed celebrity of his heyday in the 1920s, the Prince of Wales retained, in 1935, a considerable influence upon London's smart set, in which life's goal was entertainment, supported by shrewdly conserved private fortunes. This world, into which Virginia was about to be welcomed, seemed scarcely to acknowledge the existence of the Depression, or the hardships being inflicted upon thousands of Jewish families in Austria and Germany. The smart young people with whom Virginia mixed were indifferent to the decline of the world to which their parents still clung: 'the passing away of old things . . .' that D. H. Lawrence, a traditionalist in wolf's clothing, had lamented to Lady Cynthia Asquith back in 1915. The present, in 1935, was what counted. Regretting the past was out of fashion.

Edward VII, as a far more enlightened Prince of Wales than his disquietingly nationalistic grandson, had loosened several of the barrier ropes in Victorian society by choosing not to restrict his friendships to scions of ancient aristocratic tribes. David (nobody who knew the Prince well ever called him Edward) further accelerated the progress towards social fluidity through a flurry of affairs with married women, all of whom had American blood. It is not clear that an American divorcee such as Virginia Cherrill, from a modest background and without any great fortune to her name, would have gained entry to London's smartest circles back in the Twenties. By 1935, however, the Prince of Wales had moved on from the American Thelma Furness (Gloria Vanderbilt's aunt) to the Anglo-American Freda Dudley Ward, and, finally, irrevocably, to Pennsylvania-born Wallis Simpson. American divorcees, with or without privileged background, were on the way to becoming social fixtures in London by the time of Virginia's arrival. What they lacked, however, was the quality that made Virginia a treasure to her new friends: an incorruptible integrity of spirit.

The Markses had promised her a warm reception; not even they anticipated what a success their transatlantic friend was about to enjoy. Virginia Cherrill, the London gossip columns announced in May 1935, was the hit of the season; no party was complete without this charming young woman. Drawing up a list of England's ten most eligible bachelors, one reporter noticed a unifying link. All but one of these illustrious gentlemen (Lord Morven Cavendish-Bentinck, the exception, was not much drawn to female company) were regular escorts of Miss Cherrill. It was just as well for Wallis Simpson, one can't help thinking, that the heir-apparent never caught Virginia's eye. But then – given that the Prince of Wales was never known for his wit – the future King probably wouldn't have been offered more than the time of day by laughter-loving Miss Cherrill.

The social barriers of the old caste system had begun to sag by the time that Virginia reached England; the warmth of her reception was, nevertheless, quite remarkable. How was it that a young woman, twice divorced and with no such fortune as Doris Duke's or Barbara Hutton's to act as enticing bait, managed to saunter so easily in, to be embraced not only by members of the smart circle surrounding the Prince of Wales, but the traditional, more judgemental world of their parents? Tallullah Bankhead, a US senator's daughter, had never achieved so much (acting as a prank-loving ringleader of the 'Bright Young Things' was Miss

Bankhead's finest social achievement). Greater divinities of the screen – Garbo, Dietrich, Harlow, Lombard – failed to grace England's social pages, either by dancing elegantly at hunt balls or by feigning enthusiasm at the outcome of a day's partridge shooting. The reason is not hard to discern: few American film-stars perceived the charm of hearty games, chilly bedrooms or bathrooms floored with cracked lino. Cheery stoicism was not their forte. Virginia, on the other hand, took to the English lifestyle as if she had been rehearsing for her role in it all her life.

The trick, as Virginia seems to have sensed from the first, was to behave as one of the gang, to accept British oddities and put on no airs, to laugh at her hosts' jokes, imitate their (newly smart) dressed-down style, join in their childish after-dinner games and never, on any account, dispute their views upon politics. Reverence for their history, a subject for which her veneration was great, never failed to please.

Virginia appears to have cracked the code of British upper-class etiquette without difficulty; the puzzle remains of how she arrived where she remained, perched insouciantly at the top of the social tree? Perhaps it was simply – as with becoming a film-star, so with marrying the man who became the world's own matinée idol – that Virginia never took British high society (nor, for that matter, herself) too seriously.

'The Markses were wonderful about introducing me to all their friends,' she volunteers. 'And Simon Marks knew everybody. Did I tell you he asked Robert Lutyens – Sir Edwin's son – to design new stores for M&S? Simon was always doing things like that, looking for ways to help people along. I think he gave my name to a few friends who needed fresh faces at their parties. Simon was a wonderful man.'

There's no doubt that the well-connected Markses provided many valuable introductions, but the key to Virginia's swift welcome into aristocratic society was her friendship with Edwina Mountbatten.

Simon Marks who, with his wife, Miriam, helped Virginia settle in England and made her a lifelong fan of his department stores.

Virginia had first encountered this charismatic woman when Edwina visited California during her honeymoon. She met her again, when Lady Mountbatten returned to Beverly Hills – without her husband, on this occasion – during the summer of 1934. (Edwina, back then, was spending much of her time with Harold 'Bunny' Phillips, her lover and regular travelling companion, while embarking on a new affair with Stephen 'Laddie' Sanford, the polo-playing heir to a carpet fortune.) Virginia's unaffected manner appealed to Edwina; a friendship, although never an intimate one (Edwina did not forge alliances with women whose beauty made them her competitors) developed. Edwina may have been the first to suggest that a young woman emerging from an unhappy marriage might do worse than come to England; certainly, Edwina provided the family contacts that placed Virginia, almost from the moment of her arrival in London, in late March 1935, at the centre of high society.

'Edwina,' Virginia says, 'told her sister, Mary Cunningham-Reid, to ask my friend Rosie and me down to her place near Newmarket: Swynford Paddocks, a lovely old house. Swynford gave me my first taste of English country life. It was quite a novelty.'

I wonder whether Virginia's hosts, Alec and Mary Cunningham-Reid, chose to inform their American guest that this elegant Jacobean manor was the house in which, just over a hundred years before her own visit, the newly married Lord Byron had created an uproar by flirting with – and possibly having sex with – his hostess and half-sister, Augusta Leigh.

Such a background history was appropriate to a house that was known, during the reign of the Cunningham-Reids, for its raffish ways. Virginia, who preferred generous, long-suffering Mary to her caddish husband, became a frequent guest at Swynford, but her reminiscences give little away.

'Mary was such a dear,' Virginia murmurs, 'and she had so much to put up with.'

Given the 40-year-old Captain Cunningham-Reid's reputation as a relentless ladykiller, it's tempting to wonder whether Virginia herself added to her hostess's burden.

'Absolutely not. I *never*,' the old lady declares, with a note of outrage that makes me smile, 'never, ever, went to bed with a man whose wife would have objected. And everybody knew that Mary adored Alec, even though he did treat her like a swine.'

Virginia's assurances seem borne out by the fact that she remained a popular and frequent guest at Swynford: wealthy Mary, rather than her philandering and impecunious husband, controlled the purse-strings and the invitation-lists at her home.

Captain Cunningham-Reid appealed to Virginia and Rosie Nicholl less than one of their first fellow-guests at the hospitable house. Sir Robert Throckmorton, tall and dark-haired, with a full mouth and eyes that always looked slightly fatigued, was the owner of Coughton Court, a romantic Tudor house in Warwickshire. Regularly described as one of England's most eligible bachelors, Sir Robert was admired by his own sex for being a fine shot, an entertaining companion and a generous host. Virginia evades questions about her precise relationship with this charming flirt, but the scrapbooks and letters indicate that she soon became a regular visitor to Coughton Court.

'Bobby came from one of the oldest Catholic families in England,' Virginia announces. 'They were involved in the

Sir Robert Throckmorton (Bobby), snapped by Virginia on one of their jaunts abroad.

Gunpowder Plot. Only I never could get him to talk about his history. He didn't seem to care about the past one bit.'

Instead, to her slight disappointment, Sir Robert wanted to hear all Carole Lombard's *bons mots*, and to exchange gossip about Laddie Sanford, his fellow polo-player. Sanford, together with his wife, Mary Duncan, a former American film-star, was due to accompany Sir Robert to India on a big-game shooting tour towards the end of the year. Virginia was urged to join their group.

'Darling Bobby', Virginia wrote later, on the back of one of the little black-and-white photos of him that she had preserved, together with a mass of his teasing notes that sent 'a kiss on the bobby' to 'Dear Cutie Pie' or declared, with unsigned simplicity: 'I love you Throckmorton His Mark'. Wherever Virginia travelled, be it to Biarritz, to Budapest, or to India, Sir Robert was always one of the party. At the least, these two were fond friends; possibly, they were something more.

This easy friendship was among several enduring ones that began at the Cunningham-Reids' relaxed and sociable home. Rosie Nicholl, who visited Swynford Paddocks almost as frequently as Virginia, brought along Margaret Whigham, the tall, dark-haired daughter of a Scottish industrialist. Back then, Margaret's chief claim to fame was that Cole Porter had mentioned her by name as a young beauty in 'You're the Top!'. Today, she is better remembered as the Duchess of Argyll, a vain and extravagant woman possessed – it was alleged at the time of her widely publicised divorce – of a voracious sexual appetite. Vanity, stubbornness and the habit of uncontrollable extravagance lost the ageing Duchess many of her friends, but Virginia and Rosie always stood by her. Neither of them, to their dying day, were prepared to speculate in public upon the identity of the notorious 'headless man' who had been photographed in a situation of uncommon intimacy with the Duchess; both women, as Rosie's daughter confirms, knew that the man in question was Virginia's old friend, Douglas Fairbanks.

'Margaret was not an especially intelligent woman,' Virginia concedes, under pressure. 'But, you know, I never could help liking her, and she did say the funniest things. Can you imagine: at the time of that hideous divorce case from the Duke, she wrote to say that we all ought to thank God for the Profumo scandal, for giving people something else to think about! She couldn't help sounding vain; it was a question of having too much beauty – and not quite enough of anything else.'

Teresa asks Virginia to identify a smartly dressed, broad-faced man who sprawls in a deckchair on the Cunningham-Reids' lawn beside a slender beauty in a white sunhat. On the reverse of the photograph, Virginia has identified the two only as 'Max' and 'Litzi', May 1935.

He, Virginia explains, is Max Ausnit, the owner of the biggest steelworks in Romania. He might, she says uncertainly, have been involved in making armaments; all she can say for sure is that Max was as generous as he was rich.

'People called him "le rouge" because of the colour of his hair. And his brother Gregor – I never met him – was black-haired, so he was called "le noir". Max was larger than life. He loved houses, good clothes, good parties – and most of all, he loved Litzi. You can't see properly in any picture just how beautiful Litzi was.'

Litzi, Virginia explains, came from a Roman Catholic family; there had been a terrible uproar when the exquisite young Livia Pordeau ran off with Jewish, recently divorced Max, the father of a twenty-year-old son.

'None of her family would speak to her. Max wouldn't let Litzi read any newspaper from Romania, because of all the bad things that were written about them both. But the Ausnits adored each other and, to me, they always seemed like a perfect match. Max loved to see people eat, and Litzi loved her food. You'd never guess it, to look at her. She really did have a figure like an hour-glass.'

Laughing, Virginia starts to describe an occasion upon which, taking Litzi and Virginia off to his favourite Paris restaurant, the Tour d'Argent, Max urged the two ladies to make themselves at home with the menu. Between them, they devoured seventeen courses; Max was delighted.

'He said: "God, but I'm a lucky man! There are only two women in all Europe who can eat as much as that – and I can afford you both!" That was Max, all over.'

Towards the end of the summer of 1935, Max swept off all their friends – those whom he and Litzi had made in England – to stay at the Villa Chinière, his newly built home in Biarritz. Here, the guests were invited to sun themselves and gamble – at Max's expense – at the casino that overlooked the curving, soft-sanded

Max and Litzi Ausnit at home in Biarritz with V (snapping them) reflected in the window.

shore; evenings were spent drinking champagne and dancing under a pink-lit ceiling at the Chambre d'Amour nightclub. Photographs of the group suggest that Virginia had found a new admirer, the handsome playboy son of a Belgian financier.

'Bobby Loewenstein,' she says. 'But you don't want to hear about every single man I danced with or went to lunch with, do you?'

I notice, once again, how astute Teresa is. She doesn't respond. After a moment, Virginia again picks up the thread.

'Bobby Loewenstein was often around at those parties; he was very polite, very well dressed, quite brittle. I always thought of him as a lost soul. You know, one of those people who laugh a little too much, too quickly? The problem for Bobby was that he inherited a fortune when he was just eighteen. He never seemed to have anybody helping take care of it all; he just floated along with whatever took his fancy. He was simply too rich. When the war came along, he joined up with the RAF as a pilot. I remember being told that he was exceptionally brave and somehow it didn't surprise me at all. Bobby needed a cause.'

Max Ausnit had acquired a large number of influential friends in England; the summer after her visit to the Villa Chinière, Virginia was asked to arrange for their entertainment. Previously, when attending race week at Ascot, the Ausnits had stayed at a big hotel. In 1936, due to the fact that his wife was pregnant, Max had chosen to rent a large country house for the summer.

'And he wanted to give a big party there and for me to organise it. Litzi dropped the baby, easy as a bag of sugar, the same week as the party. Three days later, she was back in the enclosure at Ascot, looking like a model. Incredible woman, but not even she could have arranged a dance for five hundred people just when she was giving birth.'

An unexpected aspect of Virginia emerges as she cheerfully relates how she, herself still a relative newcomer to England, had arranged one of the grandest social events of the summer.

'I wrote out invitations, chose the marquee, got the band from the Embassy, everything. It did go well. Max was so pleased that he sent me a car as a present! Not any old car, either: I was living in Swan Court, Chelsea, by then, and I saw this Bentley drawing up outside, and then the porter announced it was for me. Scarlet and white, with white leather seats – can you imagine how vulgar! So I called Max and I said: "Thanks, my dear, but I can't. I'll look like a kept woman." I mean, you could see it coming from ten miles away. "And anyway," I told him, "it's got a glass division behind the driving seat. I can't afford a chauffeur."

'"Don't be so silly," Max said. "*We're* paying for the chauffeur."

'"Well, it's too flashy," I said. "So I'm sending it back."

'Three hours later, another one rolled up! Dark green, this time, with pigskin upholstery and gold fittings – and that was Max's idea of a little thank-you present.'

In July 1935, Californian readers of *Motion Picture* were informed that Miss Virginia Cherrill was about to marry 'Lord Michelin'; in London, that same month, the *Express* hinted knowledgeably that a certain 'Miss Tyrell' might shortly announce her engagement to Lord Inverclyde.

Who Lord Michelin may have been – or if he even existed – is unclear, and Miss Cherrill, in the summer of 1935, was still the legal wife of Cary Grant (the divorce was completed in July 1936); these inaccurate snippets confirm only that, three months after her arrival in London, Virginia was flying high. Cecil Beaton, a young man whose social antennae seldom let him down, photographed her at the wedding of the aristocratic racing-driver Earl Howe; a month earlier, she had been staying with the Astors at Cliveden, together with the ubiquitous Bobby Throckmorton and another, more exotic bachelor, Felipe de Rivas, a muscular, languid-eyed polo-player with whom several well-bred young wives enjoyed a heated friendship.

'. . . And I've told you how the Queen's consort short-sheeted me!' crackles the tape. I can hear Teresa draw breath. What's coming now?

The story proves to be an innocuous one, the memory of a schoolboy prank. In 1935, young Prince Philip of Greece had been dispatched to an English prep school. Cheam was picked because of its proximity to Lynden Manor, the home of his father's cousins, the Marquess and Marchioness of Milford Haven. What interests me is the fact that Virginia identifies herself as a regular guest at Lynden Manor: evident, here again, is the link to Edwina Mountbatten. George Milford Haven was Edwina's brother-in-law.

'George was an enchanting man,' Virginia says. 'Very good-looking, brilliant – I mean, almost a genius – about anything to do with maths and engineering, but full of fun. He used to make me do tests of strength – arm-wrestling – just to give everyone something to laugh at. I was useless, even when his arm stopped resisting, because Georgie would always pull faces and make me start to laugh. He and Nada – she was Russian – were so sweet to me.'

A family day out at Cowes. The Mountbattens and Milford Havens, 1922. (Left to right) Louis (Dickie) Mountbatten, Edwina, Nada and George Milford Haven.

When asked, Virginia says she can't even count the number of times that she stayed at Lynden Manor, but that it came to feel like home.

'Lynden was a heavenly house for anybody who liked English history. Some parts of it were thirteenth century – can you imagine! And Prince Philip was there every school holidays, fooling around with Nada and George's own son, David. That was when he gave me an apple-pie bed, the little bastard. Otherwise, Philip was a nice kid, quiet, kept to himself. His family were living in Paris, back then. I think he was pretty lonely.'

At the end of her first nine months in England, as Virginia completed work on *Troubled Waters*, her second film with James Mason, George and Nada Milford Haven invited their American friend to bring her 'pooksie self, you darling' along to a Christmas charity night that was being held at the Albert Hall. The theme, they felt, might appeal: it was be a celebration of the art of cinema.

The evening brought a surprise in its wake, when the guests of the Milford Havens, having begun with champagne in the Mikado Room at the Savoy, moved on across town to Kensington and the Albert Hall. Here, to her consternation, Virginia heard that Cary Grant had already arrived. He was asking for her.

'I wasn't at all sure I wanted to see him, but Georgie and Nada said they were going to rearrange the seating, to make things easy. They were quite excited about the idea of a reunion. So then Nada stood up and they all filed out of the box and Cary came in, smiling and looking just as I always remembered.'

The Milford Havens were not alone in sensing romantic possibilities. Reporters noted that the separated but not yet fully divorced Mr and Mrs Grant had spent the rest of the evening engrossed in each other's company; one bold journalist asked if a reconciliation might be on the cards? No chance, said Cary, and when a photographer snapped the couple, he gave the man a hundred-pound bribe not to sell the picture to a paper. No point in giving people ideas, Cary smiled. Miss Cherrill and he were the best of friends. They had been enjoying a pleasant conversation, nothing more. He had a film to do, and she was about to commence rehearsals for a play. Mention was then made of the fact that *Sylvia Scarlett*, his most recent movie (it was later judged to mark his breakthrough into serious acting), was due for imminent release. Virginia must have been amused by the way this was slipped into the account: Cary was nothing if not professional.

Had he suggested anything more? Had she been tempted?

'I loved Cary,' Virginia states. 'You know I did. Leaving him broke my heart. But he wasn't my favourite husband and it wasn't a good marriage. Even if he had asked me – and I'm not saying that he did – I could never have gone back.'

Instead, with a determination that demands more respect than any of her hectic social activities, Virginia turned down an invitation to visit India with Bobby Throckmorton and his friends, in order to appear alongside Phyllis Monkman in rep – during the depths of a freezing English winter – at the Alhambra Theatre in Glasgow, and then at the Blackpool Opera House.

'And you know what?' the old lady announces with a laugh. 'I loved it!'

1. Jim Cherrill and his daughter, Virginia, 1911, in Chicago.

2. Virginia just before she won the Golden Apple beauty award at the Chicago Artists' Ball (1925).

3. Charlie Chaplin.

4. The 342-take scene from *City Lights*: Chaplin and Cherrill.

5. The Fox Studios present: two new contract players, March 1931.

6. John Wayne and Virginia remained good friends after making the abysmal *Girls Demand Excitement* (1931).

7. Cary Grant.

8. Virginia and Cary in fancy-dress at the Biltmore with two fellow guests (unidentified), 1934.

9. Virginia and – a newcomer to films – James Mason, in *Late Extra* (1935).

10. Jai and Virginia having fun.

11. Virginia at the time she was being romanced by Jai (the Maharaja of Jaipur) and Grandy (the Earl of Jersey).

12. Virginia and Bhaiya, the young Maharaja of Cooch Behar (1937).

13. Virginia stands between Grandy (3rd man standing from left) and (to the right of him) Jai, at a Sawai Madhopur tiger shoot.

14. 'Jai was so generous: he just heaped things on me.' Beaton took this eleven years after Virginia first visited India.

15. Virginia and Jo in England; note the Maharani's Western and very contemporary attire.

16. The Georgian Ball at Osterley. Douglas Fairbanks Sr and his wife Sylvia, flanking Mrs Fairbanks's sister, Vera Bleck.

17. Lord and Lady Jersey at home: selling Osterley to the tourists in June, 1939.

18. 'A real English rose': Esme Harmsworth, shortly after her return from Lisbon with Virginia in 1941.

19. Virginia and American officers walk through the ruined streets around St Paul's Cathedral.

20. 'And there he was.' Florian Martini, the young Polish pilot who won Virginia's heart.

Winning hearts in England: Virginia in the thirties. (This photograph was treasured by the Maharaja of Jaipur, who kept it on his desk.)

10

❧

A COMPLICATED LOVE LIFE

(1935–1937)

He had rubies and pearls and the loveliest girls
But he didn't know how to do the rumba.

'THE MAHARAJAH OF MOGADOR' (1947)

The Maharaja of Mogador (who ends up, in the 1947 song, by being robbed of his wealth by a savvy girlfriend) was a fictitious hybrid, based upon tales of the Twenties and Thirties, when London and Paris were annual fixtures in the social calendar for those among India's home-grown rulers who relished an international life.

Indira, the widowed Maharani of Cooch Behar (now part of Western Bengal), helped to set the raffishly imperious tone for the behaviour of Indian royalty when abroad. Entering her husband's tiny state for the first time by open car, back in 1913, Indira, herself a Baroda princess, had signalled an end to the old-fashioned system of purdah that compelled women to hide away behind walls, shawls and screens. Equally at ease when wearing the sari (for which she pioneered a new fashion among her compatriots), or dressed for a day's hunting in the English shires, the Maharani insisted that her own children should be educated in England, where she herself spent as much time as possible.

Friendships that were forged in the classrooms and upon the playing fields of Eton and Harrow were maintained by social tradition. Each winter, the maharajas welcomed their British school-chums, together with more recent friends, to socialise and shoot big game in India. Superb shots themselves (Ila, the eldest daughter of the Maharani of Cooch Behar, was personally responsible for the deaths of the fourteen leopards that comprised her mother's favourite boudoir rug), the rulers displayed their sporting skill with equal aplomb upon annual summer tours of England's polo fields. 'Jai' Man Singh, the handsome young Maharaja of Jaipur (now part of Rajasthan), took pride in obtaining the most coveted English trophies, at Cowdray, Windsor and Cirencester; between their triumphs on the field, 'Jai' – the Hindi word for victory – and his team found time to attend a round of parties at which Virginia, by the summer of 1935, had become an admired and well-liked fixture. It was almost inevitable, as the summer drew to a close, that Virginia Cherrill's name would be among the list of beautiful women who were invited to join the sporting parties travelling out to join their Indian hosts at the end of the year.

Virginia, judging from the sheaf of pleading letters to 'Mrs Grant' that Teresa has preserved – each handwritten on the thick, deep blue monogrammed paper from Smythson's that the maharajas ordered in bulk – was spoilt for choice. 'We've got a house party,' she was reminded on 14 December 1935, by 'Pip', the tiny, rich, and staunchly Anglophile Maharaja of Rajpipla (located in what later became Gujarat). On 16 December, Indira of Cooch Behar's eldest son, Bhaiya, wrote to beg Virginia to visit his palace during her first voyage to the East. A week later, the Maharaja of Jaipur sent his own final appeal to the beautiful young woman whose photograph stood in place of honour upon his desk: 'Wish you were here to make Xmas really gay. Longing to be with you, Jai.'

By Christmas 1935, Virginia had completed her brief immersion in *Troubled Waters*, the forgettable follow-up to *Late Extra* in which – once again – her co-star was James Mason. Why then, with no less than three of India's ruling families clamouring for her company, did she choose to spend the coldest month of a freezing winter going on a tour, not of the Indian states, but of Glasgow, Blackpool and Southsea? The play in which she was there making her stage début was nothing wonderful; the actors appearing alongside her, Peter Haddon and the ageing Phyllis Monkman, were not among her special friends; Virginia's role – she played a talentless but spirited violinist – was described by one critic as 'absurd'. We know, at least, that the novice actress gave of her best in a thankless role. 'Virginia Cherrill is utterly charming,' gushed one critic, 'and takes unto herself a perfect genius for the absurd self-dramatisation which the part demands.' Charm failed to save a bad play. *Uneasily to Bed*, due to poor attendance figures, closed at the end of a month.

Eagerness for stage work seems an unsatisfactory explanation for that chilly month Virginia spent toiling in rep. A more plausible motive surfaces in a letter sent to her, on 22 February 1936, by Indira of Cooch Behar's son, Bhaiya. What a relief it was for him to hear, Bhaiya wrote, that his friend Virginia had not, after all, been involved in a lawsuit (and how thankful she must feel herself!).

With a lawsuit threatened, might Virginia have fled from London to escape public embarrassment? Could that be the reason why she had slipped from sight into provincial theatre-life, rather than risk visibility among a cluster of her smartest friends, the regular winter guests of India's royal families? Who, in Southsea, Blackpool or even Glasgow, was likely to raise the spectre of a scandal?

No other allusion is made in Virginia's papers or tapes to anything like a lawsuit in the early months of 1936; evidently, the immediate problem was overcome. It's impossible to know just what the situation involved, but it seems fair to guess that a beautiful young American film-star had been causing a certain amount of marital havoc during her first summer in England. Virginia may have been anxious to escape being cited in a divorce case. The tape recordings reveal nothing; circumstances suggest that the potential litigation had something to do with George Child Villiers, the young and – at that time – still married Earl of Jersey.

Early in the spring of 1935, shortly after her first visit to the Cunningham-Reids, Virginia and Robin Filmer-Wilson, one of her fellow-guests at Swynford, agreed to make an informal expedition to Osterley Park. This magnificent eighteenth-century house, remodelled for the Child family by Robert Adam and owned by the 25-year-old Earl of Jersey, stood on the western fringes of London. It was well known that 'Grandy' (George Jersey had been addressed, since his Eton schooldays, by this shortened version of his courtesy title, Viscount Grandison), together with his beautiful young Australian wife, Patricia Richards, spent little time together at Osterley. The preferred home of the Jersey family had always been Middleton Park, in Oxfordshire.

'Our plan was just to wander about the outside of Osterley and take a look,' Virginia explains to Teresa. 'We'd heard the Jerseys were often away; we hadn't expected to find anyone there to stop us. But then Grandy came out under those wonderful columns at the front, and when he saw Robin and me, he came running down the steps. So we had to come clean and own up to the fact that we were trespassing.'

'A bit of an odd fish' was how Grandy Jersey described himself in rambling memoirs that he wrote in his later years. Virginia,

Osterley, the home of Lord Jersey, on a winter day in the Thirties.

however, was quite charmed when the tall, gaunt, sallow-skinned young man, trailed at the heel by a mild-mannered Alsatian hound, welcomed the two intruders as if they were long-lost friends. Instead of being ushered out and off the grounds, Virginia and Robin Filmer-Wilson were welcomed into the house. Lord Jersey led them on a tour of the splendid, if chilly, state-rooms; over tea, he shared with his guests the difficulty of trying to feel at home in an underlit, badly ventilated icebox.

'Osterley really was a bit of a mausoleum,' Virginia comments now. 'And his grandmother – Margaret Jersey was a wonderful woman, but she didn't know diddle about decorating – had put the most terrible wallpaper in some of the rooms. She was living in central London, by then; none of the family found Osterley an easy house to live in. But what struck me on that first visit was how isolated Grandy seemed. His wife, Pat, was away. He didn't even know really where she was. None of the servants were around. We felt quite bad about leaving him when it was time to go.'

Addresses were exchanged; plans were made to meet again. Shortly after this, having noticed Virginia's enthusiasm for his dog, Lord Jersey insisted on buying her a puppy.

'Juny, my little Sealyham that I had for years: I didn't tell Grandy that I wanted Juny because he reminded me so of Cary's dog. We spent a whole day, picking Juny out, at a kennels just off the new Watford bypass. But that's not the point . . . it wasn't the dog that made such a bond between us.'

The point the old lady wants Teresa to grasp takes me by surprise. I hadn't known that Grandy Jersey was interested in art; neither had I fully appreciated the extent of Virginia's own knowledge of that world. Grandy had raised a substantial sum in 1935, by selling off the contents of Middleton, the old, recently demolished family home in Oxfordshire; now, he wanted to use this money to start a new collection.

'He just wasn't sure quite where to begin. So I told him what Edwina Mountbatten had said to me: look at the Impressionists. Grandy himself had a good eye; all I did was to give him an idea. I told him how much I'd always loved the Potter Palmer collection in Chicago. Maybe I mentioned the big collection Edward G. Robinson was putting together back in California; I don't know. People from Grandy's world weren't looking to buy those kinds of works for their homes; they thought the Old Masters fitted in best. But Grandy was interested. He picked up on it straightaway.'

Picture-viewing and purchasing, Virginia explains, became the basis for a comfortable friendship that developed between herself and the lanky, diffident young Earl – he was two years younger than she – during the summer and autumn of 1935. Lord Jersey's day job at a bank was not a demanding one; more often than not, he would take his afternoon off to go to a gallery with Virginia.

'Pat Jersey didn't have much feeling for modern art,' Virginia tells Teresa. 'So I'm sure our friendship didn't trouble her, not back then, anyway. It wasn't in the least romantic. Grandy would advise me about what to do with the bit of money I had – he was always shrewd about investments – and I'd go along with him to see what they'd got at the Lefevre Gallery, or Dudley Tooth. I could always pick something out, but Grandy soon started making the selections himself.'

Teresa asks her for some clue to the kind of works they were buying; I gasp when Virginia casually mentions two Cézannes. These afternoons at London galleries mark – as Grandy's family have since confirmed to me – the genesis of a significant art collection.

'And then we bought Gauguins, Sickerts, Renoirs, Sisleys, Dufy and Utrillo – God, *everybody* bought Utrillos. Grandy had one over his fireplace for years. And Morisot . . . Bracquemond . . . Valadon: what *was* the name of that woman painter he liked so much?'

Teresa offers a few educated guesses: Virginia, rejecting them, sighs and passes on.

'So, there you are. I was Grandy's art adviser – and he was my money man. That's how it all started out. Of course, I did know that his marriage wasn't in a good state. (It was so funny, the way Robin Filmer-Wilson ended by marrying Pat Jersey, and I got together with Grandy, all after that first visit, wasn't it!) But, back then, my mind was elsewhere. I'd fallen for Jai.'

'And Jai was crazy about you,' I hear Teresa encouraging her. 'Come on, Virginia, you *know* he was. Remember when you told me how Jai asked you to marry him?'

'I certainly do. So why are you asking me again . . . ?'

(Does this canny old lady realise that she is being recorded? If so, how much does she embellish, or hold back, delete? I've listened over and over to these recordings. I can never entirely make up my mind.)

My favourite version of Virginia's first encounter with the mischievous and seductive 23-year-old Maharaja of Jaipur recounts how she paused to watch two sleek new Bentley cars racing, flat out, at dusk, along Piccadilly. The adversaries were Jai of Jaipur and his most fervent admirer (and keenest rival), Bhaiya, the 19-year-old Prince Regent of Cooch Behar. The automobile race was typical of a genial relationship that was suffused throughout with intense sparring.

The Maharaja of Jaipur ('Jai'), snapped by Virginia.

'Jai and myself used to race about Calcutta, and Jai once missed a bullock cart by literally six inches while travelling at eighty miles an hour,' Bhaiya boasted to Virginia (a few months after Jai's victory in the race to Piccadilly Circus). 'Everyone in my car (following) looked the other way . . . I call Jai dangerous, and Jai calls me dangerous, so I expect we both are.'

The more probable narrative relates that Virginia met Jai, Bhaiya and Pip (the ruler of Rajpipla) at a reception given by George and

Nada Milford Haven to mark the beginning of a summer of sport, parties, and as many flirtations as the young maharajas could possibly manage to crowd into their hectic summer calendar. Back at home, tradition compelled the Indian rulers to behave themselves; once in Europe, they embraced the Western style of life with the glee of escaped prisoners.

Of the three, there has never been any doubt that handsome, athletic Jai, one of the finest (some said *the* finest) polo-players in the world, was easily the star. Pip of Rajpipla – small and dapper was a party-lover whose preferences, when in London, ran towards shopping at Asprey and quaffing cocktails at the Savoy. Harrow-educated Bhaiya of Cooch Behar, closest cohort to Jai, was completing, in 1935, his first year at Trinity College, Cambridge. A high-spirited, intelligent and impulsive young man, Bhaiya's flair for creating scandals recalled the days when his beautiful and promiscuous mother (Indira's notorious number of lovers had earned her the name 'Maharani of Couche Partout') had appeared at a party in Paris attired – so it was rumoured – in nothing but a magnificent emerald necklace.

'Everybody I knew called Bhaiya's mother "Ma" – including Bhaiya,' Virginia recalls. 'But it was "Ma" for Maharani, and that was always clear. Not even Bhaiya dared cross his mother. She certainly terrified me. But Bhaiya's real problem was Jai. Jai was so handsome, so amusing, so fearless: there wasn't anything at which he didn't excel. He treated Bhaiya like a younger brother, but that didn't help. Bhaiya wanted to *be* Jai. And, of course, he wasn't.'

Bhaiya's envy isn't hard to comprehend. He himself came from a family blessed with wealth, charm and great physical beauty. His sisters, Ila and Ayesha, were sporty and attractive; his slender younger brother, Indrajit ('Digga'), had inherited a large share of their mother's personal magnetism. Bhaiya, at the age of nineteen, was, by contrast, round-faced, bespectacled and overweight.

Subdued at home by the commanding presence of Maharani Indira, he suffered, on his jaunts to Europe, from the pervasive sense that he must always, when compared to Jai, be found wanting. It cannot have helped him to know that Jaipur's young ruler was widely rumoured to be on intimate terms with 'Ma', his own mother.

Virginia's sweet and unassuming nature made her a magnet for men like Grandy Jersey and Bhaiya, who suffered from low self-esteem. Sending what amounted almost to a love-letter in January 1936, Bhaiya told Virginia that she had made a great impression on him, and that he had felt, from the first light touch of her hand upon his, that they were destined to be friends.

'And we were friends,' Virginia insists. 'Only Jai and I were all wrapped up in one another, from the very moment we met. I didn't have much time to think about Bhaiya.'

Asked by Teresa to chart the progress of the relationship with Jai, Virginia sounds blissful. She describes how they would go dancing together at Ciro's – a favourite haunt for all the maharajas – and then walk together, arm in arm, wandering through the streets of Mayfair and Piccadilly, until after dawn. Witnessing Jai's triumphs upon the polo fields at Windsor and Cowdray, dining alone with him at the Savoy, drifting, in his easy company, from Le Touquet to Paris, to Biarritz and on to Budapest, Virginia felt increasingly bewitched. She describes it as having been one of the happiest summers of her life – had she only been able to put Cary Grant out of her thoughts [plate 10].

'I think, from the first time that Jai slept with me, he knew the truth. I adored him, no question, but he wasn't Cary. And the divorce papers weren't even finalised. I couldn't forget – and I never was much good at pretending.'

She didn't do too badly: at some point during this halcyon summer, Jai asked Virginia to marry him. (It is not clear whether he knew that she was still, technically, a married woman.) Unwisely, she chose Bhaiya for her first confidant. Bhaiya seized the opportunity to enlighten her about the traditional life of a maharaja.

Brought up in the West, Virginia's sense of India was vague. She had observed Jai's immaculate Savile Row suits; she had seen him studying the form at Ascot and Newmarket racecourses, foxtrotting sleekly across restaurant dance-floors, picking out gifts from Asprey for a weekend hostess. This style of existence, she assumed, must also be his way of life in India.

'And then Bhaiya let drop the fact that Jai had been choosing presents for his wife, Jo, and their little boys. He told me that Jo was only thirteen when she married Jai, and that Jai's first wife, the mother of his oldest children, was Jo's *aunt!*'

Bhaiya also took it upon himself to explain the system of purdah that still existed in Jai's old-fashioned state.

'I didn't even know what the word meant until Bhaiya spelled it all out,' Virginia tells Teresa. 'I thought purdah was something you ate.'

Scant evidence survives in Jaipur today of Jai's passionate courtship of Virginia Cherrill. Fortunately, Virginia herself preserved a bulky sheaf of her correspondence from India. A handful of the letters and cards are from Jai; thirty are from 'Jo', his young second wife, the Maharani Kishore Kanwar, born in the neighbouring state of Jodhpur. The remainder, a further twenty letters, are from Bhaiya. All, evocatively, are laden with heavy golden lettering and designs; supplying stationery for the maharajas must have been an honour over which some bitter stationers' battles were fought in Bond Street and Knightsbridge.

Studying this gilded correspondence, together with Teresa, I am shocked to find Bhaiya's capacity for malice. Responding to a wistful letter from her, in February 1936, he admitted that he had tried to harm her reputation. 'I will never forget what a cad I felt after I met you,' he wrote.

The details are nowhere clear, but it seems that Bhaiya had decided that the best way to undermine Jai's romance was by ridiculing it to his mother. Jai, he had informed Ma, felt nothing for this American gold-digger. The relationship was not one that they should consider to be serious. The deed had been done; too late, Bhaiya expressed remorse.

'I . . . told my mother,' Bhaiya wrote, 'that I was, after all, wrong about Jai's love for you.'

Virginia, while hurt, was gracious. Thanking Bhaiya for his apologies, she congratulated her young friend on his having acquitted himself well in his first durbar – Bhaiya had just been officially invested with the power to rule his state – and sent him an amulet meant to attract good luck.

'I can't tell you how thrilled I was to get your sweet long letter,' a grateful Bhaiya gushed in return; a page later, however, he returned to the attack. Speaking as Virginia's devoted adviser, he wanted only to spare her from 'misunderstanding' by explaining why Jai would not – and should not – marry her. 'You see', he wrote, 'Jai's life is laid out for him and he must stick to the schedule, yet it would be inhuman not to be natural, even though very occasionally.'

By 'natural', it was apparent that Bhaiya meant having an affair. Virginia Cherrill was a beautiful young woman; she was not a suitable candidate to become the wife of a maharaja. The time had come for Virginia to reconcile herself to becoming one of Jai's pleasant memories, for 'I really think', Bhaiya piously concluded, that 'he is too nice and too great a gentleman to forget'.

In April 1936, Bhaiya paid a visit to Jaipur and took note, while visiting the Rambagh Palace, of Jai's large desktop photograph. Virginia had inscribed it, at her lover's request, 'To the captain of the team'. Jai spoke frankly to Bhaiya during this visit. He told him that he adored Virginia and intended to marry her. Writing to Virginia once again, Bhaiya changed his tone. He gathered that Jai would be travelling to England soon; perhaps there would be a happy reunion? He, meanwhile, always kept her sweet amulet safely beside him, a treasured memory of a valued friendship. He did so hope that she might now send him as well a lovely photograph of herself, just like the one that she had presented to Jai. 'I like having photos of real friends', Bhaiya wrote. 'Please forgive me if I have offended you in any way . . . Well best wishes, I wish I were Jai.'

Whether by intention or not, Bhaiya – however contrite – had already caused considerable damage. Arriving in England for the summer of 1936, Jai found that Virginia had filled her diary with engagements. Her most regular escort had become the Earl of Jersey [plate 11].

It isn't clear just when Lord Jersey decided that his brief marriage had run its course – or when his wife began the relationship with Robin Filmer-Wilson that ended in their marriage. Grandy had seemed a lonely figure at Osterley in the spring of 1935; a year later, he was urging Virginia to bring her mother across to England. A married man, Grandy had picked out the woman he wanted for his second wife, while still wedded to his first.

'I never gave Grandy any encouragement,' the old lady declares. To me, Virginia's recorded voice here sounds a touch defensive.

Blanche Cherrill arrived in London in March 1936, bringing with her Anita Blair, a vivacious young woman with curly dark hair and a bright smile. Anita, for the next sixteen months, travelled almost everywhere with Virginia as her companion – and her screen. Whether sallying out from Blanche's quietly elegant apartment at 120 Mount Street, just off Park Lane, or from Virginia's new flat in Swan Court, Chelsea, or from Grandy's own, discrete Swan Court home – Grandy and his intended inhabited separate floors of the building – this unlikely pair of couples (Blanche and Grandy; Anita and Virginia) formed an inseparable quartet.

A small black-and-gold photo album was employed to record Blanche's first visit to England. Virginia's absence from the shots suggests that it was she who held the camera. It's hard to determine how much Blanche was enjoying herself. Stoutly dressed for unreliable British weather in a large hat, sturdy coat and sensible shoes, her broad face remains impassive as a Buddha's. Nothing stirs Mrs Cherrill: whether photographed at Stonehenge, at Hampton Court or – upon a chilly April day – amidst the partly erected walls of Grandy's new Oxfordshire home at Middleton Park, Blanche's face is always unsmiling; her back is always turned, resolutely, to the view.

The tapes reveal little more about this period than does Blanche's guarded stare. Virginia volunteers nothing; Teresa, sensitive to her reticence, limits her questions to the vague. Piecing together scraps of evidence from the scrapbook and Grandy's unpublished memoirs, I find a picture gradually emerges of an old, half-forgotten scandal, of adultery, of public repudiation and of discreet liaisons.

On 14 April 1936, Lord Jersey was 'discovered' in bed at his Swan Court flat with Mrs Olive Clivden, a Canadian dancer who, for a small fee, had been (not unwillingly) persuaded to participate in this staged act of adultery.

It's somehow mitigating to discover that Grandy, in his unpublished memoirs, writes with great affection of Olive Clivden and of the brief affair that they enjoyed, following their first, pre-arranged date. It's less easy to respond warmly to the way in which Grandy then went on deliberately to humiliate Pat Jersey, his young wife. His friends were shocked; ten years later, Grandy paid for his caddishness when he was denied entry to Brooks's, one of London's most traditional gentlemen's clubs. (James Lees-Milne, who had put Grandy's name up for election, was appalled by the snub; Grandy, understanding the reasons, was not.)

Publicly, throughout 1936, Grandy continued to describe himself as a married man, and to deny that he had any intention of deserting Pat. But what could have been more overt than a letter to *The Times*, Britain's foremost newspaper, announcing his withdrawal of all financial support from his wife?

> I, the Rt Honourable George Francis, Earl of Jersey . . . hereby give notice that I hereby expressly withdraw all and every authority which my wife, Patricia Richards, Countess of Jersey, may have at any time either expressly or by implication or otherwise acquired to contract for me, or in my name as agent, or in any way to pledge my credit, and that I will not be responsible for her debts, whensoever or howsoever incurred. *Dated this first day of May, 1936.*

There can be no doubt that such a letter was widely read and discussed: Pat Jersey, a lively and beautiful woman, attracted considerable support and commiseration for the position in which her husband had placed her. This outburst of public sympathy for his spouse may explain why Grandy chose to spend much of the summer of 1936 conducting Virginia, her mother, and their ubiquitous friend Anita Blair, on an agreeable tour of some of the more remote areas of Britain.

Between May and July, the party, snugly ensconced in Grandy's new Bentley (Virginia's automobile gift from Max Ausnit arrived a little later in the summer), toured the extensive Jersey estates. In Wales, they visited Baglan House, Grandy's family home near Swansea; continuing through South Wales, they visited his uncle and aunt, Lord and Lady Dynevor. Moving on to Kent, they stayed with another aunt, the witty and worldly Beatrice Dunsany, wife of Eddy, a noted playwright, poet, and – a bond with Virginia – a passionate dog-lover.

Following Grandy's extraordinary letter to *The Times*, his family might have offered a chilly reception to the young American film-actress who appeared – neither the Dynevors nor the Dunsanys were naïve – to be their nephew's mistress, and the hidden reason for his published letter. Perhaps, pragmatically, they decided that this cheerful, unpretentious and effortlessly beautiful young woman was just what stiff, unfeeling Grandy needed. They took to his new girlfriend at once – and for good, as a considerable batch of fond family letters, written to Virginia over many decades, testifies.

Slowly, as Virginia herself was surely aware, she was being prepared for the role of a future countess. Revisiting half-built Middleton for a third time in June, she met Grandy's pretty little blonde-haired daughter, Caroline Child Villiers. Further introductions followed: to the older of Grandy's two sisters, Joan, and her sedate banker husband, David Colville; to Grandy's likeably rakish brother Mansel – married at that time to a girl almost as beautiful as Virginia herself; and to Ann, the Earl's lively youngest sibling.

'We all got along pretty well, although Mansel and Ann were my favourites,' Virginia states. 'They were fun, and warm . . . not like their brother.'

Teresa asks what Virginia means.

'Grandy was a cold fish. The absolute opposite of Jai. You can't imagine two men more different. I couldn't ever understand why he was so determined to marry me. I told him, over and again, that I didn't love him. He didn't seem to mind. He just wanted a wife.'

Born in 1910, Grandy Jersey was the eldest of four children – two boys and two girls. As a child, he had seemed the least likely of the brood to survive. Rheumatic fever and a heart condition prevented him from completing his formal schooling. Aged thirteen, shortly after he inherited his father's title and considerable fortune, the new Earl was removed from Eton. From then on, he was to be home-educated by a young tutor, one Ronnie Slessor, in the old house at Middleton that Grandy shared with his widowed mother, Lady Cynthia (herself the daughter of an Irish aristocrat). In 1925, just a year after her husband's death, and despite a gap of ten years in age,

Lady Cynthia raised the eyebrows of her in-laws by announcing that she intended to marry Ronnie Slessor. Their response was not to his social status – the Slessors were judged to be of good background – but to Ronnie's age (he was just twenty-five), to his profession and to such a hasty remarriage for a widow. Three of Cynthia Jersey's children, Mansel, Joan and Ann Child Villiers, responded well; Grandy – he had adored Ronnie, looking upon the young man both as older brother and substitute father – felt betrayed. Aged sixteen, he lacked the authority to take action. Ronnie, to his stepson's intense discomfort, now became the master of Middleton and Osterley, his family homes. Ronnie, the family confirm, was not entirely tactful in handling his newfound authority.

In 1931, during the same week that he turned twenty-one and assumed legal control of his inheritance, the young Earl ejected his mother, Lady Cynthia, his stepfather, Ronnie Slessor, and their two small children (Dinah and Henry) from Middleton Park. It was made clear that no financial support would be offered to them and that Ronnie Slessor would be excluded from all but the most formal family gatherings. Grandy's more literary friends took note of the fact that his new Alsatian (the puppy had been a gift from Ronnie) was given the name of Claudius. The allusion to Hamlet's hated stepfather, the murderer of his own royal brother, seemed less subtle than savage.

Grandy, as Virginia soon discovered from his more outspoken relations, did not prove much more generous to other members of the family. His sister Joan was told to look to her husband David Colville for her support; when Mansel and Ann asked their brother for an occasional handout, Grandy proved reluctant and chary. The Child Villiers siblings lived, as a result, on a modest scale, while the Slessors, on the verge of penury, valiantly struggled to keep up appearances. This was nothing new, in British society, but the case of a young man keeping a devoted mother short of cash and comfort presented an unusually stark contrast.

Virginia does not discuss Lord Jersey's finances with Teresa, but it is difficult to suppose that such a generous woman approved his attitude. The contrast between sober, tight-fisted Grandy and lavish, mischievous Jai can't have left her unaffected as, in the first week of July 1936 – after arranging the Ausnits' great summer party to Max's satisfaction – Virginia resumed her affair with the young Maharaja.

Jai of Jaipur, according to the recollections of Bhaiya's younger sister, Ayesha, spent the summer of 1936 conducting a clandestine flirtation with her own schoolgirl self, based upon the understanding that marriage would eventually follow their chaste London courtship. Perhaps Jai planned to add two wives to his collection. Certainly, during the late summer of 1936, his pursuit of Virginia became increasingly ardent. Photographs in her pale blue scrapbooks capture Jai chatting to Virginia at a racecourse, dancing with her in a nightclub, and lounging at her side, once again, in Le Touquet and Biarritz, surrounded by the usual stellar crowd: the Ausnits, Bobbies Throckmorton and Loewenstein, Rosie Nicholl and – passing through, under the Milford Havens' guardianship – a relaxed and laughing young Gloria Vanderbilt.

Posing beside Grandy for the camera, Virginia always looks stiff; the photographs that show her with Jai reveal a different body language, a posture of ease and – it's hard not to construe – sensual pleasure. Her divorce had been finalised; by September, when Jai and she were staying out in Budapest with the Ausnits, she had agreed to consider marriage. First, however, she wanted to observe Jai, not in his role as a playboy of the Western world, but as himself at home in Jaipur.

'I had to case the joint,' Virginia explains to Teresa. 'A whole group of my friends were going out to India in December. I agreed to go out and to take Anita along with me for company. Jai liked Anita. She was good fun.'

Before this voyage, however, Virginia had resolved to undertake a return journey to California: in part to keep her mother company; in part, to catch up with some old friends. That rationale, at any rate, was her claim; it seems a remarkable coincidence that, a week after she left Southampton on the SS *Bremen*, bound for New York, Grandy Jersey should also have decided to pay a visit to America.

Virginia and the Earl? First reports of their romance came from London, where the Earl squired Virginia (who was once Chaplin's leading lady and later Cary Grant's wife) about London. Then recently, Virginia came to Hollywood after her British movie-making, and told enquirers here that the rumor that she'd marry him was all so much hooey. BUT – all of a sudden, the Earl himself arrives in Hollywood, and right now he's Earling Virginia all over the town, and so far, he hasn't denied that his intentions towards the Cherrill are matrimonial . . .

Motion Picture, undated cutting from 1936

Virginia may have been placing her bets with care, calculating that if the relationship with Jai failed to work out, she could always settle for Grandy. Certainly, Lord Jersey had as little trouble in tracking her down in California as had Cary Grant when Virginia fled, before their marriage, to New York. It seems unlikely that a shy Englishman would have travelled so far alone without any hint of encouragement; did Blanche, desirous of a splendid alliance for her daughter, perhaps provide it?

Virginia's conversations with Teresa slip quickly past this particular Hollywood visit; Grandy, writing his private memoirs many years later, felt less need for discretion. Proud of his brief flirtation with Hollywood's nobility, he related how Virginia and he had shared a bungalow at the Garden of Allah ('a block with some oriental name at the top of Sunset Boulevard'), dined at the Brown Derby, admired the Himalayan backdrops on the MGM set for Frank Capra's *Lost Horizon*, and spent some days out at Palm Springs, lounging by the pool in the company of a towel-draped and cheerfully sloshed Humphrey Bogart. (Virginia, identifying the two men in her scrapbook of photos, playfully dubbed them 'Desert Rats 1 and 2'.)

Grandy enjoyed a little coup of his own during the visit: one of their neighbours in the Garden of Allah's poolside bungalows turned out to be a former schoolmate. David Niven, then in the process of shooting *The Charge of the Light Brigade* with Errol Flynn, evinced a keener interest in Virginia than in his old friend; their meeting at the Garden of Allah appears to have marked the start of one of Virginia's most enjoyable irregular liaisons, conducted (over

David Niven, one of Virginia's 'favourite' lovers,
seen here in one of her favourite shots.

the next few years) during her annual returns to California. The relationship was never a serious one: still, as Virginia, by then in her early eighties, phoned up Teresa one night to boast: 'It isn't every ageing beauty who can lie in bed watching two of her favourite lovers act their socks off in the same film.' (The work in question was *The Bishop's Wife*, a comedy from 1947, starring David Niven and Cary Grant.)

A dinner given for Virginia and Grandy by actor Robert Paige confirmed the suspicions of Hollywood's newshounds that a marriage was in the offing. Virginia Cherrill, it was announced, would become a countess, just as soon as Lord Jersey's divorce came through. Cary Grant, approached for his thoughts, ridiculed the idea. So, when they were invited to comment, did Grandy and Virginia.

Returning home in each other's company, the couple became more cautious. A 'chance' shipboard encounter was staged for the benefit of their fellow-voyagers; later, both Grandy and Virginia would tell inquisitive British journalists that their friendship began when they met in the autumn of 1936, as fellow-passengers on board the *Queen Mary*. Disembarking at Southampton, Virginia informed a handful of pressmen that she had no intention of marrying anybody 'for a very long time', while Grandy pointed out – quite correctly – that he was still a married man.

Grandy, however, had set his heart on making Virginia Cherrill his wife; hearing that she was intending to travel to Jaipur at the end of the year, he telephoned Jai and got himself added to the visiting party.

'I couldn't stop him,' Virginia protests. 'And it's true that I didn't feel too badly about his joining the party. It meant there'd be one other person around who wasn't completely in love with the wholesale slaughter of tigers. Loving animals was one thing Grandy and I really did have in common. We just dreaded having to take part in one of those awful massacres.'

Virginia on her travels.

11

❧

DECISIONS

(1936–1937)

'I think we are going to be very happy.'

'There will be tiger shooting, deer stalking, leopard shooting, pig sticking, an elephant drive, and other fascinating diversions', proclaimed a 1930s brochure for a 'Shoot Your Own Tiger' holiday. For 750 guineas, the traveller with Orientourist Holidays, of Regent Street, London, could be guaranteed a royal Bengal tiger shoot, entertainment within the homes of some of the leading families of India and the certainty of bringing back to Britain – already cured – the skin of his, or her (many of the best shots were women), particular prized prey.

Big-game hunting, together with polo and a little sightseeing, was what Virginia's fellow-passengers were keenly anticipating as they steamed towards Bombay. The Grand Duchess Marie Bonaparte (one of Virginia's companions on the *Nourmahal* trip to Tahiti) had brought along her brace of Purdey guns; Laddie Sanford had been honing his skills while stalking in the Highlands. Bobby Throckmorton, twirling Virginia around the steamer's dance-floor, let drop the fact that he was hoping to bring down five tigers this year. As one of the finest polo-players on the Jaipur

The most alluring cruise ever planned

SHOOT YOUR OWN TIGER

TO **INDIA** —as Guests of the Ruling Princes
January–April, 1938

*One of the holidays on which – for a price – a plutocrat could
go shooting with an Indian prince. Rosita Forbes arranged
these lavish tours.*

team, and one of the best shots among Jai's friends, Bobby had a
reputation to maintain. When she asked her friend what he
intended to do with the skins, Bobby replied that he planned to
pass them on to a couple of young godchildren to adorn their
nursery walls.

'I just gasped,' Virginia tells Teresa. 'I mean, what could I
possibly say!'

Stepping off the boat, she was greeted by her personal bearer ('a
fine, most dignified man'), who explained that he been assigned by

the Maharaja to conduct her wherever she wished to go, and to protect her throughout her stay. (It was an experience that the bearer evidently enjoyed: every Christmas, for the next forty years, Virginia received his small, handwritten card, wishing her well, and hoping – quite fruitlessly – for her imminent return.)

The passengers were given little time to recover from their long journey. Trying to put long-ago events in order, Virginia describes a full day that consisted of watching polo, followed by a state banquet ('My friend Anita and I were the only women with appetites big enough to eat both the dinners, the Indian one, and the English one'), and culminating in a ball. A little card has survived, of the kind in which a name is marked by the card-holder opposite each designated dance: Jai's name features twice; Bhaiya's, five times. Grandy – the Earl was an awkward dancer – does not appear upon the list.

'That was the night Anita took one look at Bhaiya's gorgeous younger brother and fell in love,' Virginia sighs. 'And if anything could have made Ma [the Maharani of Cooch Behar] dislike me even more, that was it. Digga was only eighteen, you see, and his mother's pet. I got the blame for bringing them together. Even Jai was quite annoyed.'

And what, Teresa wants to know, did Virginia think of Jaipur, and how was she treated?

It felt, Virginia tells her, like something out of the *Arabian Nights*.

'When we arrived, there were elephants to carry us up to the front of the palace, and flaming torches, and fireworks, and guards in the most beautiful uniforms, with turquoise-and-gold turbans, standing to attention all along the façade. And one afternoon, I remember everybody playing musical chairs on the lawn at the Rambagh Palace, with the State Band on the terrace, and bearers with fans, and peacocks and monkeys everywhere – it was extraordinary; quite unreal.'

Virginia goes on to describe how Jai would spend part of each day in formal attire, while holding audiences ('he had to let people kiss his knee'), and how, in the evening, he always changed into the same semi-Westernised outfit: black patent sandals, white silk trousers and a narrow black jacket.

'The women were expected to dress like princesses and, of course, everything I'd packed was wrong. I didn't yet own any proper jewels, and Ethel Butterworth had to keep lending me her second-best necklace. But Jai was so generous: he just heaped things on me. I came back to England laden down like a dancing-girl with stuff I could never wear: bracelets and toe rings and anklets. There's a Beaton picture, somewhere, of all my plunder. He made me spread the things all over a table for him to photograph. Cecil loved jewels [plate 14].'

Jai, it becomes apparent, was doing everything in his power to please Virginia. 'He had the most beautiful silk saris made up for me, although I never felt comfortable about being a foreigner and wearing Indian clothes. And there was one evening that I remember when he took me up alone, quite late, to the Amber Fort, a big yellow castle set into the side of a hill, above a reservoir, outside Jaipur.'

This exotic setting, so Jai told her, was where, high upon the hillside, in the tower of a yet more ancient fort, the treasure was stored of the royal families of Jaipur, but nobody, with the exception of each new ruler, was ever allowed to touch these opulent riches.

'And I do remember looking down at the city of Jaipur from up at the Amber Fort, and seeing the moon hanging above those wonderful pink walls, and the dusty plain spreading out beyond: it was like something from an opera set. I found it strange that all the people in this huge region should be under the care of just one person, however much he cared about them. Jai kept talking away about what he was planning to do, after we married, and I kept remembering back to Carthage, and just thinking how different he and I were.'

The entertainments that Jai had prepared for his guests revolved around banquets, sightseeing, gem-buying and sports: with these, most of the visitors were well satisfied. But Virginia was not.

'I'd been living at the Rambagh Palace for a whole week. We'd been taken to see ruins, and the observatory, and then off on a trip to Jodhpur, to the north, and I still hadn't once set eyes upon his wives or his children. I warned Jai that if he didn't take me himself to meet them, I'd find somebody who would. An artist called Charles Baskerville was out at Jaipur, painting the family: I knew Charles would do it for me, if I twisted his arm.'

After two weeks of adamant resistance, Jai gave in. Late one night, after leading Virginia through a maze of narrow passageways, he brought her into a room that, to her surprise, was decorated in modern, Western style. Here, a slight, dark-haired young woman with huge brown eyes and full red lips came hurrying forward. Greeting Virginia in perfect English, she asked, with great politeness, how she liked Jaipur. Jai then introduced the young woman as Jo, the Maharani Kishore, a princess of Jodhpur, and the mother of his two youngest children, Joey and a baby, Pat.

'Jai's first wife, Jo's aunt, was pretty trying,' Virginia says. 'Always stuffing herself full of medicines and grumbling about her health. But Jo herself was a darling, so pretty, and such fun! She asked straightaway if I was going to come and live in the zenana, after I married Jai. I told her that it wasn't clear that there was going to be a marriage. And then she asked Jai to leave us alone, and the two of us sat down and talked. We were up half the night!'

The meeting marked the beginning of a significant friendship. Reading Jo's letters (Virginia's have long since disappeared), we catch hints of an intimacy so close that there was talk, at the gossip-ridden Jaipur court, of a love-affair. Taking turns to cuddle baby Pat (always referred to as 'your friend cha-Pat' in Jo's letters to Virginia) in the gardens of the zenana, the two women exchanged confidences. Jai, his young wife confessed, did not often visit her at night; she did not know what she should do to please her husband. Virginia was persuaded to offer a few tips; her suggestions seem to have worked.

Virginia in Jaipur with 'Mickey' and 'Bubbles',
Jai's two oldest children.

'Oh Virginia,' an elated Jo wrote to her new friend, a little later in 1937: 'I have become so "sexy" that I can hardly wait for the night to come, but the trouble is that Jai has to keep fit for polo, so what do you think I ought to do???' Her newfound sexiness was, she added cheerfully, all Virginia's fault, for 'I was such a good innocent little girl. I can quite hear you saying: "You big dope!"'

Virginia, meanwhile, poured out to Jo all the unhappiness she still felt about her failed marriage to Cary. Locked away in the privacy of the women's gardens, Virginia disclosed something she would admit to nobody else: that she wished she had never left Cary Grant.

Jo, romantic to the core of her slender being, trembled with sympathy. 'Darling, honestly it breaks my heart to think you are not as happy as you ought to be', she wrote in a letter to be conveyed to her new friend's room by their regular messenger, Virginia's bearer: 'I wish I could do something for you. Please believe me, Virginia. I promise you that I'll always be devoted to you, and I am ready to do anything and at any time for you, and I'll never let you down. It doesn't matter what happens, because I know perfectly well that I couldn't have a more loving sister than you . . . I love you and I always will.'

Virginia's hardest task, however, was to explain to her friend that she did not intend to marry Jai. This refusal puzzled Jo: if Virginia loved Jai enough to sleep with him, and travel with him, why could she not become his wife?

'I simply couldn't cope,' Virginia admits, when Teresa, too, asks for her reasons. 'I couldn't cope with the gossip, or the etiquette, or the idea of locking women away behind bars. I hated the caste system. I tried to speak, one day, to a sweet little girl who was working in the palace gardens; somebody came and told me to keep away from her; she was one of what they called the untouchables. I once saw a camel lying in the bazaar with its back broken; nobody gave it a glance. The dogs just ran wild through the streets until they got distemper, or starved to death. And the way everything had to be shot! Pure butchery! Tigers, elephants, leopards: it was awful, *awful*.'

Both Virginia and Grandy had been dreading the tiger shoots; these ritual hunts, as the highspot of the visit, were reserved until the end of their stay. Noting, in his unpublished memoir, that the first of three shooting days had taken place at Sawai Madhopur (today a wildlife reserve), half a day's ride by elephant from the city, Grandy mentioned that the party had been housed within 'a luxurious tented village'. He failed to add that Jai was sharing his own accommodation with Virginia.

'We had a pretty good tent with two bedrooms and running water,' Virginia recalls for Teresa. 'Jai rang the bell and a servant brought in a pan of hot water for washing. And there was a loo, although it wasn't much of one, just a hole in the ground.'

Refreshed by their night's sleep, the sporting party were escorted to their posts. The arrangements, as Grandy's account makes clear, were designed to ensure that the tigers had not the slightest chance of escape. Five of the royal beasts – only maharajas and their special guests were permitted to shoot the Bengal tigers – had been located in a terrain of thicket and trees. Twenty keepers stood ranged behind that area, ready to drive the prey forward across an open ride. Above this stretch of cleared ground, the marksmen safely perched atop steel platforms, some twenty feet in height, 'too high', as Grandy dryly observed, 'for a tiger to climb'. To the rear of the platforms, a wall of cliff rose to a height of several hundred feet: once again, Grandy took note of the fact that the weighty animals stood no hope of scaling the side of such a precipice.

While not quite spelling it out in capital letters, Grandy was describing the preparations for a well-calculated slaughter. Bobby Throckmorton, a celebrated big-game shot, was the first to hit a target; after that, Grandy wrote, 'we all poured lead into the tiger'. Five royal beasts had been marked out for the bag; at the end of a successful morning, five sleek bodies were carried away to be skinned. The smell, Grandy noted, after the ritual visit during which each guest picked out a skin to take home, was 'ghastly'.

The photographs taken at Sawai Madhopur, triumphant scenes in which the royal house-party stand guard over the handsome corpses, betray almost nothing [plate 13]. Former film-star Mary Duncan Sanford leans back against Bobby Throckmorton while her husband, Laddie, grins over the shoulder of Anita Blair; Virginia, dashingly dressed in jodhpurs, tight boots and open-necked shirt, stands at ease between her two admirers, Grandy and Jai; in another photograph, she and Grandy stand over one of the royal beasts. Neither of the pair looks especially happy in their offensive pose.

Two animal lovers enact a charade of triumph: Grandy and Virginia.

The massacre sickened Virginia; the state of purdah distressed her; the fever of malice and gossip that ran rife through Jaipur's royal household – and to which Virginia's own relations with the Maharaja, and with his young wife, were subjected – filled her with complete dismay. And yet, when Grandy Jersey returned to England at the end of the month, Virginia elected to stay on. Jai wanted to make the most of these last days of her visit; the two of them agreed to travel back to Europe alone, in their own privacy.

No information survives about this stolen honeymoon, unmentioned in the recorded interviews with Teresa. A tiny album of annotated holiday snaps, pushed to the back of a neglected drawer in Virginia's last home, offers the only testimony. Turning its pages, we can follow the couple from Karachi all the way to the mouth of the Euphrates, up to Basra, Palestine ('a real sheikh', Virginia has written fondly beside her handsome lover as Jai smiles into her lens); and on, to stroll beneath the great columns atop the Acropolis in what seems, from the dusky light, to be an early evening in Athens. The final snap – but who took it? – reveals the couple at the railway station in Vienna, clasped in each other's arms and looking as if neither can possibly bear to let the other depart. They aren't smartly dressed; Virginia has her spectacles on and a muffler around her neck; Jai huddles within a winter coat.

Perhaps, at parting, the prospect of any real separation seemed unbearable. Arriving back in England at the beginning of March, Virginia wrote a letter to Jo, explaining that, while there would be no marriage, Jai and she both wanted to continue their present relationship. Jo gave her approval. All she wanted, she declared, was the happiness of her closest friends.

'Virginia,' Jo wrote the following January, 'there are only two people in this world whom I love and will always do so from the bottom of my heart, no matter what happens, and those two people are you and Jai. I am ready to do anything for you, even give up my life if that is necessary.'

Back in her Chelsea flat, Virginia was summoned downstairs to visit Grandy Jersey, who had been confined to bed by a severe attack of jaundice. (Virginia herself, although she makes no mention of it when talking to her friend Teresa, had been attacked by malaria during her Indian visit, and would suffer from recurrent attacks of the disease.)

'Grandy looked awfully yellow,' she says. 'I told him he ought to get some rest, since he looked sick as a dog, but he asked me straightaway, "Are you going to marry Jai?"

'And I said: "No, I'm not. I couldn't stand it."

'And then he said: "That's lucky, because I've written to your mother and told her to come over for our marriage."'

Virginia, still disinclined to take the invalid seriously, reminded Grandy that he was not yet divorced.

'He said he'd worked it all out – and then he handed me a diamond ring.'

Virginia starts to laugh. 'Everyone thought I got it from Jai for going out to India: our relationship wasn't London's best-kept secret. And I'd always reply: "No, I got it from Grandy, for coming home." Grandy thought that was very funny, at the time. But I never consented to a marriage. I promised to help out in every way I could, but I told him, straight out, that I didn't love him. Grandy didn't care. He said I could do whatever I liked, so long as I'd agree to be his wife. But I didn't agree.'

Looking for ways in which Virginia fulfilled her promise to 'help' Grandy Jersey, the clearest example appears to have been her increased involvement in the rebuilding of Middleton Park, a project in which Pat Jersey now showed – understandably – no interest whatsoever. Grandy, to judge from the drab way in which he was allowing Derek Patmore to refurbish his newly acquired – and modern – house in old-fashioned Farm Street, Mayfair, possessed little sense of how to make a home comfortable. Commissioning Edwin Lutyens, towards the end of the great architect's career as a designer of country houses, he found that the celebrated master was more interested in the overall design of the château-like Oxfordshire mansion (contrived, at Grandy's wish, with four satellite lodges), than in making it easy to inhabit.

Sir Edwin Lutyens had been suggested to Grandy by an architecturally minded friend who favoured Jersey's scheme –

an extraordinarily ambitious one, at a time when the days of the great English country house seemed numbered – to demolish the old family house and build an up-to-date palace in its place. It isn't clear at what point Lutyens's son, Robert, also became involved in the project.

Middleton Park, Sir Edwin Lutyens' last and grandest design for an English country house.

'Did I bring Robert in to help out at Middleton?' Virginia wonders, uncertain of her memory. 'We certainly had fun going over the rooms together and planning things out. Robert was always teasing me about my American quirks: modern bathrooms, concealed heating, chairs you might actually want to sit down in. Dear Robert, he was a charmer – great fun. I liked him much better than his father.'

Virginia's feelings about the elder Lutyens were reciprocated. She was, Sir Edwin noted to a friend after one of their rare meetings, a brainless little American woman, and very common. His son, however, seems to have adored her.

Their connection is easy to trace. Robert Lutyens's beautiful Polish wife, Eva Lubrzynska (a former girlfriend of Vladimir Nabokov's), was related to the family of Virginia's friend Simon Marks. This link had already led to some of Robert's most substantial commissions: to create (among many others) two flagship Oxford Street stores for Marks & Spencer, to remodel Simon Marks's own house at Hyde Park Gate and to design a luxurious apartment (to be inhabited by Simon's closest family), in Brook House, the newly rebuilt Mayfair home of the Mountbattens. (Edwina, whose family owned the building, had retained a magnificent penthouse for the use of herself and her husband.)

Virginia has stated that she still had no intention herself of marrying Grandy; she showed, if this was the case, a most altruistic thoughtfulness for the way in which his guests were to be accommodated at Middleton. Each of the twelve bedrooms designed by Robert Lutyens incorporated Virginia's practical suggestions: cheerful colours; a comfortable chair in which to relax; proper lighting arrangements; and the spacious ensuite bathroom which – some envious neighbours sniffed – made Middleton Park closer to a smart hotel than to a gentleman's country home.

'Robert and I made a good team,' comments Virginia. 'And I loved his wife. Eva was a wonderful woman, fascinating to look at, and so clever. She worked with Madame Curie, you know, back before the Great War . . .' A sudden pause, a silence, invades the tape. And then, plaintively: 'Where's Florek . . . ?'

'He went out with the dog,' I hear her friend replying. Teresa sounds a little put-out by Virginia's sudden change of direction. 'Something I can do . . . ?'

'I was wondering if Florek's parents could have known Eva's, back in Poland . . .'

'Maybe they did,' Teresa says, humouring her. 'Who knows? Now, where were we? You still weren't sure you wanted to marry Grandy . . .'

'Marrying a married man wasn't my top priority,' Virginia drawls. 'Besides, I had my mother back in town, again, and Jai was bringing Jo over for the Coronation. Did I ever have my hands full!'

Following the abdication of Edward VIII, his brother George was set to become Britain's (reluctant) King. The Coronation was to take place in May; every hotel room in London, within hours of the first announcement, had been booked. Wealthy home-owners were able to demand extortionate rents for the week of the crowning – and did so. The competition to toss extravagant parties became fierce. Virginia's unaffected manner and startling beauty ('She has the white skin of a Madonna lily', one admiring journalist noted) ensured that she found herself much in demand.

The maharajas of India, already conscious that their days of glory were under threat, were anxious to pay their respects to the British Empire's brand-new King. A browse through the lists of London's visitors at the time seems to attest that every state upon the continent was represented in Britain's capital: the Maharani of Cooch Behar, together with all of her family, was staying at the Dorchester; Jai had rented a large private house in Mayfair for himself and for his excited young wife, the Maharani Kishore ('Jo') paying her first-ever visit to Europe.

Such concerns, then, formed Virginia Cherrill's main occupation for the summer; Jo, exquisitely dressed and armed with the names of all of London's best shops, counted upon her new friend for advice and companionship. She was not disappointed. Sitting at Jo's side, Virginia set off for Asprey to help select presents for the young Maharani's extensive family back in Jodhpur, as well as for the ladies of the zenana; together, they ventured down to Sussex, to applaud Jai's team on the polo field at Cowdray Park; together, they peered through binoculars at the finishing lines at Ascot and Goodwood; together, they travelled one day to admire the Pavilion at Brighton, the elaborate domes of which – it was imagined by Virginia – might offer a comforting echo of home to her friend from India [plate 15].

'Jo wasn't all that impressed. She wanted to know why I was taking such trouble to show her the Pavilion, after they'd already gone and shown me the Taj Mahal!'

Whenever possible, Virginia saw to it that her mother was included in the party. Indians, she had noticed, respected mothers; Blanche was treated by both Jo and Jai with the courtesy due to a resolutely unassuming woman whose sole concern appeared to be guaranteeing the happiness of her daughter. Anita Blair, who had spent the winter in England, pining for the handsome young brother of Bhaiya, was often on hand to act as a companion for Virginia's mother. The older lady had a soft spot for Anita, both as an inveterate fellow-bridge-player, and as a female compatriot who respected one of Blanche's most poignant and cherished dreams: namely, that her antecedents would one day enable her to qualify as a Daughter of the American Revolution.

One intimate glimpse of Blanche's second summer in England has survived in a series of photographs, taken during a May boating trip upon the Thames, a morning's cruise down to Reading. Blanche sits in the bows of the river launch, chatting to Litzi Ausnit; Jo and Virginia pretend – unconvincingly – to steer at the helm; flirtatious dark-haired Anita leans back into the embrace of a good-looking French doctor. (Madame Docteur was taking the photographs.) At Reading, where the party disembarked for lunch, a photo depicts Virginia conducting a cheerful argument with Jai, while Jo, dressed in Western-style trousers, looks shyly on. ('Trying to get a drink', runs Virginia's caption.) In another snap, a laughing

A May boating trip with Jai, Jo and the Ausnits. Anita Blair is being embraced: Blanche (in hat) at back of the boat. Virginia's dog has joined the party.

Virginia places an elegantly shod foot on the rotund stomach of a prone and giggling Bhaiya [plate 12].

Bhaiya's crush upon Virginia was ill-disguised. He had filled her dance card at the first of the Indian balls. In March, he had informed her that his real age (Bhaiya was just twenty-one) amounted to being ('at least') *thirty*-one, back in India. 'I miss you a great deal, darling,' he added, after lamenting the fact that, during her visit, they had spent so little time together. Writing to Virginia once again (two years later), in the autumn of 1939, Bhaiya recalled the summer of the Coronation as having been one of the happiest times in his life. 'The memory of May, June, July '37 will for ever be imprinted in me and they can't take that away from me, nor the memory of red roses.'

Life, as the romantic Bhaiya had evidently forgotten, had been less fragrantly scented, back at the time. The fault had been largely his own.

Virginia had already experienced Bhaiya's capacity for trouble-making; she was, nevertheless, unprepared for just how badly the young Maharaja could behave when he abandoned self-control. The cause of his sudden outburst is unclear; it took place during a party at Jai's rented Mayfair home. Later that same evening, there was a further furious scene inside a taxi, when Virginia accused Bhaiya of spreading treacherous rumours about Jai, Jo and herself.

Evidently, Virginia's accusation had been just. On 18 July, Bhaiya sat down in his mother's suite at the Dorchester and wrote his friend a letter. While giving no secrets away, it suggests that Bhaiya was, in his own confused way, head over heels in love.

> *Virginia darling,*
> *As every time I see you I never seem able to make sense, I am sitting down here to write and tell you some things I would like you to know. Please remember that in no way am I trying to clear myself of the many mistakes I have made.*

You say that I am lying, when I say you should not doubt me; as proved from ten days ago I am untrustworthy. But it is not that [my underlining] I want you to know — I never want you to doubt my love for you.

I am afraid I cannot explain the incident of ten days ago. It is just one of those things that happen . . . but I want you to know I love you. I know you are far too good for me.

Also please try to forgive my fooling. It is hard, I know, but I always did fool — I guess I am one. But above all, I want you to know this. I never lie to you . . . Possibly, you are right when you said I was too young . . . but darling please . . . believe me when I say that I have never known such happiness as when I am with you. Darling, this is damn silly but I just feel like it. See you tomorrow.

Love, Bhaiya

Forgiveness (as usual, with Virginia) was granted. Three days later, on 21 July, Bhaiya and his formidable mother attended a party (it was arranged in the show flat of a new building, Dorset House) over which Virginia, the hostess, presided in a modest brown dress, her attire enlivened by a small brown turban that, so she playfully told the press, echoed those worn by traffic policemen in Bombay. A red paisley scarf knotted around her waist constituted the hostess's one concession to ornament; Virginia's intention, we can surmise, was that the ageing Maharani Indira should feel herself to be the star of the glittering gathering. Bhaiya, as a token of renewed affection, was presented with a tiny silver charm to wear around his neck.

'You know the girl who gave me the locket I wear around my neck,' he wrote to Virginia on 16 May, two years later. 'Well, I am still crazy about her. Always will be.'

Bhaiya's younger sister, Ayesha, writing up her account (many years later) of her schoolgirl romance with Jai, portrayed her mother, the Maharani Indira, as a fierce opponent of their plans to marry. Reading Virginia's description of her own difficult relationship, that summer of 1937, it seems that the situation was touchingly misunderstood by the young Ayesha. Indira (beyond, that is, the possible memory of her own rumoured affair with handsome Jai) had no reason to oppose an alliance between her daughter and one of the richest and most progressive young rulers of India. She had every reason, however, to fear that Jai might, instead, wed the beautiful American actress with whom he continued to conduct an all too well-publicised romance.

So why, then, did the Maharani allow Virginia to give a party in her honour? The answer seems clear: Miss Cherrill no longer posed a threat.

A week before that July cocktail party at Dorset House, Virginia and Grandy had announced their engagement to the press.

'Virginia gives up films for love!' shrieked the *Daily Mirror* (omitting to add that Virginia had failed to make a film for over a year).

Photographed in Grandy's newly refurbished home at 18A Farm Street, Mayfair – the smart little bachelor house stood almost in the shadow of the Jersey family's former, and far grander, London residence, in Berkeley Square – the couple staged a darts competition in the new games-room. Awkward questions – Grandy's divorce had been finalised just five minutes before the engagement announcement – were fended off.

Where had the two lovers first met? (Virginia and Grandy glibly cited the return trip from New York on the *Queen Mary*.)

And was it an instant love-affair? (The couple grew reticent. It had not, they explained, been quite like that: 'not love at first sight – but nearly'.)

Where did they plan to honeymoon? (Nowhere; they hated planes.) 'I think we are going to be very happy,' Grandy ventured. Virginia smiled.

Such an interview, from a journalist's point of view, was flat stuff; the reporters were obliged to pad out their columns with accounts of the Earl of Jersey's celebrated family, his 9,400 acres of land; his five homes (these now included two houses in Farm Street, one of which was about to form a generous wedding-gift to his wife), and the elaborate celebrations that Grandy had recently hosted at Osterley for the marriage of his sister Ann to Alexander Elliott. (Virginia, Jai and Jo were among the 600 guests.)

The day after their engagement had been announced, Grandy took along his fiancée to meet his grandmother at her London house in Montagu Square. After Grandy had left, Lady Jersey enquired of Virginia if she knew the best way to handle her grandson.

'He'll do anything you say, and pay for it,' the older woman advised. 'But never make George do a thing he doesn't want to do.'

And then, Virginia recalls, Lady Jersey started talking about people she knew, and who she thought was a real lady, and who wasn't.

'I thought she was trying to tell me something, so I asked her, straight out: "So what about me?"'

'And she was so funny! She said: "My dear, *you* are an American, and that's as different as if you were a Ubangi, and had a plate in your mouth."'

It was as well that Virginia's sense of humour was good. She and Lady Jersey got on well. The old lady, she tells Teresa, owned by far the sharpest brain in the family.

'And my God, but she was indiscreet! It was like learning an entire private history of the grandest families in all England, to spend an afternoon with that old girl. She'd throw off the name of the Aga Khan or some Austrian count as the unnamed father of somebody I knew. "Oh, it's no secret!" she'd say. Well, it was always secret enough to give *me* a jolt!'

Grandy's divorce was finalised towards the end of July, just a week before the ceremony at Chelsea Register Office, for which the groom arrived ten minutes late. The bride wore a short blue dress, a tilted hat and a corsage of orchids, a flower that Virginia particularly disliked, but that her mother had purchased as a gift. Posing for photographs, she clasped to her breast Juny, the white

Virginia's third registry office wedding. Juny is more camera-shy than his owner.

Sealyham terrier that had been Grandy's first gift. (Did Lord Jersey know that Juny had been chosen for a pet because he reminded Virginia of Cary Grant's playful little dog? Had he read Cary Grant's response to an inquisitive reporter: that he had been incredulous at the news of the engagement, but if Virginia had found what she wanted, then he was happy for her . . . ?)

Pat Jersey paid off old scores with a honeymoon gift of her own to the newly-weds. Shortly after the ceremony, Grandy's small daughter, Caroline, was delivered by chauffeur to the door of 18A Farm Street, together with instructions that the little girl was not to be returned for a week. Jo and Jai, dining at Farm Street the following night, were touched to find Caroline sitting beside Virginia at the table. Virginia (Jo decided then and there) must make haste to have a baby of her own: the joys of motherhood became henceforth a favourite, and recurring, topic in Jo's long, and loving, letters.

On 2 August, the two young couples, together with Caroline, set off to inspect progress at Middleton. Caroline, bored by adult chatter, ran off to explore the gardens, and to climb atop one of the large

Lady Caroline Child Villiers, snapped by Virginia at Middleton in August, 1937.

stone lions that linked old Middleton to its newest incarnation. Jai, meanwhile, was given a tour of the house's interior and allowed to admire Robert Lutyens's *pièce de résistance*: an astonishing pink marble bathroom with a shower, sheathed in purdah glass that allowed the new lady of the house to gaze out across green acres of parkland while simultaneously preserving her modesty. Jai approved. Prompted – one suspects – by competitiveness over Virginia, he offered a lucrative commission of his own: to supervise construction of some forty guest rooms at his splendid Rambagh Palace. (Sadly for Robert Lutyens, this project would ultimately prove to be no more than fine, and idle, talk.)

The party lunched from hampers beside Middleton's newly finished swimming-pool. Later, while Jai, Jo and Virginia stretched out together to doze the afternoon away beneath one of the garden's ancient cedars, Grandy, a notebook perched upon his knee, sat apart. Details were being finalised for a formal wedding ceremony, scheduled to take place on 11 August at Osterley. Having hosted his sister Ann's Osterley wedding the previous month (the Earl was standing in for the father that Ann and he had lost so early in their childhoods), Grandy felt eminently well prepared.

The classically assembled photographs of bride, groom and parents display Virginia, the new chatelaine of one of England's loveliest houses, standing in the drawing-room at Osterley, flanked by her husband and her mother. One picture shows Grandy and his own mother, Lady Cynthia Slessor, posed apart from each other, their arms hanging at their sides, indicative of a recent spat before Grandy had agreed that his stepfather might join the wedding party. The bride, attired in the same simple costume that she had worn previously at the Chelsea Register Office, clasps her mother's hand. Blanche, here, looks radiant, to a degree that makes me wonder if Virginia had married Grandy, in part, to gratify the social ambitions of Mrs Cherrill.

'The Osterley wedding did make Blanche happy,' Virginia confides to Teresa. 'Of course, she'd have liked it even better if I'd worn a white dress and veil. But I wasn't going to do that, even for her. I'd been married twice already, for God's sake.'

The Osterley reception, 11 August 1937. Left to right: Unidentified, Anita Blair, Blanche, John Child Villiers, Barbara Child Villiers (front), David Colville, Sally Colville (front), Joan Colville, Mansel Child Villiers, Grandy, Edward Barran, 'Jo', Alexander Elliott, Ann Elliott, Cynthia Slessor, Ronnie Slessor. Virginia holds Juny.

And Virginia? Do we have any clue to her feelings on the day when – having admired the impressive row of presents that had been laid out for public view in Osterley's Long Gallery, shaken hands with the family tenants, and accepted the congratulations of the guests – she stood under Osterley's splendid portico at her husband's side, to watch an evening display of fireworks that culminated in a diamond-like tracery of linked initials: an open 'V', severed by the sharp vertical line of a 'J'?

'And were you thinking "Jersey", just then, or "Jai"?' Teresa teases the old lady, who simply laughs.

How did Virginia Jersey feel, as she took off her finery, later that night, as she laid aside the heirloom jewels, patted away her make-up, and climbed into a single bed?

229

Perhaps we can guess.

Filling her sky-blue scrapbook for 1937, the new Countess glued into it a photograph of the formal Osterley wedding-group. On the facing page, she affixed a small cartoon that she must have snipped from a newspaper.

The cartoonist's subject is a couple of newly-weds on the first morning of their honeymoon. Like Virginia, the pretty young bride clasps a tiny dog to her breast. Staring at her seemingly oblivious husband across their breakfast table, her expression registers cold dismay.

A more revealing picture, taken at the Osterley reception.
Note the body language. Left to right: Lady Cynthia Slessor,
Grandy, Virginia, Blanche Cherrill.

12

A GRAND MARRIAGE

(1937–1938)

'He was a very strange man.'

Marrying into the nobility had become quite a tradition with American girls by Virginia Cherrill's day. (Winnaretta Singer, the sewing-machine heiress, transformed herself into the Princesse de Polignac; Consuelo Vanderbilt married the Duke of Marlborough; Barbara Hutton, after divesting herself of Jai's polo-playing friend, Prince Alexis Mdivani, promptly tied the knot with Count Haugwitz-Reventlow.) Few, however, could match the splendour of Virginia's alliance.

Today, the name Jersey signifies little more than a Channel island and a breed of dairy cow; in the mid-Thirties, before the final post-war dispersing of the family's ancestral estates, the Child Villiers family still prided itself on its role in history. James Villiers, created Duke of Buckingham, had presided over the court of James I and, subsequently, over the royal army of James's son. (In Virginia's day, the great painting by Rubens of the Duke's apotheosis still dominated the collection at Osterley.) Middleton was already being hailed, before completion, as the last great country house to be built in England; Osterley, the Jersey's principal home, was venerated by many as Adam's masterpiece.

Virginia is ready to admit to Teresa that the match delighted her mother. (She seems, almost, to intimate that she married Lord Jersey in order to please Blanche.) For herself, she continues, she would have been just as content to stay single.

'For a start, I had Pat Jersey's gang lined up against me like a firing squad.'

Confirmation of this statement appears in an item penned by 'Cholly Knickerbocker', the pseudonym for Maury Paul, one of New York's most acid-tongued tabloid journalists. Announcing to his New York readers, in July 1937, that the film-star Virginia Cherrill was due to marry an English earl, Paul also passed along the news that the British aristocracy were determined to ostracise the young screen actress, as a gesture of support towards the first, discarded wife of Lord Jersey.

The predicted boycott never took place. It is apparent that Virginia already commanded a circle of loving admirers: Bobby Throckmorton, teasing slender Virginia for worrying that she had looked overweight in her blue wedding-dress, sent a present of chocolates to his 'Dear Fat Girl' the following month, accompanied, he told her, by 'love and passion'. But how could even the stuffiest members of the nobility hold out against a beautiful young woman who let it be known that she preferred milk to wine, who took pride in telling journalists that an admired new blouse had cost her the equivalent of three dollars, and who, a full six months after her wedding, proudly exhibited her first use of a coronet, on the corner of a doll-sized handkerchief?

'It probably helped that Pat Jersey married Robin Filmer-Wilson only a couple of months after we got married,' Virginia muses. 'Pat and he were crazy about each other. Grandy and I even went to their reception. No bad feeling existed by then, so far as I can recall. Pat had married Grandy when she was eighteen, way too young. People always said that her mother had set it all up.'

Asked whether she herself attracted envy from fortune-hunting ladies – Grandy Jersey was one of the richest men in England – Virginia sounds surprised. It wasn't, as she points out, any secret that Grandy was tight with his money.

'I've no complaints on that score,' she quickly adds. 'I don't know why, but Grandy was never mean with me. I could get money out of him for Mansel and the sisters, and even Grandy's mother; he wouldn't ever give it them direct, but he'd do it if I asked him.'

Confirmation of this is provided when I visit Henry Slessor, Grandy's bluff and friendly younger half-brother. Ronnie Slessor, he tells me, was so short of money that he helped to pay the school bills of Dinah and Henry, his own two children, by selling beautifying cosmetic gloves for ladies.

'"Glovelies"!' cries Henry, roaring with laughter. 'Followed, less successfully, by "Spritelies" – until the factory got blown up in the War. My dear father wasn't cut out to be a businessman, I'm afraid. Virginia did her best for us. We all adored her. She was *such* a friend to my mother.'

Grandy's younger siblings, Mansel and Ann, shared the Slessors' enthusiasm for Virginia's informal style, her kindness, and her intense sense of fun; David Colville, on the other hand, married to Joan, the elder of Grandy's two sisters, was himself the son of an ambassador and of a lady-in-waiting to Queen Mary.

'David couldn't stand me,' sighs Virginia. 'English men can make you feel about a centimetre high, when they set their mind to it. David Colville was an expert at that.'

It isn't hard for me, at this point, to understand why, while David Colville shuddered at Virginia's impulsive ways, Grandy Jersey, a chilly, introverted man, had been drawn towards her warmth and spontaneity. I find it more difficult to understand why Virginia chose to marry him. She was neither a snob nor a fortune-hunter. Was the marriage, perhaps, a useful camouflage for

two people who relished sexual freedom? Could that be the answer? The tape-recordings offer some confirmation.

'The great thing about Grandy,' Virginia confides to Teresa, 'is that he kept things clear. I could do just as I wished, so long as I was discreet – and so could he. Sex was never a part of it. We didn't share a bed, and we never asked each other awkward questions. Now and again, I'd pay him a visit.'

'But didn't Grandy want an heir?' Teresa asks.

'Yes,' Virginia says. 'That was part of the deal – unfortunately.' Her voice rises a little. 'Can you check in the old scrapbooks again, Teresa? I wanted to show you a picture of my Juny on the steps at Middleton.'

'Juny . . . ?'

'*Juny!* You can't have forgotten . . .'

Teresa admits that she had, just for a moment, failed to remember the name of Virginia's favourite dog, an animal she herself never knew, dead for over forty years.

'I'll forgive you,' Virginia declares, but she sounds wistful.

The allusion to Juny becomes more poignant when Teresa and I discover, among the letters dating back to the Thirties, a sheaf that purport to be written by a Sealyham terrier and an Alsatian hound: Juny and Claudius, it becomes apparent, were the couple's chosen substitutes for the children that they longed for and lacked. To Grandy's descendants, it is hard to accept that such a stiff, aloof man as George Jersey could have impersonated a dog: witty Lord Dunsany, they insist, was surely the family correspondent who sent Virginia playful reports from 'The Bone Mart' and 'The Dog Basket'. How – they ask – could Grandy have grown sensitive enough, following the death of Virginia's Sealyham terrier in 1940, to pen his grieving wife a letter upon transparent paper, in watered-down ink, from the paradise in which the spirit of Juny might now imaginably be dwelling? Such delicacy was not, the family assure me, Lord Jersey's style.

The subject of the canine letters never comes up in Virginia's conversations with Teresa. I lack supporting evidence for my conviction that these playful epistles – they are either typed or hand-printed in blocklike letters – originate from Grandy's desk; it seems beyond belief, however, that Lord Dunsany, dwelling in Kent, knew well enough the intimate details of his nephew's marriage to have been their principal author. In one missive, for example, Juny asks his spouse to be more circumspect about an Indian lover. Juny has overheard a conversation 'between a gull and a local duck'.

> *Naturally, I didn't intend eavesdropping, but when I heard India mentioned, I pricked up my ears . . . Now, when I tell you that the gull made a very funny story of it, and made you and me look awfully silly – he and the duck were cackling away like a couple of barnyard fowls – you will realize how upset and hurt I was that you should go around with such incredibly stupid people as that . . . I dread to think of my reputation in India . . . why not a pie dog in India would sniff at a lamp post after me. Now do please be careful when you get home . . .*

Despite the signs here that Grandy is offering his wife a veiled warning, there is also evidence of an eccentric good-humour that is representative, in Virginia's opinion, of English couples.

'They're all like that, I'm telling you. None of them share beds, and the dogs always come first. Ours was a typical English marriage.'

'Typical' is not how most of us would describe Virginia's chilly union to the head of one of the most eminent families in England. There's plenty of evidence to show, however, that she fulfilled her new role, both as a family member, and as Countess of Jersey, with warmth and goodwill. In October 1937, she dragged an unwilling Grandy along to the cheerfully chaotic 'Hooligans' Ball', given in their unfurnished Bayswater flat by Ann and Alexander Elliott; later, Virginia made sure that her husband sent the young couple a lavish housewarming gift. She opened fêtes, became the energetic patron of a West London hospital for sick children, and took a keen interest both in the Jersey estates and the welfare of those who helped to run them ('You were always so sweet to father, and he

20, SOUTHWICK STREET, W.2.

Having finally succeeded after weeks of hard work in bringing some semblance of order into their new home,

Mr Alexander and Lady Ann Elliot

feel that it is now quite ready for their hooligan friends to come and smash it up again and that Tuesday, October 26th at 10 o'clock would be as good a time as any other for the process of demolition and destruction to take place. Our dear friends will be poisoned (we hope) by as nasty an assortment of food and drink as human ingenuity can devise, while the servants have kindly agreed to lend their portable gramophone to add its hideous din to the general chaos. Kindly wear your black ties and most valuable studs and bring your gold cigarette cases and cheque books—we must make something out of this! Should you have the common courtesy to answer this invitation please stamp your envelopes.

Grandy's sister and her husband gave a typically 'Thirties housewarming: Virginia went along.

did have, if I may say so, a soft spot for you', the daughter of Henry Little, Osterley's land agent, wrote to Virginia after her father's death in the 1950s). Nevertheless, it is easy to see why a traditional husband – one as conventional as David Colville – might have taken disapproving exception to a woman who refused, after marriage, to give up her lover. Grandy showed no such concern; this, we must assume, was the bargain to which he had agreed after his divorce from Patricia Richards was finalised. Virginia was prepared to marry him, but only if she was allowed to retain an unusual degree of independence.

'It was simply awful saying goodbye to you this afternoon,' the young Maharani of Jaipur wrote to Virginia on 3 September 1937, a month after the wedding of the Jerseys. Jo had just dined at Farm Street with Grandy and Bobby Throckmorton; Virginia, meanwhile, had overcome her dislike of planes enough to fly off – with Jai – to join the Ausnits and their guests for ten days in Biarritz. 'We had quite a good dinner,' Jo continued, 'but the place seemed completely empty and dull without you, this is what Grandy and I thought.'

It does, even in the context of a period when marital faithfulness was not highly rated, seem remarkable that Jai and Virginia were able to holiday abroad, in a very public place, so soon after her wedding. David Colville was shocked by Virginia's freedom, but Grandy made no objections, while Jo, made familiar of necessity by her Indian marriage with the habit of sharing, felt neither outrage nor jealousy. Grandy was not a lively companion; all Jo desired was the chance, herself, to spend more time with his wife. 'Do talk to Jai about my coming here every year,' she pleaded in the same letter to Virginia:

> because I will miss you so much when I go away, and I do want to
> be with you for four or five months a year at least. Darling, I don't
> know how to thank you for all what [sic] you have done for
> me . . . remember, Virginia, I'll always believe you, and I am
> 'yours for ever' no matter what happens . . . Look after yourself,
> your Ladyship. Well good-bye and God bless you, darling. All my
> best of love, Jo

Jo's hopes were pinned upon the persuasive skills of the friend to whom, she now wrote, she had confessed 'more than to anybody else'. Jai, however, was adamant. Progressive, as were all the maharajas, in his desire for an independent, self-governing India, Jai was also a staunch traditionalist. There was no question of Jo being granted her desire to spend half of every year in England. By the beginning of October 1937, his young wife was back once more in purdah, an object of reverence to be stared at during the endless succession of ceremonial days: 'people coming to see me every day and every time of the day that suits them, but not to welcome me, just to gaze . . .'

Virginia's attempts to help emancipate Jo met with scant sympathy when she turned for support to Bhaiya. Back in Cooch Behar, and living on a stringent alcohol-free diet, Bhaiya was feeling low. ('Cooch Behar is very dull – no 'alk'; no Bag o'Nails; nothing but work and sleep. I haven't seen a film since I've been here.') Bhaiya took the view that Virginia was dabbling in matters of which she had no real understanding. 'You seem very annoyed with Jai,' he wrote. 'You misunderstand. A wife to an Indian doesn't mean the same as to you all. You think Jai is cruel to his wife, but I assure you that he is devoted to her.' Softening his tone, he added that he was longing to see Virginia when she and Grandy made a second visit to India for Christmas 1937. Bhaiya added, as a warning to leave Anita Blair out of this return trip, that his mother remained enraged by Anita's affair with her younger son, and that she believed Virginia had helped to set it up.

It isn't known whether Virginia answered Bhaiya's letter; we do know that his warnings didn't prevent Anita Blair from accompanying the Jerseys to Jaipur at the end of the year.

The letters that Jo wrote to Virginia during the autumn of 1937 offer a rare glimpse into a friendship between two young women who did their best, at all times, to offer one another support. Virginia, always ready to act on behalf of Jo, tracked down a new lady's maid for her, during a brief visit to Paris; subsequent letters transmit a flurry of affectionate messages between Jo's French Madeleine, struggling to acclimatise herself to life in Jaipur, and

Elizabeth ('Liesl') Dietrich, who had arrived in London just before the wedding of the Jerseys, and would serve Virginia faithfully for the next thirty years.

Madeleine was beginning to get used to Indian food, Jo wrote on 1 November; nevertheless, she missed Paris; she was hoping that her friend Elizabeth would write to her soon. As for other news, the Sanfords had already arrived for their Christmas visit and Mary (Mrs Sanford, like her compatriot Virginia Cherrill, was a former film-actress) had been visiting Jo in the zenana. Jo wanted to reassure Virginia that, much though she liked Mary, there was here no competition. ('Listen, baby, you are one in a million. Is that ok?')

A few tart asides in Jo's letters suggest that the young Maharani was feeling apprehensive. 'Ma' (Bhaiya's mother) had become a frequent visitor to Jaipur, she noted; while making much of Jo, the Maharani Indira was also in secret correspondence with Jai about sundry topics upon which he declined to speak. Hearing that, on at least one occasion, the ageing matriarch had decided not to come to Jaipur, Jo offered a single crisp comment: 'Thank God'.

'There are lots of muddles here,' Jo wrote to Virginia again, on 22 November; she sounded anxious. The English, she thought, were laying plans to corrupt Jai; 'all the people here are giving cocktail parties, with the idea of getting Jai onto wine and women'. Even the Prime Minister of Jaipur, Sir Henry Beaumont St John, seemed bent upon turning the young Maharaja into a full-time playboy, 'so that they can all keep him under their thumb and then kick him out'. It was just as well, Jo wrote primly, that Jai's polo required him to stay fit. And now, please, would Virginia hurry up and send information about her own arrival?

'I took one trunk with me for my first visit to Jaipur,' Virginia tells Teresa. 'Travelling with Grandy, I took thirty-seven!'

Grandy's unpublished memoirs, by conflating the two trips to India, of 1936 and 1937, give nothing away. Brief mention is made

of the fact that Jo – 'poor Jo' – was compelled to sit at the back of
the train to Delhi in a darkened purdah car; otherwise, everything
is smoothed away into a series of pleasant anecdotes and travellers'
tales. A few formal details can be gleaned from Virginia's blue
scrapbooks. The Jaipur guests included Lady Jean Rankin, Bobby
Throckmorton, the American Butterworths and, travelling under
the Jerseys' hospitable mantle, Miss Anita Blair; at dinner, Virginia
was generally seated next to Jai (or directly opposite him), with, on
her other side, Sir Henry Beaumont St John. Her continuing
intimacy with Jai seems confirmed by the fact that she retained no
impression whatsoever of Jaipur's English Prime Minister.

Travelling to Delhi with Grandy, Virginia visited a crestfallen
Bhaiya who, following a polo injury, had been confined to his bed.

'I hardly recognised him at first, he'd lost so much weight. But
he was still the same old Bhaiya. The doctor had put up a notice
outside his room to say there were to be no visitors after midnight.
Bhaiya had changed it to say: men were only welcome, if they
arrived late, and with a woman. The other polo accident was more
serious. We were all quite alarmed by the injury to Jai.'

Polo was a cause of frequent accidents. Bhaiya had broken his
collar-bone; Jai just escaped breaking his back. Virginia remembered
seeing him carried to his room at the Rambagh Palace on a stretcher.
While brave enough to insist upon being taken out with the house-
party for the ritual tiger shoots, Jai was ordered straight back to bed
by Dr Huban, his English physician.

'Jai did everything he could for us,' Virginia recalls. 'He even
gave Jo and me two matching Bentleys to go off and tour in, and
that did cause trouble. People didn't like it. There was talk.'

Evidence of this trouble survives in a frantic letter written by Jo
to Virginia, towards the end of the Jerseys' visit to Jaipur. All the
signs are that both women realised a brewing scandal threatened
the future of their friendship:

Thursday night, January [1937 is indicated by Jo's reference to the London visit]

Virginia my darling, you can't imagine how happy I was to see you here after London and to have you with me even for a short time . . . Oh God! I don't know what I'm going to do without you, Virginia. It is really breaking my heart to think that you are going away and don't know when we'll meet again. There is only one thing that can keep us a bit cheerful at the moment, to hope to meet soon. I wish we could always be together; think how marvellous it would be. However, darling, it doesn't matter where you are. I'll always be thinking about you.

Darling, promise me you will take care of yourself and keep as happy as you can and forget all those nasty things that were said about us, or we'll never be happy . . .

I hate to say it, but goodbye and God bless you, darling. I'll miss you and love you more than ever. Be happy. All my fondest love, your own Jo

Jo never again visited England. Virginia never returned to Jaipur.

'But we were always friends,' Virginia insists. 'We told each other things. I'd do Jo's shopping when she wanted special presents sent over for Jai – and Jo was always shipping me gifts for my mother, and for Liesl, and for Anita – she was unstoppable. Even Juny got sent a silver collar!'

Virginia was happy to go shopping for Jai on her friend's behalf; nevertheless, when the young Maharaja flew into Croydon Airport in April, 1938 for his annual social and sporting visit (his string of sixty polo ponies, insured for £4,000 each, had arrived a week earlier, by special steamer), Jai found that his regular girlfriend was proving unusually elusive.

Virginia's excuses were flimsy. She claimed to be overseeing the work of Robert Lutyens, both at Middleton and at the pretty old house in Farm Street that Grandy had just bestowed upon her as a wedding-gift. She also reported that Grandy's first little Farm

Street home required urgent preparations to ready it for a tenant, their stage-friend Dorothy Campbell. She told Jai, too, that she felt it heartless to go out enjoying herself while their poor friend Nada Milford Haven was in mourning for her husband, dead, at the age of forty-five, from blood poisoning (following a fall in which the Marquess broke his thigh, after slipping on the polished floor of the Mountbattens' London home).

None of these reasons need have prevented Virginia from seeing Jai in the summer of 1938: the work needed to prepare the Farm Street house for Dorothy Campbell's occupation was not considerable; Lord Milford Haven's death had occurred early in the year. Virginia, it appears, was obeying her husband's request for discretion at a time when her friendship with the Maharaja of Jaipur had become sufficiently in the public domain to encourage one famously tactless hostess, the American Elsie Mendl, to ask Virginia to bring Jai along to a party ('I want him!' Elsie declared) and leave Grandy, her own husband, behind. Virginia declined the invitation.

Jai was not amused. Back in India in July, he wrote to reproach Virginia for keeping him away from her, '. . . thanks to your own stupidity!!! Darling, please realise that, whatever others may say, things between us will never change, so please be reasonable in the future. My only few moments of happiness were when I said goodbye to you . . . wish every moment had been like that. All my love, darling . . .'

Bhaiya, meanwhile, sent self-pitying letters from near Delhi (where he was undergoing military training) of his own trials in a world that he found 'frightfully Poona: chukka, pukka, whisky soda and tiffin: still, I exist.' Bhaiya's appetite for party-going had not been curbed by army life; he told Virginia on one occasion that he was writing to her after dancing until four in the morning; he was expected, in an hour's time, to be out on parade.

What Bhaiya did not explain was why he had chosen at that time to absent himself from his home state. Both Virginia and Jo were by now well aware that the Maharani of Cooch Behar's private correspondence with Jai concerned a marriage plan for her youngest daughter, Ayesha. Bhaiya's letters never mention his sister. Did he approve the projected match? Had he removed himself in order to escape furtive scenes of domestic intrigue? It was impossible for Virginia, reading his lively, frivolous letters, to guess at Bhaiya's secret thoughts.

Jai's wife remained the most constant of Virginia's foreign correspondents. Jo had observed how affectionate and happy her friend had seemed when playing with the royal children in the zenana, and how at ease she was with little Caroline Child Villiers. Motherhood, following Virginia's marriage, became the most regular topic of the young Maharani's loving epistles. 'Say, Countess, you had better do something about the first m.k.[sic] of Jersey', Jo had urged, back in November 1937. Later, she begged Virginia to go to a good doctor, or to seek advice from her own incomparable Dr Huban in Jaipur. 'Isn't there any sign of Jo-Jo II?' she pleaded upon one occasion; and on another: 'Please Virginia, I am dying for you to have a baby (a tiny little gora-log)'. Sending a gift of a sari, she drew Virginia's attention to the fact that it was embroidered with those traditional baby-harbingers: storks.

The absence of a baby in the Jersey household owed nothing to lack of hope and even effort. Grandy sorely wanted a male heir; his wife longed for a child. Virginia had already miscarried once, during her marriage to Cary Grant; in London, she began to pay regular visits to Dr Greta Graff, a reputable gynaecologist with a practice near Harley Street.

In the early spring of 1938, the gossip columns of the London papers announced that Lady Jersey, together with a bevy of other beauties who included Grandy's sister and his former wife, was expecting a child. Ann Elliott gave birth to a daughter. Pat and Robin Filmer-Wilson's boy was born towards the end of that year. Virginia, in her fifth month, miscarried once again.

'Grandy,' she tells Teresa, 'was quite cut-up about it.'

So, to judge from the expression on Virginia's face, as she posed that August for a portrait by the fashionable Russian artist, Savely Sorine, was Grandy's wife. Sugary though Sorine's style is (his companion portrait of Grandy is a stronger work), he displays admirable honesty in recording the strain upon the features of the young Countess's face. Virginia looks wistful, and suddenly older than her thirty years.

Other possible causes for distress and exhaustion can be adduced: Virginia was struggling to meet Grandy's deadline of turning Middleton into a habitable home for a big Christmas house-party. Her house in Farm Street required furnishing with more than the trunk of richly coloured old rugs that she had brought home from India and a few well-chosen pieces of antique furniture; at Osterley, where funds were urgently needed for major repairs, she was working alongside her husband on a scheme – advanced for that time – to open the house and gardens to visitors, while introducing the public to works by some of those contemporary painters whom the couple most admired. It seems likely, too, that Virginia was disappointed by the news from Josef von Sternberg, the great director whom she had known and admired since her early days in Hollywood: ill-health, von Sternberg wrote in the summer of 1937, was forcing him to cancel plans for a film in which Virginia had been promised her most significant role since the making of *City Lights*.

The loss of an unborn child presents a more substantial reason for Virginia's evident sadness towards the end of that first summer of her marriage. Photographs taken during her annual late-August visit to the hospitable Ausnits at Biarritz – Virginia's companion that year was her old friend Rosie Nicholl – reveal her looking taut, fragile and thin as a string. Snipping out news items for her scrapbooks, she pasted in a report on the 'accidental' death (suicide was then a criminal offence) of a beautiful young socialite named

Nina Pierson. Miss Pierson's blurred photograph shows that she bore a strong physical resemblance to Virginia.

'It really was a shame,' Teresa agrees, as we discuss the significance of Virginia's continuing lack of a child.

Calculating the difference in ages, it occurs to me, for the first time, that this loving friend – Teresa – might herself have somehow fulfilled the role of a daughter.

'Not quite,' Teresa corrects me. 'You're forgetting that I had two wonderful parents of my own. We all adored Virginia, but no – I was her friend. I was never her substitute child.'

Back in 1938, other children offered a degree of solace. Nurses at the Hanwell Children's Hospital in Isleworth, close to Osterley, were touched by the affection lavished upon their small patients by pretty, tender-hearted Lady Jersey, their most regular visitor. Grandy's lively little daughter Caroline – unlike many a child in a similar situation – eagerly looked forward to days spent with her stepmother.

'Virginia,' comments Lady Caroline today, 'always made me feel I was somebody special – and she was the best present-giver in the world.'

Colin Campbell, then a young boy (his mother, estranged from her military husband, lived at Farm Street as a tenant of the Jerseys), felt precisely the same. Answering an impulsive telephone call from a complete stranger late one evening, he recalls for me how Virginia once looked after him when he'd suffered an attack of measles as a small child. 'We had a silly game. She nicknamed me "The Breath of Death" after the doctor had warned that I was infectious. She'd hug me and say: "And how's my Breath of Death today?" It became our private joke. What a pity you never knew Virginia: she was enchanting!'

Virginia's visit to the Ausnits had been her only journey away from England since the Christmas excursion to India. Meanwhile, Blanche was reported by Anita Blair, out in California, to be in bad shape: Mrs Cherrill had put on weight, took little exercise and immensely missed her daughter. The solution, both for her mother's condition and her own unhappiness, Virginia decided, lay in a change of scene. With Grandy's consent, travel arrangements were put in hand; in mid-September, Virginia, Blanche and the ubiquitous Anita Blair set off, by boat, for their first-ever visit to Italy.

From the few scraps of evidence that survive – an absurd series of passionately inscribed snapshots of himself mailed to Virginia from a smirking young Italian identified only as 'Ettore'; an ardent note inviting Anita and Virginia to revisit all their admirers at the British Embassy in Rome; a couple of images of a large, ineffably glum Blanche standing beside an even larger touring-car – it seems that the young women enjoyed the jaunt more than did Mrs Cherrill.

In England, where the sense of impending war had reached the level of subdued panic, Grandy was summoned to a Red Cross meeting in Oxfordshire at which it was made clear that he was expected to surrender Middleton – should the situation arise – for use as a wartime hospital or school. Agreeing with a heavy heart (the unfinished house was intended to become the Jerseys' principal home), Grandy began to think that a vacation might raise his own spirits. He would have preferred Virginia herself to return, but a cable from Claudius the Alsatian, hinting that 'naughty Jezebel' had better come home to 'jealous dog', produced no response. Resourcefully, Grandy hired a utility van, invited his brother, Mansel, to join him as co-driver, and set out to join the trio of holiday-makers at Florence. The purpose of the van, Lord Jersey explained to journalists, was to bring back, not an errant Countess, but some of the antique furniture that his practical wife had purchased abroad for their new home. Virginia, he further enthused, had a wonderful eye; he had absolute confidence in her good judgement. (One vice to which such a proud man would never publicly admit was jealousy.).

It fell to Grandy to escort Blanche and a grieving Anita Blair (the news had reached her that young Indrajit – Digga – of Cooch Behar had finally been prevailed upon by his mother to sever their relationship) to meet their homebound liner at Genoa; Virginia, meanwhile, remained in Florence, to shop for furniture while keeping company with Grandy's younger brother.

'I always got on well with Mansel,' the old lady reminisces happily to Teresa. 'I was trying to cheer him up. He and his wife were going through a bad divorce and poor Mansel: he had the mother-in-law on his tail. That woman – Grandy always knew how lucky he was with Blanche.'

Returning to England to prepare for her first Christmas party at Middleton, Virginia found an urgent missive awaiting her. Jo had received confirmation of the news she was dreading: Jai intended to marry, as his third wife, Ayesha of Cooch Behar. Jai's sister, Chand, liked Ayesha and approved the match; the Maharani – Ma – had given her official blessing to the union. 'I bet she [Ma] is happy now she is hoping to get what she has been wanting all this time', wrote Jo. 'Hope this hasn't worried you too much, but I had to tell you.' As for herself, Jo added, 'I haven't got anyone now except you, Anita and Grandy, whom I can call my friends.'

Jo's distress becomes understandable when we recall that Ayesha belonged to the younger generation of Indian royalty, born and bred during a time of cultural transition. Ayesha had never experienced purdah; partly schooled in England, she would be at ease in Jai's dual world in a way that Jo, an old-fashioned princess, could never achieve. Formally, Ayesha would submit to the tradition of purdah when she married Jai; beyond the state boundaries, however, she would be allowed to join the house-parties and shooting expeditions (Ayesha was herself an excellent shot), to travel around Europe, to dance in nightclubs: to behave, in short, as her pioneering mother, Indira, had done before her. As young Ayesha took Jai's hand, Jo would be expected to slip gracefully back into the woman's world of the zenana, into the prison from which she had dreamed, with Virginia's support, of making her escape.

Towards the end of her sorrowful letter, Jo asked Virginia to accept a parting gift. She doubted that the two of them would ever meet again; instead, the grieving Maharani wanted Virginia to keep beside her a bronze sculpture, a cast of her own slender arm, a token of their enduring love.

'And I did keep it with me,' Virginia affirms. 'In over fifty years, I've never forgotten Jo.'

Others have. Eclipsed by the stronger personality of her husband's third wife, still lingering off in the shadows, stands Jo. Her letters have never been published; official histories dismiss the Maharani as a traditional zenana bride. Ayesha's memoirs pay affectionate tribute to 'Jo Didi' as a kind, cultured and sisterly mentor, well placed to advise a younger and more modern wife on court etiquette.

Jo, to judge from her lively, loving and well-informed letters to Virginia, may merit a little more attention than she has, until now, received. It is unlikely that she could ever have matched the energy and courage that Ayesha showed during the years following the birth, in 1947, of Indian independence, when the maharajas surrendered their former powers. Jo could never have entered politics, as Ayesha did, in later life; it is hard to imagine her living an emancipated life, taking responsibility for herself. Nevertheless, some acknowledgement should be made of the noble and resigned anonymity of the Maharani Kishore's role in the final years of royal Jaipur, and even, perhaps, of her pathos.

Virginia and her friend the Maharani Kishore ('Jo') in the zenana garden at Jaipur.

13

A DECADE'S END

(1938–1940)

> They all had breakfast in their rooms and none of them
> ever touched a morsel. It all came straight back down the
> stairs, and went out to feed the pigs.
>
> HENRY SLESSOR, REMEMBERING CHILDHOOD VISITS TO
MIDDLETON PARK

'I know that you and Grandy are always at Middleton for Sunday',
wrote one of their friends in 1939. That image, while an
exaggeration, confirms the picture given in Grandy's memoirs of
a home that was, during the short-lived reign of the Jerseys, both
used and loved.

Entertainment there, until the house became more habitable,
had usually taken the form of day excursions. 'We used to have
summer barbecues beside the new swimming-pool,' remembers
Henry Slessor, Grandy's much younger half-brother. 'Everybody
you ever heard of in the movie world seemed to be there. Grandy
must have been around, but Virginia's the only one I remember
seeing, and she was usually running about, making sure that
everybody was happy and content. She and I grilled sausages
together. Virginia could make the smallest thing feel such fun.'

Henry Slessor was a small boy back in the summer of 1938; it's unsurprising that he fails to remember the names of the glamorous guests at these early and informal gatherings at Middleton. Grandy, sounding a little nostalgic in his recollections of the house he had once intended to be his chief family home, was able to be more specific. In his memoirs, he mentions the names of – among others – Douglas Fairbanks Sr and his second wife, Sylvia Hawkes; Rex Harrison; Lilli Palmer; their own pretty Farm Street tenant Dotty Campbell (formerly, as Dorothy Field, the star of several musical comedies); and Johnny Weissmuller. (Tarzan's party trick, as Grandy remembered it, 'was to fill his mouth with birdshot, and spit it quite a distance at the bare back of a lady in a *décolleté* dress'.) Since Grandy's own idea of a good practical joke was to tie a kipper to the exhaust pipe of a guest's departing car, his comment upon Weissmuller's behaviour was not necessarily disapproving.

These particular guests had come only for picnics around the pool; by Christmas 1938, the last furniture vans had lumbered away down Middleton's long elm-canopied drive and out, past the pretty old-fashioned church in the park, on to the Oxford road. Grandy's new home was finally ready to receive its first house-party, a sizeable family gathering with, for garnish, a wistful-looking Russian prince who, perhaps, had nowhere particular to spend an English Christmas. The guests seem to have enjoyed themselves: photographs taken outside on the final day show a cheerily informal group. The hosts, both of them looking pleased but fatigued, sit, flanked by their beloved dogs, at the feet of Grandy's siblings.

Later, the Jerseys would speak dismissively and a little misleadingly about Middleton. Virginia told American friends that she had never liked the place. Grandy sometimes claimed never to have spent more than a single night in his new Oxfordshire home.

'I used to sleep with all the dogs lying around me, in a beautiful Louis XV bed.' This comment is the only specific statement about

Middleton that Virginia ever makes to Teresa. Grandy's written recollections dwelt on the exotic visitors from Hollywood imported by his wife, and on the modern features of the Middleton décor that seem most to have gratified him: a set of leopard-upholstered (curiously for two animal-loving owners) chairs; a dining-table fashioned of mirror glass; concealed cocktail cabinets and an up-to-the-minute gramophone system that piped music through the three linked garden-side rooms that were most regularly used for entertaining.

Visitors were mixed in their response. One local reporter snidely observed that Lady Jersey's new 'dream home' would have looked more appropriate in Hollywood; another journalist enthused over the blend of Virginia's American taste with the fondness of Robert Lutyens for art deco, and expressed regret that the two of them had not gone jointly into business. ('Middleton is altogether charming . . . the house reflects taste and skill in the American manner.') More scholarly critics praised the Jersey mansion for combining classical elegance with modern comfort; almost all admired the use of four elegant satellite lodges – this had been Grandy's own idea – to accommodate and provide a degree of privacy for the house's workforce. These auxiliary buildings, in an aristocratic era still replete with garret bedrooms, badly lit back staircases and gloomy servants' halls, appeared admirably progressive.

It's possible that the detachment of the Jerseys concerning their new home was their way of dealing with the likelihood, in the face of an impending war, that they would soon have to yield it up for sacrifice. As early as April 1938, Virginia had been taking notes upon how to make rooms gasproof and seeking advice about building a bomb shelter; six months later, Grandy had been invited to volunteer his unfinished Oxfordshire home for future public use, in emergency conditions.

War, in England, had become a topic for daily discussion. The hard shallows of society in the mid-Thirties were yielding to something that felt, almost, like emotional depths. Crossing the ocean late in February 1939, to care for an ailing Blanche, Virginia was astonished to find, out in Hollywood, that her friends cared less about the prospect of war than hearing what she had thought, while in New York, about appearing on the popular radio-show *In Town Tonight*, alongside her former husband. The show's compère, Freddy Grisewood, had made much of the fact that Cary Grant happened to drop his favourite gold pencil and that Virginia had retrieved it for him: this, as she smartly informed her inquisitive friends, meant not a thing.

'Cary and I always got along well,' the old lady reminds Teresa. 'We could still make each other laugh. I was just happy that things were going well for him.'

Virginia, evidently, is alluding to Cary Grant's film career. In private, the actor's love-life remained unsettled. Journalists still tirelessly drew attention to the fact that the only quality that a succession of blonde girlfriends appeared to share was an uncanny resemblance to Virginia Cherrill.

Blanche recovered her health; Virginia, while caring for her, was struck down by a serious viral infection. Grandy sent anxious telegrams from snowbound Middleton; Jai, unaware of Virginia's illness and worried by a new surge of political rebellion ('awful times') in Jaipur, wrote to evoke wistful memories of her last visit to India. 'I wish to God you were here', he confessed, on 4 March 1939: 'There is nothing I long for more than to have a real friend by me and, darling, you know how I feel towards you . . . Please, darling, write to me. You can understand the conditions I live in here. I need you in every way . . . all my love for ever, Jai.'

Virginia may have reciprocated Jai's feelings, but, adrift in the bright flippancy of Hollywood, where the talk was all about the ongoing shooting of the predicted hit of the year, *Gone With the Wind*, war-threatened England was where she longed to be.

'Chill much better now', she cabled to her husband on 8 March; five days later, she announced her intention of starting for home. Grandy worried about the safety of crossing the ocean at a time when war seemed so imminent, and when Virginia (safely placed in California) stood a good chance of escaping any personal danger. After failing to dissuade his wife with accounts of a bleak winter ('Better defeat streptococcus with Californian sunshine than return Oxfordshire snowstorms'), he allowed his favourite accomplice to speak with more force. On 15 March, Virginia received a further cable from Middleton; it was signed by one 'Claudius Earsup': 'Strongly disapprove sea travel until situation clearer don't anticipate war but don't risk being at sea [in] outbreak stay where you are.'

'Grandy was always worrying about my safety,' Virginia tells Teresa. 'He was good that way.'

Listening, I wonder if Teresa shares my growing sense that Grandy did, in his own strange way, adore his second wife.

Neither her husband nor his beloved hound could persuade Virginia to take their warnings seriously; by early April, the social columns were announcing Lady Jersey's praiseworthy return to England, a country to which – she told reporters – she had come to feel a debt both of loyalty and love.

Virginia could be fearless about putting herself at risk; this did not mean that she took the threat of war any more lightly than her husband. Grandy, having joined the Honourable Artillery Company (part of the Territorial Army) shortly before his wife's return in April, began attending regular anti-aircraft practice sessions on this venerable regiment's grounds at Armoury House in the City. Virginia, briefly in France with her friend Eva Lutyens for a May lunch-party that was being given by another Eva – the daughter of Marie Curie – was astonished by the insouciance of their fellow-guests. The French army, she recalls, were doing manoeuvres in the park of the Château de Sceaux, close to Eve Curie's house: 'The men were making parachute drops. And the lunch guests kept pointing at them and calling out "*Pas pratique. Pas pratique*". Their complacency killed me, but you couldn't say anything. They just laughed. They didn't believe that anything was ever going to threaten France. To them, it was just a joke.'

Virginia had returned from America out of an admirable spirit of patriotism; she returned as well because she knew Grandy needed her support at Osterley. Work had been going on for over a year to prepare the house and gardens for public access; this venture, Grandy hoped, would help to fund the beautiful, but alarmingly derelict, old house's need for repairs and renovation: the modernisation of the originally bewitching vision of Robert Adam.

'Grandy used to say Osterley was so old-fashioned that it took twelve different people to produce a boiled egg for breakfast. We never thought of living there, but – partly because old Lady Jersey felt so strongly about it – we did want to make a go of the house. Grandy worked very hard. He chose pretty much all the modern paintings that were to be on show for the public, and he hung every one of them himself.'

Grandy also took responsibility for writing a guidebook that enticed visitors in with promises that they would see 'The Runaway Bride's Chamber' (the bedroom of a former owner's wayward daughter) and that they would be repeating the experience of Queen Elizabeth I, a devoted visitor to Osterley.

'She was, but nothing was left of *that* old house except the stable block. I don't suppose she spent much time in there!'

Virginia, meanwhile, gave over her attention to redecorating some of the areas that were to be on public view, and to overseeing an arboretum of historic trees to be grown from seedlings. She stole this pretty idea from the presidential garden at Mount Vernon, says Virginia; Grandy, who loved trees, was charmed by the concept.

'It never happened. The seedlings were still in one of the greenhouses when the War broke out. We never knew what became of them. It was quite sad. One had been brought over from George Washington's oak . . .'

Osterley was a project that drew Virginia and her husband closer together, as they worked upon a common interest, dedicated to a mutual purpose [plate 17]. The week before the official opening in June, they called in the press and posed, side by side, looking out across the lake upon which – as Grandy did not miss the chance to point out – seventeen rare forms of water-lily now floated. Lord and Lady Jersey, wrote the dutiful hacks, were an ideal modern young couple: hard-working (Grandy had taken care to mention his daily trek to work at a City bank), public-spirited (in the graciousness of sharing their home with the public for a shilling a head) and, in their life-style, democratic (Virginia leaned a bicycle gracefully against her hip).

Virginia and Grandy promote the opening of Osterley in June 1939.

While the journalists reported upon what they had been shown, Virginia – in another aspect of her life – was allowing herself to enjoy a last London summer of intimacy with Jai. ('Please, darling, try not to say anything about Ayesha to him . . .' Jo warned in her covering letter to 'Toots'. 'It doesn't do any good, so what's the use?' Jai handed his wife's epistle in person to Virginia at their first London meeting.)

Virginia heeded her friend's advice. Ayesha, the bride-in-waiting, was never mentioned by the lovers. Together, Virginia and Jai dined at Ciro's and the Coq d'Or, attempted silly, nonsensical anagrams of Virginia's name ('Rani of Motidnivigri' scrawled on a scrap of paper) and – keen to catch the hit of the season – watched pretty Lilli Palmer (clad in a costume of enticing brevity) play a schoolgirl wife in *Little Ladyship* at the Strand Theatre. Afterwards, the two then went home . . . together?

'Girls like my mother and Virginia didn't necessarily *sleep* with every man they flirted with,' Colin Campbell assures me. 'When they talked about their "beaux", or their "lovers", they didn't always mean what we might think today.'

Teresa never confronts her friend with questions that compel a direct answer. Jai and Virginia had once been lovers; had passion gradually given way to some more profound affection? Might such a possibility account for Jo's relaxed response upon hearing that Virginia had given a summer party for Jai at her Farm Street house? 'He said . . . it was great fun,' Jo wrote. 'So I thought: all is well . . .' Could this plausible shift in the relationship explain why Bhaiya, conscious of the imminent public betrothal of his own sister to his friend, felt happy to tell Virginia, in July 1939, that he himself was 'still crazy' about her, and 'always will be'. Perhaps, Colin Campbell has put his finger upon the truth; possibly, Jai and Virginia's renewed intimacy amounted only to a deeply loving flirtation. Virginia, herself, discloses nothing. Jai, so his eldest son,

'Bubbles', told Virginia, when he visited her many years later, kept a large photograph of her exquisite face upon his desk until his death.

'She was *so* pleased when Bubbles came to see her,' Teresa sighs.

Sinister portents continued throughout the summer of 1939; in Bucharest, a bomb was hurled at the house of Max Ausnit, while Bhaiya, in a further July letter, foresaw – without much regret – an end to the rule of the maharajas: '[The] States have not many years to last, so you had better give me a job as footman or, better still, barman . . . look after your sweet self.' Osterley, meanwhile, was set to act as host-house to one last great celebration before – as some feared – the final descent of the British Empire's decaying ship of state.

Grandy had won approval from the Press for his wish to restore (and even to grant public access to) one of the treasures of Georgian England. In May 1939, he was approached by the newly formed Georgian Group, whose aim it was to protect threatened eighteenth-century buildings. A ball held in 1938, in the immaculate Georgian surroundings of London's Mecklenburgh Square, had helped raise funds and promote the group's endeavours; when plans to repeat the event fell through, Oliver Messel, a leading light in the group, appealed for help to Lord Jersey.

'Oliver Messel did all the hard work,' Virginia insists. 'All we had to do was to draw up a guest-list, and act as the hosts. And of course, it was wonderful publicity for the house. Osterley did look so beautiful. Grandy was thrilled. I rather enjoyed it myself!'

Messel had a flair, not only for design, but for attracting publicity; Cecil Beaton was booked to photograph the event for *Vogue* magazine; Messel's creation for Virginia's exquisite Georgian gown, a confection of silver and sky blue brocade, was released to various fashion pages the week before the Ball. Fed with advance morsels

A last hurrah: Raising funds for the Georgian Group,
while promoting Osterley.

of information – Douglas Fairbanks Sr would be among the guests; Virginia, the hostess, would be wearing magnificent heirloom jewels (she didn't) – the gossip columnists went to work. Would the Osterley ball outshine a dance held by the Marlboroughs the previous week, at Blenheim; would it be superseded a few days later by Barbara Hutton's gala at her newly built Winfield House in Regent's Park? Which of these extravaganzas would take the crown?

Barbara Hutton, then on the verge of divorcing her second husband, Count Haugwitz-Reventlow, was able to gather a few tips for success from her friend Virginia's party; she, together with Lilli Palmer, Cecil Beaton, Syrie Maugham, John Fowler, Grandy's mother, the Dean of Windsor, the ship-owning Embericoses, Dorothy Campbell, and the ever-present Miss Anita Blair, joined the score of personal friends who were invited to dine by candlelight – while a small orchestra played minuets by Handel – in the Long Gallery at Osterley. Following the meal, Grandy and Virginia led their dinner-guests down the steps of the great columned portico at the entrance to Osterley, to dance foxtrots and quicksteps in a vast red-and-white-striped marquee (designed by Messel); to have their fortunes read by a mysterious stranger in an elegantly designed grotto (Messel's work, once more); and to watch the scintillations of fireworks shimmering across the lake, a display – choreographed by the tireless Mr Messel – that echoed, and then exceeded the celebrations, just two years earlier, for the Jerseys' marriage.

Over a thousand guests attended. Most, entering into the spirit of the occasion, chose eighteenth-century clothes to complement the elaborate masks created by Messel. A few did not. The chaste wimple of Lady Diana Cooper failed to pass muster as authentically Georgian. Douglas Fairbanks's voluminous raccoon coat looked more in keeping for an evening at Great Neck with Jay Gatsby than for a night with Grandy Jersey, the evening's host, himself immaculately costumed as Robert Child, for whom the Adam brothers had worked on Osterley [plate 16].

A little sniping was inevitable: the young reporter from the *Architects' Journal* jeered at Osterley's floodlit façade for looking like a filmset ('flat as painted plywood'), and the gala evening itself as a surfeit of brittle chatter ('like the trained sibilance of supers') which he proceeded to satirise in approved Firbankian style: 'Of course, it's madly Adam.' 'My dears, there's wrestling round the front.' 'Of course, those crinolines and that wig are a godsend to her.'

Virginia, gracefully attired as Sophia Child (through whose marriage, to the fifth Earl of Jersey, Osterley had passed into Grandy's family), received a better press. She, cooed one reporter, was a perfect hostess, 'a joy to the eye'. Her radiant smile concealed, however, a little private concern. Jai's name had been among those upon the list of her personally chosen dinner-guests; alarmed by further news of political troubles in his state, the Maharaja had flown home early, the week before the ball. When Virginia heard next from Jai, he had married Ayesha.

Virginia as Sophia Child at the Georgian Ball.

'I was always happiest when I was back in Illinois,' the old lady often declares to Teresa during their conversations. By the time of the Georgian Ball, however, four years had elapsed since her last visit home.

In August 1939, Virginia returned to Carthage for a long-planned reunion of 100 members of the Wilcox clan. The family gathered around her, fond and admiring; one of the youngest cousins snapped their glamorous visitor standing in front of a car, bare-legged, in a short-sleeved summer dress. Virginia's hair is casually pushed back; her only concessions to vanity are a simple bracelet and a dash of lipstick. She looks like what, in essence, she always remained: an uncomplicated young woman from a simple

Virginia in Carthage, August 1939.

rural background. It's apparent, glimpsing her like this, why she always maintained such an easy friendship with the people who worked for her; she asserted – for she felt – no lines of division.

Virginia enjoyed her visit. She was still lingering there, putting off her return to New York, when the War broke out. Her crossing had been booked for 9 September; on 4 September, news broke in the press that a British liner, the *Athenia*, had been torpedoed while crossing the Atlantic. Over a hundred passengers had lost their lives.

'Grandy and Cynthia, his mother, both kept cabling me to cancel the booking. It never crossed my mind. And when it came to it, nothing happened.'

Nothing, in so far as the major warring powers were concerned, would happen until the following spring. This peculiar postponement did not mean that life, during the months of the so-called 'phoney war', went on unchanged. During September, Warsaw's struggles were widely reported in the British press; in Romania, Max Ausnit, the director of the country's largest steel and arms works, was arrested on trumped-up charges of fraudulence. The factories were confiscated; Max was invited either to pay a fine of one million dollars, or face imprisonment. (These illegally seized factories of Romania played a crucial role in the coming War, as a chief supplier of armaments to Hitler.)

'And they did send Max to prison, but only after King Carol tried to seduce Litzi Ausnit, and she slapped him. Litzi herself managed to get out to France; they caught poor Max at the border and brought him back. I can't count the number of times they tried to finish Max off; they really hated him for being a Jew and marrying Litzi, who wasn't. But Max had friends, too . . .'

In London, under a sky heavy with the grey bladders of enormous barrage balloons (key to the air defence of London), Virginia stood side by side with Grandy's first wife outside the Ritz, posing for the camera with their fund-raising baskets of flowers for the Red Cross; Cecil Beaton, offering belated thanks for the Osterley ball, praised Virginia for 'your integrity, calm, courage and kindness' – and suggested popping round to Farm Street to photograph her collection of Indian jewels. Flipping through the society magazines, Virginia was less intrigued by accounts of Ivor Novello's latest musical (as well as a tribute to Charles Trenet's songs) than by reports of a play taking New York by storm. *The Man Who Came to Dinner*, playing to entranced audiences at the Music Box Theatre, stirred up complex memories of her old Hollywood days, and her former life with Cary.

'It was all about Aleck Woollcott, whom I'd met when he used to stay at Harpo's place. I felt strange when I read about that. It all seemed so far away from the life I was living in London. I think that was when I realised just how English I'd come to feel.'

At Christmas, although the main house at Middleton had been occupied since early September 1939 by a host of schoolchildren evacuated from the capital, Virginia and Grandy travelled to Oxfordshire. The lease was up on old Lady Jersey's London home in Montagu Square; for her last years, she wished to return to the familiar surroundings of Middleton Park.

'We helped her move into one of the lodges. And then we went in for tea with the schoolgirls who were sleeping in dormitories at the big house. Poor little things; they'd never lived outside London before. I couldn't make out whether they were more scared by the country silence or by the planes. You could hear the bombers roaring overhead all the time at Middleton. Strangely, back in London, I never heard a thing.'

A Christmas card survives, a blurred photograph of Middleton, inscribed to Lord and Lady Jersey, with neatly crayoned signatures from each of the young convent evacuees: Winnie Miller; Tammy Murphy; Mary Reilly; Janet Hug . . .

Baglan House, the Welsh home of the Jerseys, had also been requisitioned for use by the Army; Grandy, pre-empting a probable strike upon his major home, decided to volunteer Osterley for use by specific banks, ones with which he had both personal and professional links. (Clerical employees seemed less likely to cause damage, shrewd Grandy judged, than either soldiers or schoolchildren.)

'Although we did have soldiers at Osterley,' Virginia pipes up. 'I almost forgot. Teddy Hulton was one of my "beaux", as we said, back then. You know: he owned *Picture Post*. Teddy and I were both attending some fund-raising cabaret one night at Grosvenor House, and we started talking about the war effort. He and his colleagues wanted to start a training course for Home Defence; they'd found three vets from the Spanish Civil War who were willing to run the show. They needed a big piece of open land, near London. And I said: "Well, what about Osterley! Ask Grandy."'

Virginia's account, I realise, explains the oddity of some of the scrapbook photographs that I had assumed were connected to a fireworks display, perhaps at the Georgian ball. The gardens of Osterley remained sacrosanct, at the insistence of the Jerseys; the park, from March 1940 on, became a noisy playground for patriotic gentleman in City suits. Snapped for the pages of Edward Hulton's thriving new photo-news magazine, the voluntary Defence Guard can be seen honing their skills in camouflage and the hurling of grenades; in one memorable image, they take vigilant aim at an airborne fleet of furry teddy-bears.

'Teddy Hulton's idea of a joke? I don't suppose so: he didn't have much sense of humour. We didn't manage to stay in touch, although he did take Grandy out for a thank-you drink. I think that was while Grandy's regiment was stationed, oddly enough, at some hotel in Knightsbridge. The Rembrandt . . . ?'

Mayfair, placed in the heart of London, was not the ideal place to reside when enemy planes began to target the city. A shift of location from Farm Street was judged to be prudent. In March 1940, Virginia Jersey spotted an intriguing announcement: *Tudor Palace for Rent*.

'Can you imagine anything more romantic for an American girl who was nuts about English history? I took the Underground out to Richmond that same afternoon and went to see the man who was moving out. The whole thing was perfect. I couldn't believe my luck.'

Richmond Palace for Rent

WHAT is left of the Old Palace at Richmond, where Cardinal Wolsey lived and Anne of Cleves died after her divorce from Henry VIII, and where Mary Tudor spent her honeymoon with Philip of Spain, has been empty for the last three years.

Now a tenant is required and for $15 a week he will be able to live in the 400-year-old palace, with its ancient panelling, secret door and passage, and will, moreover, have the right to search for the $10,000,000 worth of hidden treasure reputed to be under the premises.

Soon after the present palace was built in 1499 (the original manor dated back to 1300 and was rebuilt by Edward III. and by Henry V.) Henry VII. buried a hoard of gold bullion and jewels in an underground tunnel which could only be reached by a secret door hidden in the panelling. *Vancouver Daily Province 4/4/40*

Virginia and Grandy, from the time they had spent at nearby Osterley, were already familiar with the charms of Richmond: the broad green, the riverside walks, the pretty, winding lanes. This visit, however, was Virginia's introduction to what had once been a royal home. Henry VIII (following an uncharacteristically equable divorce) had given Richmond Palace to Anne of Cleves for a dwelling place; Henry's daughter, Queen Mary, honeymooned at Richmond with Philip II of Spain; Elizabeth I, imprisoned at the Palace as a girl, returned to it to die.

The Gate House building, which Virginia had come out especially to view, comprised part of the original entrance block:

a last relic of the grand old Tudor Palace, it faced out, looking across the level land of Richmond Green.

'I fell in love on the spot,' Virginia tells Teresa. 'Everything about the place seemed perfect: the oak staircase, the panelled rooms, the lovely old bricks. People said that it was haunted, but I never saw anything. The Old Palace became my favourite home, no question.'

Urged by his excited wife, Grandy agreed to the modest lease. Lord Jersey, moving with his territorial regiment from camp to camp throughout the war (symptoms of a weak heart rendered him unfit for active service), would seldom be able to enjoy life at Richmond. To their friends, the Old Palace was always identified with Virginia.

Plans for a speedy removal from Farm Street were interrupted by a new development, one that had been long anticipated: Virginia was once again pregnant.

'Grandy pretty much ordered me to go back to the States,' Virginia says. 'He thought I'd be safer there, and that my mother could help with the baby. Grandy always had a high opinion of Blanche's practical skills.'

Teresa sounds surprised by the implication that Virginia might consent to be instructed where her baby should be born and reared. Later, we both wonder whether Virginia could have had other motives for visiting America during Britain's dark summer of 1940, as Italy joined forces with Germany, and a newly Nazified France broke off relations with England, a country that dared to support de Gaulle and the Free French.

America, in the summer of 1940, was still keeping itself at a distance: Roosevelt, approaching his third campaign for office, actually chose the slogan 'I Hate War' as a sure way to attract votes. (It did.) Virginia was one of a hundred outraged Americans based in Britain who signed a letter – it was to be broadcast on coast-to-coast radio in the States – demanding that the President should immediately undertake a commitment to the Allies.

It's hard to know how close Virginia was able to reach to Roosevelt himself. The blue scrapbooks reveal that she had kept up her friendship with William Rhinelander Stewart and Nelson Doubleday, two members of the President's old inner circle of advisers and informants. A news item about Virginia dining with Rhinelander Stewart and his wife just two nights after her July arrival in New York confirms only that she pursued that particular contact. Perhaps, she was just catching up with an old friend; possibly, she hoped to exchange more significant information than social gossip.

The official purpose for her Atlantic crossing, however, was to provide the prospective heir to Middleton and Osterley with the best possible chance for survival in the midst of extremely dangerous times. Lady Jersey, 'looking as lovely as ever on her arrival at the Drake Hotel', Cholly Knickerbocker informed his New York readers, in July 1940, '. . . is expecting a visit from Mr Stork'.

Two months later, while staying at her mother's home in West Hollywood, Virginia – once again – miscarried.

She had come to America ostensibly, or even primarily, for the sake of her unborn child; welcomed by an increasingly needy mother and by a mass of friends, freed from the privations of life in a country at war – a nation in which she had no true home of her own and now no real family: surely Virginia must have felt tempted to follow Grandy's advice and stay where she was undoubtedly most secure?

'I didn't,' she admits, 'feel ready to go back straightaway to England. It was the third baby I'd lost and I didn't want to face questions about – you know – an heir to the title. It mattered so much to Grandy – and yet, physically . . .'

Her voice trails off. I can hear barking in the background and a man's voice – Virginia's husband, I immediately imagine – shouting at the dog to quiet it down. When Virginia starts to talk again, it's about the impending visit of a favourite relative, a Wilcox nephew.

Disappointed though Virginia evidently was by the outcome of her pregnancy, she seems to have kept busy during her two months in California. She drove up from Beverly Hills to the ranch where her friends Carole Lombard and Clark Gable were living in newly wedded bliss; she caught up with an inebriated Humphrey Bogart (her friend was still playing, for the most part, supporting roles, usually as the villain) and joined Bogey as an original investor in Romanoff's, a new restaurant being launched by a self-styled Russian prince (one who was born in Cincinnati). In September, Virginia helped Mrs Charles Boyer and Mrs Jack Warner auction off a batch of glamorous gowns donated to aid the war effort. (America, while officially inactive, was often privately supportive, fortifying the fight for survival in Britain.)

'One dress had belonged to the Duchess of Windsor,' Virginia remembers, 'and a couple of them had been donated by my old friend Marion Davies. Marion was always so generous.'

California had not lost its attraction for Virginia; she did not need a newly married Anita Blazier (née Blair) to point out – as Anita so often did – that Blanche Cherrill thrived upon her daughter's companionship and pined in her absence.

'But I had to get back to England,' Virginia tells Teresa. 'I couldn't just stay there doing nothing. I had no child to care for. In the end, I knew where I wanted to be.'

Press reports from that time show that Lady Jersey made no secret of her intentions: 'Virginia Cherrill . . . tells us that she is longing to return to England and share the lot of her friends and compatriots,' one Hollywood magazine revealed. Fifty years later, Teresa reminds Virginia of the perilously altered conditions under which she planned to travel. Roosevelt, triumphantly back in office in the autumn of 1940, displayed his true feelings about the war: American ships were ordered to attack all enemy craft in the

Atlantic. The ocean, overnight, became a territory of waged battle: wasn't Virginia afraid to embark upon such a hazardous crossing?

'My only real worry was about how to locate a ship that would take me. I got to New York and found the liners had all cancelled their services. The French wouldn't sail because the Germans threatened to torpedo them. And the British were the same. I couldn't blame them; I just didn't know what to do.'

Virginia's improbable saviour was the personal lawyer of Barbara Hutton. 'Sol Rosenblatt. He was a dear man, very fat, with a big tummy, kind as an angel. Sol used to come over a lot to England to do work for Barbara; he and I always got along well. He took me to this benefit for war relief, up at Cape Cod, and I explained my problem. Sol said: "I can get you on a ship, but it's a freighter going by way of Portugal. You can try for a flight back to England from Lisbon. Or else you can sit around here for months. Care to take the chance?"'

Virginia ate her dinner, thought about Sol's offer, and decided that she had no alternative. The following morning, 1 November, Rosenblatt drove her out along the Hudson to where, due to a Manhattan dock strike, the *Siboney* lay anchored.

'It wasn't easy to be taken on board. The captain was a Czech, and he didn't like foreigners. There were only twenty passengers. One was a British courier, with his briefcase chained to his wrist; another was a journalist, travelling to Switzerland for Associated Newspapers. That was my Danny' [Clifton Daniel, who later married Margaret Truman and who went on to be Editor of the *New York Times*].

Gay Talese has described, in his account of Clifton Daniel's long and successful career, the departure of the *Siboney*. Champagne flowed, writes Talese; smiling crowds waved the great ship off. Virginia offers a slightly different account.

'Usually, crossing the Atlantic, you go up on the beautiful deck and have big suites and everything. This time, instead of going up the gangplank, we went down. Sol got worried. I mean, there was nothing sailing except this one big freighter. He thought we'd be torpedoed, for sure. I told him to stop fretting. I said that I'd be fine.'

The shock came later. Waking at sea from an exhausted twelve-hour sleep ('I hadn't been to bed for two days; I was a wreck'), Virginia glimpsed the name upon some of the old-fashioned fittings in her cabin.

'I couldn't believe it. I looked at that name – *Ward Line* – and I said: "Oh Virginia, what have you *done*!"'

PART FOUR

Wartime

14

INTERLUDE

(November 1940–February 1941)

'The biggest place of all for spies was the Palace Hotel, just outside Lisbon.'

'It was just one god-damned disaster after another,' Virginia tells Teresa, who evidently knows as little as I do about the notorious history of the Ward Line.

A little research shows that Virginia's dismay was well founded. The catalogue of the Ward Line's disasters, beginning with a wreck off the West Coast in the year of Virginia's birth, proves to have been breathtaking in its extent. The Line's infamy reached a climax in the mid-Thirties when three of its ships went down in less than six months.

Of these three, the first to capture the headlines was the *Morro Castle*. The pride of the Ward Line fleet, this luxurious giant of a ship caught fire – arson was suspected – while cruising off the coast of New Jersey, in September 1934.

'The ship was in sight of shore.' Virginia's voice has dropped to a whisper. 'Oh Teresa, can you imagine how dreadful? People actually saw it all happening; they watched the passengers burning to death.'

Shocked holiday-makers at Asbury Park witnessed clearly the final hours of the liner, which burnt out and sank within fifty yards of the resort's boardwalk. An inquiry revealed that – while the lifeboats were commandeered for use by a panic-stricken crew – at least 134 passengers lost their lives.

Memories of the *Morro Castle* disaster were unpleasantly revived, only four months later, when another Ward Line ship, the *Havana*, ran aground in January 1935. The *Havana*'s replacement, SS *Mohawk,* during that same month, was just six hours into her maiden voyage when she collided with another boat and sank – with the loss of the lives of 47 passengers – at the exact location of the *Morro Castle*'s disaster. 'Ward Line' became a major news story – and the dirtiest word in shipping. Changing its name became finally the only way for the Line to survive: Ward Line transformed itself, at speed, into the Cuba Mail.

'Only, they were in such a hurry that they forgot to change the old names on the taps and towels! I couldn't believe it when I woke up in my cabin that morning, to be greeted, first thing, by the words "Ward Line". I thought, just then, that I was finished.'

The *Siboney*, despite Virginia's fears, proved in the end to be seaworthy; the true threat, during her attempt at crossing a torpedo-strewn Atlantic, came from another source.

'We were about ten days out, nearing the Azores, when a U-boat suddenly rose up alongside us. The whole surface was covered with kelp and seaweed. It must have been under for quite a while, but it stayed up, hovering alongside us, for at least two full days. We had this British courier travelling on our ship who kept his briefcase chained to his wrist. I kept wondering if the Germans knew about him and were planning to come on board. That was scary. But, of course, it would have been an act of war. I mean, we were all lit up, prow to stern, absolutely signalling out that our ship was American. I don't think they would have dared.'

Teresa doesn't question Virginia's assertion, but it's hard – given Roosevelt's newly aggressive naval policy – not to see the *Siboney*'s flaunted lights as offering more of a challenge than a defence. The German intention, however, seems only to have been to observe, or to induce unease. The U-boat dropped away after the Azores, and was never encountered again by the *Siboney*.

The military submarine was also anxiously watched by a young English passenger who, before they reached the Azores, had joined the *Siboney* and had been placed under the care of Virginia.

'We stopped along the way at Bermuda,' Virginia explains, 'and a banker came aboard, a Mr Butterfield.'

The owner of Bermuda's principal bank had a particular and sensitive mission; he was seeking an English lady who might be willing to act as a chaperone. Lord Rothermere, the British newspaper magnate, had just died while staying at his holiday home on the island; a suitable person was required to escort his grand-daughter back to London.

'I told him I'd be glad to do whatever was needed, but that I wasn't English by birth. Mr Butterfield didn't see that as a problem. So I agreed to help out, and that's how I met Esme Harmsworth. She must have been about sixteen years old, and she really was the most beautiful girl I ever saw, perfect, a real English rose [plate 18]. She and her younger brother had been evacuated out to America that summer. Esme got sent to some family friends in New Jersey, and it seems she didn't have too good a time, so her grandfather rescued her and whisked her off to his place on Bermuda, where, unfortunately, he died. Esme was a darling. She and I stayed together until we got back to England . . .'

'And the first thing she did then was to try to marry me off to Mansel, her divorced brother-in-law,' says Esme Harmsworth (now Lady Cromer). 'Milk?' She pours out, with care, my cup of tea. 'Subtlety wasn't always Virginia's strongest suit; she just sent him along to take me to a party! Mansel was charming, and handsome, too, and he did propose to me quite soon after that. But I didn't give him a "yes" or a "no" – and then, of course, he went out to Spain in the RAF and got taken prisoner. I'd married my husband by the time Mansel came home in 1943. So that was that, I'm afraid. At least I saved him from another tricky mother-in-law!'

I tell her that I think I know what she means: I've read the news cuttings in Virginia's blue scrapbooks about a scandalously silly case in 1939, when Mansel Child Villiers's mother-in-law took him to court over twenty pounds that she had spent on clothes for a grandchild. (The judge dismissed the case.)

Lady Cromer (she is the widow of a former ambassador to Washington) is as elegant, pretty and quick-witted an old lady as I've met; it's easy to see why Virginia might have craved such a charming woman for her sister-in-law.

'Virginia was such a matchmaker!' Lady Cromer exclaims, and she takes my hand to clasp it as she speaks. 'I adored her! We did have fun! I'm *so* pleased about this book.'

'Well, me too!' I say, and I tell her – truthfully – that researching Virginia's life has added to the enjoyment of my own.

Lady Cromer nods her understanding. The past feels close enough to touch in her light-filled, trinket-strewn drawing-room. I wonder – aloud – if this is what the Old Palace at Richmond might have felt and looked like, back in Virginia's day. I suspect my hostess of humouring me when she agrees – but then she qualifies the statement.

'It was graceful and comfortable, only with more colour – Virginia had some red lacquer furniture – and lots of oak panelling. I always enjoyed my visits to the Old Palace,' she adds. 'It was so full of life! Just like Virginia herself!'

I steer our conversation back to the *Siboney*, a steamship that – as I have recently discovered – had been built to carry over 400 passengers. Forty-five cabins were booked, but Virginia remembered only twenty passengers, and Lady Cromer feels certain there were no more than thirty. Her memory is one of a sense of desolation – a ghost ship – upon which the passengers kept up their spirits by playing games and acting out charades. Meals were taken at one big table presided over by the inscrutable Czech captain, who never volunteered a word that was not entirely necessary.

'I always looked forward to the end of dinner and getting to my room,' Lady Cromer tells me. 'Virginia and Mr Daniel were up in cabins on the passenger deck, but I'd been allowed a more private room off on my own, near the dining-room. I'd picked it out because of a big porthole that I could keep open at night. Only . . .'

With a sudden and perceptible shudder, she recalls a night when one of the crew members ('a strange man; nobody could understand a word he said') managed to slip into the passage along behind her. He thrust a boot in through her bedroom door. Screaming for help, Esme realised that she was too far away for anybody to hear her cries.

'I did manage to push him back, and somehow bolt the door, but it was a horrid experience. I couldn't help thinking how easy the porthole would have made things for him; nobody would have known. I still, even now, have nightmares.'

After that, so she tells me, Virginia insisted that Clifton Daniel should walk Esme down to the cabin every night and check the passage before he left her.

'I was so grateful; Virginia was a real friend in need!'

I ask my hostess for her thoughts about the relationship between Virginia and the handsome young journalist from South Carolina who was, back then, at the beginning of a brilliant career; Lady Cromer gives me a look of friendly shrewdness.

'You're asking me if they had an affair during the voyage? I wouldn't rule it out. She was astonishingly pretty, and Mr Daniel was such a good-looking man, and very attentive. He must have been around thirty; Virginia could have passed for much less than that. Yes, they did seem like a couple. I know they stayed in touch after we got back.'

From Lisbon, Clifton Daniel set off for the Associated Papers office in Switzerland; Virginia, at times as lucky in her fortuitous connections as a fairy-tale princess, discovered that the head of Shell Oil in England had learned that she was on board a ship bound for Portugal.

'I'd met him and his wife, because they were neighbours of ours in Farm Street,' Virginia explains. 'And he told Shell's man in Lisbon to look out for me, so Esme and I were given a huge suite at the Aviz.'

'Oh, the *Aviz*!' sighs Esme. 'That really was a wonderful place. Everybody used to stay there: the Windsors, Gala Dali, Elsa Schiaparelli . . . And there were beautiful tapestries in the rooms, and canopied beds, and huge mosaic-tiled terraces. I once read that the Aviz was the grandest hotel in the world. It certainly seemed so to me.'

'The shock came when we realised that our rooms weren't being paid for by the people at Shell,' Virginia tells Teresa. 'It turned out we were being charged over fifty pounds a night for the suite. They didn't have any other rooms, and I didn't have that kind of money, and neither did Esme. So I had to think.' Virginia's voice sounds quite sombre. 'Matter of fact, I had to think quite hard – and fast.'

Beauty, combined with their considerable charm, surely helped two young women to survive for two months in what was, at the time, one of the most dangerous, albeit exotic, cities in Europe. Portugal (along with Sweden, Spain, Switzerland and Ireland) had opted to declare its neutrality; Lisbon offered a haven both for refugees and for spies. One night, a handsome young Hungarian with mysterious connections invited Virginia and Esme to dine with him.

'We were thrilled,' sighs Virginia. 'Anybody who would buy us a meal was welcome – and he took us to the most beautiful restaurant. The two of us were starving. I must have eaten everything on the menu!'

Only later did an American friend identify their mystery benefactor to Virginia as a top undercover agent for the Germans.

'That's the sort of thing that happened all the time,' Virginia tells Teresa, and then immediately starts to describe a Russian couple who were staying at the same hotel.

'I have never, ever set eyes upon such jewels as that woman possessed. The pair of them threw a Christmas party for about ten of us: caviare; salmon; lovely preserved fruits; everything you could eat. They had all that money, and they still couldn't get out of Lisbon. Nobody could. Another time, one couple offered to give us their Rolls-Royce. They'd driven it from Paris and they were trying to get to South America and they couldn't get it out. *They* couldn't get out. You have no idea how desperate it all was. All anybody ever talked about was visas and passports.'

'And the women each had their favourite consulate official,' Esme Cromer adds. 'The officials must have enjoyed themselves, don't you think . . . ?'

The immediate problem was how to survive; the last of Virginia's money had been used to pay for the splendid sojourn of the two women at the Aviz. Luck, once again – as she tells Teresa – proved to be on Virginia's side.

'The biggest place of all for spies was the Palace Hotel at Estoril, just outside Lisbon. It turned out that the men who ran the Palace were a couple of ex-jockeys who used to ride for Grandy's father. So I got hold of one of them – he was about as high as your knee – and I threw myself upon his manly little bosom and told him we didn't have any money, but that I'd pay him back after the War.'

The jockey was no pushover. A room was offered, but not one of the kind that Virginia had hoped to obtain.

'It was kept for one of the hotel's chambermaids. So Esme and I went down from our suite at the Aviz to a little brass bed at the back of the Palace.' Recollecting, Virginia begins to laugh. 'And that *was* a place!'

'The Palace was extraordinary,' Esme Cromer nods. 'Like something out of a detective novel. You had the sense at every moment that doors were half open, and that transmitters were just out of sight behind them. Somebody told me later that the head porter there – he had very long thin fingernails, clean, but sinister, somehow – had been the head of a spy ring for the Germans. It always felt as though somebody was watching you.'

'All the consulate officials hung out at the Palace, picking up information while they had drinks in the bar,' Virginia says. 'That was where the American attaché introduced us to Count Hoyos, the Gestapo man who took Esme and me to dinner. And the attaché knew all about him beforehand! That was his idea of a joke!'

Esme Cromer provides the clearest account of what happened next. It must, she thinks, have been around the end of the first week in January 1941 when the two women were told to collect their passports and prepare themselves for a sudden call.

'They kept all foreign passports locked up at the police department,' she relates. 'You had to produce them as proof, before they allowed you to leave.'

Two nights later, shortly after midnight, Esme and Virginia received a telephone summons; they were given twenty minutes to pack their bags and get themselves out to the airport.

'That Lisbon airfield was the tiniest I've ever seen,' Virginia recalls, 'and it was lit up by arc lamps, to keep saboteurs away. There were just two planes standing on the runway, and there was a queue for each. The first was a Lufthansa, covered with swastikas, bound for Berlin; sitting beside it was a little battered British plane, from Imperial Airways. It was late and we were awfully tired. We might easily have stood in the wrong queue. Imagine that!'

The journey out was cramped and, due to the need for shuttered-up windows, claustrophobically dark; a fellow-passenger explained that they were flying the long way round, out above the Atlantic, to avoid being shot down over France.

'That made sense,' Virginia admits. 'Only it took a while. And then we came in at – of all places – Bristol! You just had to land wherever you could, and London wasn't an option. Bristol was in ruins; I remember wondering about Cary's family, and if they'd survived. It was such a shock: sandbags; blown-out windows; just wreckage, everywhere. We hadn't known. They'd kept the effects of the bombing out of the papers to stiffen morale. And I couldn't get hold of anybody to let them know I was back. It turned out that Esme's family home had been bombed. So had Farm Street. And Grandy was off away in camp. It all felt pretty bleak.'

'Did you begin to wish you hadn't returned?' Teresa asks.

Virginia's response is immediate. 'Not ever! Not for a minute! Besides, we were so thankful to be out of Lisbon! I felt more afraid there than I ever did later in London.'

It was time for me to leave.

Standing on Lady Cromer's doorstep, I hesitate for a moment, before taking the hand she extends.

'Did Virginia ever talk to you about Jai?' I ask.

'Ayesha's husband . . . ?' Lady Cromer smiles. 'Not to me. There were photographs of Jai around at the Old Palace. There might have been a few more set out on view, perhaps, than one would expect of somebody who wasn't a family member.'

'And Cary? Cary Grant? Did Virginia ever talk to you about what went wrong in the marriage?'

The elegant, tall old lady glances down, not quite checking her watch. I'm conscious that I've already trespassed beyond politeness. Perhaps, she suggests, it simply became too difficult for Virginia to stay. Lady Cromer pauses, seeming to reflect. 'But she did love him. Everybody knew that. She certainly did love him.'

'And Grandy . . . ?'

'Grandy . . . ?' Lady Cromer repeats, very gently. 'Grandy always seemed to me to have the most perfect manners.'

I sense that I have been put – with great courtesy – in my place. No further questions upon this delicate topic will be welcomed or directly answered.

And they never are.

*Doing their bit: A Press photo of Grandy
and Virginia in 1941.*

15

❧

FINDING A CAUSE

(1940–1943)

'I had my fun. We all did.'

David Colville, Virginia's brother-in-law, was never one of her biggest fans. He was, nevertheless, impressed by the courage she had shown in deciding to return to England at such a dangerous time. 'It is', he wrote to Grandy on the last day of 1940, 'wonderfully plucky of her and I take my hat off unreservedly . . .'

Ruined Bristol had dismayed her (Virginia later learned that Cary Grant's entire English family had been killed in the raids on their home city). A further shock greeted her in London, where faithful Liesl Dietrich was waiting at the station to break the news that 24 Farm Street had taken a direct hit. Visiting her friendly tenant at number 18A, the house in which she and Grandy had spent the first months of their marriage, Virginia learned that the former actress Dorothy Campbell was about to remove herself, her beloved red chow and Colin, her small son, to safer quarters.

'My mother had acquired a Polish boyfriend while we were living at Farm Street,' Colin Campbell tells me. 'Nothing unusual about that: back then, all the women seem to have been in love with the Poles. Then she met a new chap, an English lord, and off we went to Chesham Place, to live in what had once been the old Russian Embassy. My mother knew Virginia would want a base in London, as well as in Richmond, and they'd always been good friends. She persuaded Virginia to take the flat below hers, on the first floor.'

The house Campbell describes was a dilapidated white stucco monster, standing on the corner of Lyall Street and Chesham Place, in Belgravia.

'Even the passageways were the size of small roads: we ended by nicknaming one "the Polish Corridor" because of all the Polish airmen who came paying court to Virginia. My mother had her own callers. She was having a fling with David Niven around that time . . . Virginia was, too? I'm not surprised. My word, but he did get around!'

'So I did still have a place in town,' Virginia tells Teresa. 'And I had Liesl to help me sort things out. Compared to some of my friends, I wasn't badly off at all.'

Virginia was more financially straitened than she cares to recall. A letter from her bank manager, sent in September 1941, called attention to a thousand-pound overdraft; selecting news items for her wartime scrapbooks, she picked out a comic drawing of a harassed nobleman hard at work outside his stately home. 'The 9th Earl 'imself, a-scrubbing the 13th Step' runs the *Punch* caption; beneath it, Virginia has added a comment of her own: 'Not to mention the 10th Countess!' Another cartoon that appealed to her sense of humour depicted a fretful Army wife sighing: 'I could try to live within his income – but what's HE going to live on!'

Grandy appears to have shared his wife's anxiety; in May 1941, several pieces of Lord Jersey's finest Georgian heirloom silver were put up for sale.

Money problems back then have slipped from Virginia's mind in later life; reminiscing to Teresa, she recalls only the pleasure she felt at settling into the Old Palace in Richmond. The flat in

Chesham Place was never more than a *pied-à-terre*, she tells her friend; Richmond, from 1941 on, became her home.

'People said the Old Palace was haunted. There was supposed to be a ghostly White Lady on the stairs, and there was a Girl in a Red Dress who floated about in the guest bedroom. If so, they didn't bother me; I never saw a thing. Dr Burn, whose family lived near by, told me that the creaks and sighs were just old timbers shifting with changes in the weather.'

Virginia's voice brightens when she talks about life in Richmond, and about the ancient widows who comprised most of her neighbours. These comic old crones were, she says, 'more damn fun than their husbands can ever have been. Friends in London used to ask what I did out in Richmond. I'd tell them I heard more juicy gossip there than I got from any of the girls in town.' Amy Croft-Murray, inhabiting a Queen Anne house that overlooked the ample green, is cited as an example of the type. Amy, Virginia announces, was a real character.

'Normally, she went about in a snow-white wig, parted to the side, but you should have seen the get-up she put on for night duty as an air warden: brown brogues, green wool socks, a red tartan cape, and a Cromwellian iron helmet to keep off the shrapnel. She shared the house with her son, Teddy, and he was pretty elderly, so Amy seemed older than God. And what a snob! But we got on well, Amy and I: the stories she'd tell me! I'm sure she made half of them up, just to see if a naïve American would be fool enough to swallow them.'

'Richmond was an extraordinary place to live back then,' confirms John Burn, whose family knew Virginia well during her years as their neighbour. Guiding me down to the neatly paved riverside walk that runs behind the Old Palace, Mr Burn seems to breathe the spirit of wartime London back into the houses – shuttered and silent on an August afternoon – that stand between the Thames and Richmond Green. Down by the side of the Old

Palace, he shows me the winding lane where raffish Mr Barnett, the garage-owner, lived with his pretty daughter Vera and her boyfriend, a prize-fighter; he points up above us, remote upon Richmond Hill, to the bulky shape of the Star and Garter hospital, where Nell Burn, a lively Irishwoman, used to take Virginia on regular visits to disabled veterans of the First War.

'Virginia cheered them up. She always made them laugh, so my mother told me.'

John Burn walks me on past elegantly Palladian Asgill House, overlooking the river from the back of the Old Palace.

'That's where two sedate old chaps lived with the Siamese cats they bred for sale. Mr Ward and Mr Webb – they were a funny pair. Mr Ward once heard my mother make some remark about wilted pansies, and took it personally. He told her to wait and see just what a pansy can do if you snip the stem and give it an aspirin. Ward and Webb gave a five-course dinner for my seventeenth birthday, just them, me, the butler and ten yowling cats. They bought me a full evening suit to wear for the occasion; said it was part of a young man's education.'

And did Virginia know these people?

'Lord, yes,' says Mr Burn. 'You have to understand: Richmond was a little world unto itself. Everybody knew everybody. There, on the corner, where Richard Attenborough lives now: that's our old home, not all that changed since the days when my father used to get midnight calls to the morgue from the police, asking him to come and identify bodies they'd fished out of the river. I told you my father was a doctor: he looked after Virginia's mother-in-law, Lady Cynthia, after the War, when they came to live at Kew. What a delightful woman! We all loved the Slessors. Dinah, their daughter, was my sister Heather's best friend . . .'

'And Grandy?' I ask. 'Did your family get on well with him?'

John Burn hesitates, considers saying something, and then shakes his head.

'He was a quiet chap, not around much. We knew the Slessors and Virginia better.'

'Grandy and I were never a cosy couple,' Virginia confides to Teresa. It's hard not to smile at such a decorous understatement.

Wartime conditions reduced the relationship of the Jerseys to that of courteous strangers. Grandy wrote to tell his wife how eagerly he had listened in on 15 April 1941, when she – together with Joyce Grenfell and Bea Lillie – took part in an All Star radio quiz; his visits home, however, were rare.

'Grandy came to Richmond about twice a year; never to Chesham Place,' Virginia states. 'He was always away in one of the Army camps that were set up all over Britain. Some were for transfers, on their way out to fight; Grandy's camps were for home defence. I'd visit, when he had leave, take him the latest gossip. He liked to know what was going on. And I'd give him any scrap of news I had about Osterley and Middleton, to keep him in the picture.'

Virginia's cheerful company brought pleasure to her husband; a touching aside in Grandy's memoirs admits to his glee when an Army chum accused him of having found himself a pretty Scottish girlfriend in Edinburgh.

'As it happened,' Grandy proudly informed his friend, 'it was Virginia who had come up to spend my leave with me.'

'Grandy did love me,' Virginia affirms. 'He just didn't know how to show emotion. It wasn't in his nature.'

Cholly Knickerbocker, the journalist who had reported with some malice upon the wedding plans of the Jerseys, back in 1937, changed his tune when he heard that Virginia had taken on, in her husband's absence, the supervision of the family estates. Lady Jersey, Cholly gushed, was truly a credit to her adopted country, as hard-working as she was beautiful.

'I didn't really have an option,' Virginia sighs. 'Somebody had to do it, and Grandy couldn't, since he was always off in camp. I used to take advice from Charlie Stonebridge, the gamekeeper at Middleton. Charlie knew everything about the estate; he'd been working at Middleton since Grandy was a boy.'

Margaret Jersey, too, required attention. Life at her lodge at Middleton was not especially lively for a quick-witted old woman; her daughters, although they lived near by throughout the war, were preoccupied with their own lives.

'I know how busy you are,' the aged Lady Jersey wrote to Virginia in 1941, 'but I'm always here!'

A habit was formed, one which seems to have given pleasure to both women. The afternoon of every second Sunday, Virginia drove from London to Middleton. After a brisk visit to her former home, by then serving as a convalescent hospital for soldiers, she walked across to the lodge to take tea with the dowager Lady Jersey – and to be teased, however gently, about her strange American habits.

'We got on very well, and she was always making gifts to me of family things, often not quite what I wanted! But she did always treat me as a foreigner. She could never forget that I'd been in films, and that I didn't have proper lineage.'

Once a month, Virginia remembers, she joined the ageing estate-manager, Henry Little, for a more professional tour of the Jersey estates. This duty proved more testing than chatting to the gamekeeper or taking tea with a good-humoured old lady. Mr Little, she explains, had a horror of informality.

'He wouldn't let me call him Henry, and he always insisted on addressing me as Lady Jersey. Back in the War, I had a little Austin Ten, which I was very fond of, but it wasn't nearly grand enough for Henry. He didn't like me to drive and he hated to be in the back, but he would never sit beside me; he thought that wasn't proper. And if I stopped at a pub to buy us something to eat, he wouldn't even sit with me at the same table: that wasn't proper, either.'

Virginia's correspondence shows that, whatever Mr Little may have felt about her lack of decorum, the old man enjoyed these outings and remembered them fondly in later years. Thawing over lunch, he'd pass on stories about his uncle's life as the agent at Osterley.

'One time, back before the Great War, old Grandpa Jersey called in Mr Little's uncle for a meeting. He announced that they were facing a terrible problem.

'"We've got too much money this year," old Jersey lamented. "And I can't come up with a way to spend it. You'll have to think of something."

'Can you believe? We both laughed about that. Imagine!'

Virginia, however, had not returned to England, at some risk to her own life, in order simply to act as an elegant chatelaine for her absent husband.

'I wanted to help out in some way with the war effort,' she explains to Teresa. 'But it took a while to find something that – to me – felt right. Esme Harmsworth went to work at a hospital; my friend Diana Barnato began flying planes. And did I tell you that Bobby Loewenstein (who'd always been such a playboy) turned into a real hero, ferrying aircraft for the RAF in all kinds of weathers? He was killed, trying to land a cargo plane during a storm, just after I came back from Lisbon. Poor Bobby: he was only thirty-one.'

Early in March 1941, Virginia's dilemma found its solution when a wealthy American girlfriend, Jean Garland, decided to take her mind off an impending divorce by throwing a big party at the Dorchester Hotel. The evening, as Virginia recalls, turned out to be great fun: 'dancing, cabaret, more dancing; it went on all night!' Her friend Jean (formerly Mrs Smith-Bingham; later, briefly, as the wife of Bobby Throckmorton, the owner of Virginia's former Farm Street home) made a point of introducing Lady Jersey that night to her 'children'.

The children were, in fact, a group of young Polish pilots, the guests of honour at Jean Garland's evening at the Dorchester. Squadron 303, Virginia learned, were famous combat aces, celebrated for having brought down 122 enemy planes (more than any other squadron in the RAF), while taking part in the great aerial conflict – the Battle of Britain – that had been fought out during the previous summer above the placid fields and downs of south-east England.

'I'd never met anyone like those pilots before in my life!' Virginia enthuses. 'They were brilliant flyers; they had beautiful manners; and they were incredibly brave. Some of them were flying up to five missions a night – they never seemed to sleep – and yet they still somehow found time to flirt and dance. And besides that, they all looked like princes.'

Meeting the pilots that evening at the Dorchester, Virginia's first impression was one of glamour. It didn't take her long to discover that the insouciant manner of the Polish airmen masked a sense of furious anguish over the fate of their country, and of intense loneliness in a foreign land. Passionate and forlorn, the airmen were only too happy to be surrounded by admiring English girls; what they craved was a feeling of security, some illusion of normality in their estranged lives. They needed, as Jean Garland had been quick to recognise, some simple human reminder of their lost families. It was, as Jean explained, of real meaning to them to have a woman who would take on the role of 'Mother' to the regiment. Fanciful though the title sounded, it carried considerable significance to the pilots, many of whom had lost their parents, wives and children.

Virginia understood just what her friend Jean was saying. As an affectionate young woman – whose warm heart went out to the sick children at the Hanwell Hospital, and to the scared little London schoolgirls who had been dispatched to Middleton; one who longed for a way to help England's cause; one who, like

Jean Garland herself, found it a delightful prospect to 'mother' such courageous young men – Virginia had found the vocation she craved. The Polish squadrons provided her, at last, with a worthy cause.

'And a family,' Virginia explains. 'I'd always longed for children. Although I'm not sure that I expected to have quite so many – or all at once!'

Jean Garland helped to arrange introductions; late in March 1941, Virginia joined her friend as Mother to a fellow-squadron of Polish pilots.

Dear Lady Jersey,
As the officer commanding 315 squadron, it gives me the greatest
pleasure to welcome you, our Mother, to our squadron . . .
Fortunately you have not got too many sons; your family is small.
Some two hundred boys only, but they are naughty, terribly naughty,
and that is the main difficulty for you if you wish to make them good
and nice . . . [Sadly – and, perhaps, deliberately – the rest of this
engaging undated letter has not been preserved.]

Shortly after receiving her official welcome, as the 'Mother' of 315, Virginia paid her first visit to Northolt, the West London airfield that had rapidly established itself as the headquarters of the Polish squadrons in Britain. Today, the old-fashioned buildings are largely unchanged, and much as they are described, back during the War, by Virginia.

'Northolt looked just like a country golf club – very proper. The airmen adored it. Northolt was their home from home. They even had a sign hanging up over the entrance to the Officers' Mess: "No English Spoken Here". And I . . . (Virginia sounds delighted) I had my own office there. I earned it. I worked!'

Not everybody took the endeavours of the Countess seriously. One interviewer was certainly writing with tongue in cheek when she reported that pretty Lady Jersey often bestowed her silk stockings upon the pilots (to keep their necks warm when they went up on night flights); another journalist found it hard to repress a smile when Virginia explained that the sound of a plane roaring low over the roof of the Old Palace was simply one of 'my Poles', signalling a last farewell before he undertook a perilous night-time mission (one from which his return could never be certain).

'Northolt looked just like a country golf club; very proper.'

Virginia's status has sometimes been dismissed as that of a glamorous mascot; her office at Northolt testifies to a more significant role. So does the fact that she was prepared to learn a little Polish, enough to write a message accompanying each of the carefully wrapped 300 presents – they included a St Christopher medal and a packet of cigarettes for each man – the gifts she brought to the Christmas dinner for the pilots that was held, in 1941, at the Alexandra Palace.

('I am very proud of my dear sons – absent and present', she wrote in her closing paragraph. 'I give each one of them my best love and wishes of victory and their future happiness. *Vasolwk sviont*.')

'I travelled about,' Virginia says. 'And that wasn't easy during the War. I went to the bases near Blackpool and in Norfolk. I adopted two thirteen-year-old cadets, twins who'd lost contact with their own mother back in Poland. I took care of them, sent money, helped get them work, permits, visas, everything – oh, until years after the War. But one of the things I did most regularly was to write letters for the airmen. Some of them almost no English. It was quite difficult for them to explain themselves. And – when I felt they needed defending – I stood up for them!'

Virginia may be referring, in particular, to an occasion at Northolt upon which she spoke out against a high-handed squadron commander.

'I couldn't stand that man. He was vain, and he was a pig, and he behaved badly to his men. He'd been involved already in a couple of scandals; the man was a shit. I remember trying to explain to him some things that he was doing that all the airmen felt were clearly wrong, and he just wouldn't listen. I got so angry that I simply walked out of his office, slamming the door so hard behind me that I broke the glass. *Very* enjoyable.'

As always, Virginia ended by getting her way; the squadron commander backed down. We shouldn't be surprised. Here was a woman so disarming that, when General Eisenhower invited the Jerseys to dine with him at Roehampton, on the night before he moved his headquarters to France, the plain-spoken Kansan offered all his medals, as a token of esteem, to his civilian compatriot.

'I can't remember why he did that; maybe I put in a request for them!' Virginia jokes, when Teresa asks what had prompted such impulsive generosity. Grandy's memoirs offer a hint; the

General was worrying, that night at Roehampton, about what punishment to mete out to a black GI who had raped a white woman. The Military Code's prescribed punishment was death; Virginia argued for leniency; Eisenhower became convinced that she was right. No conversation on the tapes records this episode, but Teresa tells me that it is entirely in character for her old friend.

'Virginia wouldn't stand for anything that smacked of the unfair. She told me about one particular time when a black GI wasn't invited to some smart London social event, simply because of his colour. Virginia found out about it and asked him to come as her partner; she made a point of introducing him to all her friends. Another time, there was some big lunch for the airmen, given by the US at Grosvenor House – and they didn't ask the Polish pilots. Virginia just brought them along anyway, as her guests. Of course, by the end of the meal, she had the chief of the US staff practically eating out of her hand.'

Teresa never tires of talking about Virginia. She says little about her own life. At this point, late on in my research, I still have no real sense of her history. It is only at this point, while we discuss the way Virginia cared for her Polish 'sons', that I finally learn the origins of a friendship that would lead, decades later – as the aged Virginia became increasingly frail and bedridden – to the taped conversations upon which my work here relies. Making my first visit to Teresa's home in California I had noticed – and failed to attach significance to its presence – an old framed print of a Polish house. Now, at last, my hostess tells me her own story.

Teresa Glinski was two years old in September 1939, when Hitler invaded Poland. Teresa's parents, and their three small daughters, were forced to flee from a cultured country-house existence into a life of enforced exile.

'It was a strange moment to be leaving,' Teresa recalls. 'My father, a pianist, had just won the two highest awards – for performing, and for composition – that the Warsaw Musical Conservatory could grant. As the car was driving away from our home, we heard an announcement about the competition being broadcast over the radio. They played the Prelude my father Tomasz had composed, the piece that won the prize. We felt proud, but it was very sad. He didn't know what would become of his musical career, outside Poland.'

The Glinskis, however, were relatively fortunate. True, they'd lost their handsome country house, their Daimler, and all their personal valuables (along with the chauffeur to whom the latter – as well as the Daimler – had been rashly entrusted). True, it was unnerving to drive throughout the night over fierce Carpathian mountains – the only open route left into a free Europe – without benefit even of headlights (invisibility being essential), upon tiny roads that twisted, perilously, above dark ravines. It was also, however, true that Tomasz had succeeded in smuggling out along with him, for his family's protection, a precious brace of Purdey duelling pistols; these weapons were sold along the way, traded for a safe passage from Yugoslavia into Hungary (before the family made their way slowly across Austria, and then across Switzerland, and finally into France).

'We had connections there,' Teresa explains to me. 'My mother was related to Misia Sert, the Polish pianist. Misia knew everybody in Paris – we were sure she'd help.'

Misia, a noted beauty whose artistic circle included Picasso, Vuillard, Bonnard and Renoir, responded only with a gift of a silk handkerchief from Hermès; the Natansons, the family of Misia's first husband Tadeusz (editor of *La revue blanche*) proved more generous, supplying enough money to transport the Glinskis to England by coal-boat. Her beautiful parents did not, as Teresa observes, look too elegant by the time they arrived, soot-smirched and exhausted, at their destination.

Settling in London, Tomasz Glinski soon found employment at the Polish Embassy; in his spare time, the count gave concerts and offered his services as a strummer for public functions. Befriended by Princess Marina, a staunch supporter of the exiled Poles, Tomasz was even summoned to play the piano at Princess Elizabeth's engagement party.

This, according to Teresa, almost became a fiasco.

'Prince Philip wanted my father to play "Stardust" for Elizabeth. It was Philip's top favourite tune – and my father had never heard it. But the Prince came along in advance and whistled it out for him, so everything went off fine.'

Virginia's Christmas at Richmond in 1941: John Child Villiers and Lady Caroline Child Villiers link arms with two Polish RAF cadets.

The Glinskis had come into contact with Virginia, Teresa states, almost as soon as they reached London, through her volunteer work for the Polish Red Cross. A friendship sprang up that endured, Teresa tells me, until her parents died.

'I saw a lot of Virginia while we were in London – and later, when our family came out to California, we saw her almost every day. I can't', she adds, thoughtfully, 'remember a time in my life when I didn't know Virginia.'

When I ask for one sentence that might best sum up her old friend, Teresa's answer is prompt: 'Easy: she was just so *funny*! We'd laugh and laugh . . .'

A love of laughter was something communicated to all who knew her by Virginia. An admiring journalist once praised her for possessing, herself, 'a most gay and original wit', but her fragile appearance also hid a taste for the kind of earthy jokes that allowed her to strike up an easy rapport with the men of the squadrons. A glimpse of that quality comes through in a story Virginia tells – laughing as she speaks – to Teresa.

A group of men go off together on a fishing trip and need to choose, from among their number, someone to cook. First night, they draw lots. Next night, they decide not to repeat the draw: the cook they first picked is far too good to be given up. Three nights on, the irritated 'cook' – feeling much put upon – broils up a sumptuous dinner of patties that he has fashioned entirely of cow dung.

'And they still eat it up, every bite. Only, one of the fishermen turns to the cook, mouth full, and says: 'You know what? I'm a son of a bitch if this isn't *shit*. But – I got to admit – it's *delicious* shit!'

And where, I'd love to know, did Virginia pick up that one? From Bogey, sitting together over lunch in a studio commissary or, years later, perched at his side, up at the new Romanoff bar? From Carole Lombard or Marion Davies, giggling together over a drink – while Mr Hearst was out of the room – up at San Simeon?

Does this fishing yarn carry an echo, perhaps, of her father's voice, or that of one of her boyish Cherrill uncles – back in Carthage days? Such foolish things – lost deep within a lifetime – are beyond the retrieval of memory. The old lady is dead – and not even Teresa can provide an answer.

A few malicious friends, marvelling over the physical beauty of the young Poles, remarked that Lady Jersey seemed eager to keep them to herself (refusing, it seemed, to permit any other pretty girls to come near them) by housing them, as her home-front hostages, out at Richmond.

'I don't think that's quite fair,' Lady Cromer comments, when I seek her view. She's too modest to point out that she herself, as an exceptionally beautiful young woman, had enjoyed an open invitation, whenever she found herself free, to come and join Virginia's gatherings at Richmond.

'I always thought she was wonderfully generous with her home. The rooms were full of lovely things, but she never seemed to worry about the risk of loss or damage. I think she just wanted those brave young men to enjoy themselves. I'm not too sure what her neighbours thought: they seemed a little more old-fashioned.'

It occurs to me later – she provides no identifying name – that Lady Cromer may be remembering the eccentric Amy Croft Murray.

'I used to ask Amy to put a couple of pilots up, when we had an overflow at the Old Palace,' Virginia tells Teresa. 'And one time there was a scene because Amy discovered that one of the airmen was a count. I told you what a snob she was, so, of course, she wanted to put the count in her best bedroom and to lodge his pal up in the attic. I wouldn't let her do it. Amy was furious. She wouldn't speak to me for a week.'

Virginia's own house rules were relaxed, but clear. She allowed the pilots to stay out at Richmond all through the week, while she herself remained in town, at her flat in Chesham Place, joining them only for a part of each weekend. Liesl Dietrich, she explains, took care of the cooking and housekeeping.

'The only thing I always told the boys who slept at the Old Palace was that they couldn't bring along their girlfriends. I didn't care what they did elsewhere, but quite a few of them had wives back in Poland. It didn't seem right that they should use my home as a love nest.'

Virginia's single restriction seems the most likely source for her rumoured determination to keep at bay all potential rivals. No evidence of such uncharacteristic behaviour shows up among her papers. One surviving letter describes a dance, for example, that had just been held for the squadron.

'They asked me to bring along some beautiful girls,' Virginia wrote to a friend in California, 'so I got hold of fifteen American ambulance drivers, all pretty as anything. The girls', she demurely concludes her account, 'have not yet recovered.'

John Burn confirms this more generous view of Virginia's treatment of potential rivals. His sister, Heather, so he tells me, was a good-looking girl herself, as was her close friend, Dinah, the daughter of Ronnie and Cynthia Slessor. Virginia, speaking on the tapes, describes these attractive young women as her preferred companions, whenever she and the Polish airmen went out dancing.

'Teddy Romanowski was a marvellous dancer and so was Sasha . . .' The tape falls silent. 'Sasha . . . Pietriz? No good, I've lost it. I used to take Heather Burn and Dinah Slessor along, and we'd go off to that place near Leicester Square, where there was a black band. And, oh! my Polish boys were the fanciest dancers, but the time it took to get them out on to the floor! They were just privates, you see. So they had to go around the tables where the Polish officers sat; as they passed, they had to stop and take their hats off and bow, and then the officers bowed back and by the time they'd done all that, the dance was over. It was slow, and terribly chivalrous. The girls loved the romance of it – and I had my fun, too. We all did. After the War, both Heather and Dinah married Poles, and so did a few other girls I knew. I could have set up as a matchmaker!'

On a chilly Friday afternoon late in 1942, a group of pilots from 317 Squadron (then based at Northolt), were tucking into rationed tea and biscuits at Virginia's home when the arrival of a friend was announced, in the usual way: ' "Mummy," they said (they all called me that). "Mummy, we've brought somebody to meet you. This is our Florek."

'And there he was.' [Plate 20]

Virginia's recollections suggest that this first encounter with Florian Martini took place, uncharacteristically, at Chesham Place. I wonder whether Colin Campbell remembers the occasion? He has, after all, mentioned a passage in the building that was nicknamed 'the Polish Corridor'.

'Sorry. I can't help you, my dear. It doesn't ring a bell.'

Eager to prove of use, Campbell offers me instead his memory of opening the door at Chesham Place to a strikingly handsome American, dressed in uniform.

'He asked if Virginia was at home. So I told him to give me his name – and he did. It was Clark Gable! He was quite small, hardly taller than me, and I was only a schoolboy then. He'd just arrived in London and the Red Cross sent him along to Virginia. He was very friendly. But I did feel he ought to have been taller . . .'

Virginia's recollections are clearer about what followed on from that first introduction to Florian Martini in the autumn of 1942. The airmen who had brought him to her home were off to spend their Friday night on the town, she tells Teresa, and to stay at the new Polish hostel. Florian, a shy man, was in no hurry to join them.

'So they wanted to leave him home with their "Mummy" – namely, me. And I thought: dear God, a complete stranger, but then, I'll have to do it. So I asked if he wanted to stay and he said: "No, no, of course not", and I said he must, because you're supposed to insist at least three times, and then they give in gracefully.'

Florian Martini's response did not run true to form.

'He didn't give in. He kept saying that he'd get a bed at the hostel, while thanking me, and bowing. His English was terrible, but he had the sweetest smile. So then he told me he had a car, and so I suggested he might come out to Richmond the following afternoon. He must have said that he'd like to visit, but I forgot all about it.'

Or did she? It's possible that a painfully shy young man, handsome enough to pass for a film-star, and described by his colleagues as one of the most fearless pilots in the squadron, was about to be tested on his social skills. The following afternoon, Virginia was entertaining a small tea-party in the drawing-room at the Old Palace; her new acquaintance was announced and ushered in to be introduced to the nineteen-year-old exiled King Peter of Yugoslavia, then completing his education at Cambridge, and his mother, Queen Maria.

King Peter, so Virginia states, was 'tremendously sweet', while the widowed Queen (her husband was assassinated in France, in 1934) was a pleasant, matronly lady, not in the least intimidating. Nevertheless, as Virginia admits, two royal personages in a small room might have been expected to overwhelm any unwary newcomer.

Florian bowed, smiled, and – after a short stay – left, having passed his first social test with flying colours. He did, as Virginia often recalls, possess exquisite manners.

'I liked him straightaway,' she says. 'I knew, the minute we met, that I could trust him. Florian was good, through and through, and he was reliable. That's what I hankered for, all my life: a sense of safety. It's the one thing I never found with Cary.'

Virginia's hunger for security surely derived from her father's fecklessness. It's clear, too, however, that Florian Martini walked through her door at a serendipitous moment in her life.

Back in 1941, a year before her first meeting with Florian Martini, Virginia had received some unexpected news. Max Ausnit's son, Richard, *en route* to refuge in Brazil from wartime danger, had visited the Mexican home of the American actress Countess Dorothy di Frasso. King Carol of Romania and his mistress, Magda Lupescu, had also been paying di Frasso a visit; the sole other guests, as reported by young Ausnit, were Cary Grant and Barbara Hutton, and they were evidently staying there as a couple. In October 1942, just one month before Virginia's first meeting with Florian, Cary Grant's 'surprise' marriage to Barbara Hutton hit the headlines.

Cary Grant was the man Virginia had always thought of as her one great passion. Her marriage to Grandy had been undertaken to please Blanche Cherrill, and because it suited Virginia herself to have an undemanding husband, a friend rather than a lover. Her heart, quickened by the courtship of Jai and, more recently, by the attentions of Clifton Daniel, remained unengaged. She was still, in 1942, bound by the past, by the memory of the one man she had truly loved. Only when Cary himself appeared to sever the connection could Virginia – I surmise – liberate herself from their shared past and look, once more, for love.

Cary Grant seems to have found it more difficult to put the memory of Virginia Cherrill out of his mind. His second marriage (wits dubbed the couple 'Cash and Cary') was short-lived. Hutton remained on friendly terms with her ex-husband (in part, perhaps, because Grant made no attempt to deplete her fortune). More intriguingly, Hutton cut short her friendship with Virginia

Cherrill. It's just possible that the daily evidence of Cary's own continuing attachment to his former wife (his persistent devotion to Miss Cherrill was commented on in the press, both at the opening of and throughout his marriage to Hutton) proved too hard for Virginia's successor to bear.

16

❧

TRANSFORMING LOVE

(1942–1948)

'He'd never, *ever*, let me down.'

Virginia Cherrill would not have responded well to a conventional biographer's approach. Analysis bores her. Wisely, Teresa never asks this woman whom she has known since her own London childhood just what it was – Cary's marriage; the coldness of her own; the experience of war and suffering; or the desire for emotional commitment – that made her decide to take charge, at last, of her own destiny. Virginia, responding to questions about her feelings for Florian, always gives the same odd, and touching, response. He made her feel safe.

Listening to the old lady's quavering accounts of dancing rumbas with glamorous Teddy Romanowski, and of throwing parties at Richmond for her band of Polish 'sons', it might seem easy to predict the kind of airman who would win the heart of a beautiful woman of thirty-four. We would expect him, naturally, to be handsome. Aged twenty-eight in 1942, Florian was indeed an exceptionally good-looking young man: slender, dark-eyed and straight-nosed, he had a wide, well-shaped mouth, high cheekbones and thick, curling black hair.

'I used to boast about him so much,' Virginia says. Laughing, she remembers an occasion, shortly after the War, when she was briefly back in Hollywood.

'I walked into Romanoff's with Jules Styne's wife, to meet some girls. Bogey was sitting at his usual stool near the door, having a drink, you'll be surprised to hear. And when I came in, he jumped up and kissed me and said he'd heard that I'd fallen for a guy who looked like him. So, of course, I told him that it was true, except that Florian was even prettier. And Bogey just laughed.'

Virginia has already mentioned Florian's exquisite manners; we might further expect that he would prove romantic, witty and devilishly unreliable. Such a description could be applied to several of the intrepid Polish pilots who had come Virginia's way.

'But not Florian,' states Virginia.

'It was about trust. If Florian told me that he was going to be at a certain place at a certain time, I knew that he'd be there. He'd never, *ever*, let me down. I'd known unreliable men; I'd had my fun, but Florian gave me something I'd wanted without knowing it. He made me feel that I'd come home.'

Virginia's recorded conversations with Teresa make little reference to Florian Martini's life before he met her; given his reticent nature, it's unlikely that he ever discussed it.

Seven years younger than Virginia, Florian was born in 1915, to Polish parents, in a Russian town called Charkow, where his father, Czeslaw, was temporarily employed by the Imperial Russian Government as an engineer. Florian's name was chosen to echo that of his mother, Florentyna Gutowska. No information survives about the subsequent career of Czeslaw Martini, but, by 1919, the little boy and his mother were living in modest circumstances in a village near Warsaw.

'Florian always doted on his mother,' Virginia says. 'She was Roman Catholic, very religious, good at languages. She was fluent in German and Dutch; she and I used to talk in French. It upset her that Florian wasn't a natural linguist. He learned most of his English from watching cowboy films, you know. He absolutely loved John Wayne. I remember the look on his face when I told him that John and I had once made a film together . . .'

Florian was twenty and – having dropped out of his engineering studies at the University of Warsaw – was attending a camp for infantry officers when he decided, together with several of his colleagues, to train as a pilot. By August 1939, the young man had been placed in a Cracow-based combat squadron; the following month, as Poland began its defensive fight against the massed forces of Germany and Soviet Russia, Florian saw his first action.

My own respect for Florian's courage grows when I visit the documents office at Northolt's celebrated airfield; here, with the help of the patient Polish archivist, I decipher the précis of the subsequent career that was required to be set down, for the record, by Flight Lieutenant Martini.

On 9 September 1939, Florian was dispatched upon a covert one-man mission to scout out fuel supplies for twenty-three army vehicles; spotted, he fled across a burning bridge, entered Hungary and was promptly taken prisoner. Somehow, he obtained a visa from Budapest and secured his release; by the end of the year, he was serving the Polish forces under French command. In June 1940, he joined the exodus that followed General Sikorski, Poland's former premier, into exile in England. Here, to his mortification, the experienced young airman found himself reduced to the rank of an unproven novice and required to undergo education in basic flying skills.

'They sent him to Speke, near Blackpool,' Virginia relates. 'It was one of the first big Polish bases: they didn't seem to know what to do with the pilots when they first arrived. But Florian had a better time than some; he met a nice young lady schoolteacher who used to take him out on weekends. I don't know what she taught him, but it can't have been English.'

Flying Officer Bochniak (left) and Flying Officer Martini (right) at a Squadron dispersal area, Royal Air Force Northolt, during mid-1942.

This scholarly relationship was already waning when, in the spring of 1942, Florian moved to Northolt, to join Squadron 317, then under the command of Stanislaw Skalski, a hawk-faced young man with outstanding qualities of leadership.

'We would follow him to hell if necessary,' wrote one of Skalski's pilots; it was a view that Florian shared of a Polish hero, who, following his patriotic return to Soviet-controlled Poland in 1947, was tortured and condemned to death as a traitor. (Skalski's sentence was later commuted to life imprisonment, of which he ultimately served nine years.)

Teresa has shown me one of the most treasured possessions in Virginia's Californian home: a box of medals, among them Poland's highest award for valour: the Virtuti Militari Cross (the equivalent to the British VC or the American Medal of Honor). Later, she unearths a small grey exercise book. Poring over it together, we realise that this journal is Florian's meticulous private record, one he shared with nobody in his civilian life. The book confirms that Flight Lieutenant Martini completed 193 combat missions and destroyed eight planes, while causing crucial damage to a further two, during his service at Northolt. This was a man with an exceptional war record.

Few now survive to testify to Florian's quiet brand of heroism. One former pilot, Werner Kirchner, praises his friend's rare combination of accuracy and fearlessness. His own survival, Kirchner states, is due only to Florian Martini's ability to intuit the precise moment – when crossing into German territory – at which to release a salvo and pull up, beyond the reach of enemy ground fire. Returning to Northolt airfield at the end of a long night mission, Florian would grin and shrug off the idea that he had done anything remarkable, eager only to get back into his Spitfire's cockpit, ready for the next attack.

Such modest courage inspired friendships that would endure for a lifetime.

'And when I make that final "pancake" landing in front of St Peter's Gate, I have no doubt I will see Flight Lieutenant Florian Martini waiting for me with his Rolls-Royce supercharged engine revving,' Werner Kirchner fondly wrote in 2001 (the year of Florian's death). "What kept you?" he will say, waving me to my position at his wing. Then, we'll take off one more time. Till then, oh, how I will miss my dear Florek.'

The pilots based at Northolt played as intensely as they worked, and men from the Polish squadrons often spent off-duty nights at The Orchard, a local haunt that also attracted stars working in the nearby film studios at Pinewood, Denham and Ealing. The landlord, charmed by his glamorous clientele, made a point of popping a bottle of champagne each time the news came in of a downed enemy plane. Every night, the Orchard's swing band played until dawn; as the sun came up, early risers in the neighbourhood would often see a row of young men stumbling out into the light and off at a careful plod, through sleepy residential streets, towards the airfield, two winding miles away.

The Orchard was only one of the refuges for the pilots; Florian had not spent long at Northolt before he heard about the beautiful Countess, a local legend, who sometimes worked at the base and whose home, a historic palace, was situated within easy reach of the airfield. A few grumbled about 'Mama' Virginia's strict rules about not bringing their girlfriends into her home; most praised a beautiful and unpretentious woman who did everything she could to make their forlorn lives more bearable. Lady Jersey, Florian's colleagues told him, was a true friend to their country. If ever a beleaguered airman needed somebody to represent his cause, he could rely upon prompt support from the Poles' American 'Mama'.

I'm frustrated by not being able to establish clearly the process by which Virginia fell in love with Florian. The taped interviews, while generally consistent, are informal. Teresa does not seek, and Virginia does not supply, precise dates and exact locations. I've no real sense of how much she confided to friends about her burgeoning romance; neither do I know whom to ask. The only former Northolt pilot I've managed to track down belonged to Squadron 315, but his memory isn't good and, unsurprisingly, he doesn't remember a pilot from the 317th. Esme Harmsworth was too busy working as a voluntary nurse at Bart's Hospital, and engaged upon the romance that led to her marriage, to notice Virginia's love-affair. Rosie Nicholl was preoccupied by her new role as the wife of Harry d'Avigdor-Goldsmid, the owner of a beautiful Jacobean house called Somerhill. The tapes are our only resource and, after all, who should be able to describe the progress of this love-affair better than Virginia herself?

Her first impression of Florek, so the old lady tells Teresa, was that he was sincere, a good man, a safe pair of hands. 'I didn't think of him for myself because I was still going about with Clifton Daniel, my journalist friend from the *Siboney*, who'd got himself assigned to London. I was never serious about Danny, but we did have fun together. I thought Florian was so nice that he might suit one of the girls.'

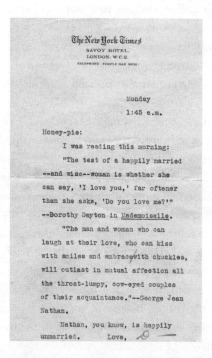

The New York Times
SAVOY HOTEL.
LONDON. W.C.2.
TELEPHONE TEMPLE BAR 9898.

Monday
1:45 a.m.

Honey-pie:

I was reading this morning:
"The test of a happily married
--and wise--woman is whether she
can say, 'I love you,' far oftener
than she asks, 'Do you love me?'"
--Dorothy Dayton in Mademoiselle.
"The man and woman who can
laugh at their love, who can kiss
with smiles and embrace with chuckles,
will outlast in mutual affection all
the throat-lumpy, cow-eyed couples
of their acquaintance."--George Jean
Nathan.
Nathan, you know, is happily
unmarried.   Love, D

'I was never serious about Danny.' A wartime billet-doux to Virginia from Clifton Daniel.

Matchmaking, Virginia confides, had always been one of her favourite pastimes; Teresa confirms to me later – with a smile – that her enthusiasm for arranging romances had been considerable.

'I used to buy tickets for Florek to take Dinah Slessor to the theatre,' Virginia goes on. 'And then, other times, I'd take them out dancing, and sometimes we'd take another of the pilots, along with Heather Burn, my doctor's daughter. Finally, after a few months, my mother-in-law took me to one side.'

'I wish you'd stop pushing poor Florek at Dinah,' Lady Cynthia told Virginia. 'Don't you know he's madly in love with you?'

'I looked at her and said: "Cynthia, you must be out of your skull. Firstly, I'm still married to your son. And secondly, I'm years and years older than he is." But Cynthia simply pointed out that she herself was twelve years older than Ronnie Slessor and that it didn't matter to either of them one bit.'

'I've never had a single unhappy moment,' announced Lady Cynthia.

'I'm sure that was true. Cynthia was absolutely lost after Ronnie died, and nobody was surprised when she followed him, two years later. Those two adored each other.'

'And so . . . ?' Teresa interrupts, patently eager to get back to the story of Virginia's own blossoming romance. 'And then . . . ?

In the background, almost lost in the crackle of the tape, I can hear a chuckle. I'd forgotten that Florian Martini has always been close at hand during the interviews at the Santa Barbara house. Sitting in the next-door room, where he plays cards or dozes before the television, he must be listening, eager to hear what's coming next.

'And so, *then*,' Virginia admits, 'I did begin to pay him more attention.'

Florian started to invite her out for drives in his car, on the Sundays when she wasn't making dutiful estate visits to Middleton. Virginia can't, now, remember what they used to talk about. Once, Florian brought along a bag of apples – food was so short, then – but when they opened up the bag, it appeared that a ravenous appetite had overcome his good intentions.

'We laughed. He'd left nothing but a bag of cores . . .'

They found that what the two of them liked best was to be out in the country; Virginia had always enjoyed the sensation of getting away from London (wartime photographs show her out riding a bicycle along woodland paths and striding across snowy fields beside Grandy's Alsatian, Claudius). Florian spoke to her wistfully of long walks through the woods near to his Polish home, back before the War.

'And then one day, Florian took me driving along the banks of the Thames, and he stopped the car by a bridge. I loved that particular stretch of the river, and so did he, watching the barges going by. It was so peaceful. I was standing by him on the bridge, and I said how much I liked to watch streams and rivers . . . moving water.'

That moment, she remembers, was when Florian said something that took her entirely by surprise.

'Too bad you're married,' he said to Virginia. 'Because if you weren't, I'd have you in front of a priest before you even knew what was happening.'

'So then I knew. That's when it properly started. And my whole attitude began gradually to change. But not overnight.'

Nobody who knew Virginia, so Teresa informs me, ever doubted that Florian Martini was the love of her life; yet the interview tapes indicate that no rash decisions were taken. As a married woman – one who possessed a high social position, considerable wealth, and a wide circle of devoted friends – Virginia needed to give careful thought to what she would be relinquishing, as well as to the anguish she would cause (not to mention the scandal that would almost certainly ensue). Florian had no money, no home, and – beyond his college training as an engineer – little chance of being able to support a wife and family. He was currently engaged, as a bomber pilot, in an existence that put his life at daily risk; should he survive, his staunchly Catholic mother would certainly oppose the alliance of her only son to a divorced Protestant woman, a foreigner, seven years older than himself. Was Virginia herself bold enough, and sufficiently in love, to make such a leap of faith?

Outwardly, throughout 1944, Virginia continued to play her role as a conscientious Army wife. Upon the rare occasions when Grandy paid visits to Richmond, his wife attended fund-raising events at his side, and listened to his worries about the future upkeep of Osterley and Middleton. (Wartime occupation of large private houses presented a greater threat to their survival, it was becoming apparent, than the bomber planes targeting Britain's cities, factories and airfields.) When Grandy left, Virginia busied herself with keeping up the spirits of her two squadrons, while working at clubs for servicemen, and the American Red Cross. News photographs show her, on one day, inspecting planes on a bleak airfield in Norfolk, and on the next, escorting three American officers through the grey and ruined streets surrounding St Paul's Cathedral [plate 19]. Her expression appears always bright and resolute.

That look of outward resolve masked profound anguish, as Virginia, falling ever more deeply in love with Florian, and spending most of her time among his bewildered compatriots, watched, as if from a ringside seat, the unfolding of the wrenching tragedy of Poland.

On 1 August 1944, while Florian and his colleagues were – at great personal risk – using the wings of their Spitfires to deflect (by tipping them, perilously, in mid-flight) the V1 missiles targeted on London, the citizens of Warsaw rose up against their German occupiers. The revolt was required to last for only a few days, until the imminent and eagerly anticipated arrival of advancing Soviet troops. When the Soviet army halted short of the city, the revolutionaries found themselves without aid, and wholly at the mercy of the Germans. Pleas from the London-based Polish government-in-exile for rescue missions to Poland were rejected by Churchill; the pilots who began flying supplies from Northolt to their stricken city were ordered to desist. The man who issued that edict, then commander-in-chief of the RAF, was the brother of Ronnie Slessor.

Later, after the War, Jack Slessor acknowledged that his decision had been misguided; at the time, he believed that he had no option. The RAF needed its brilliant Polish airmen; it could not afford for them to be shot down while attempting futile mercy missions.

'It was agonising for the pilots,' Virginia murmurs. (Is she keeping her voice low for a reason, anxious not to distress her husband with memories of those times?) 'Most of the ones I knew still had family back there in Warsaw. I'm not sure Jack Slessor understood how hard it was for them. But, of course, at the time, the British were convinced that Stalin was about to rescue Warsaw.'

By October, Germany had exercised its imposing force and Warsaw lay in ruins. The Soviet army had done nothing; even the use of Soviet airfields had been blocked, during most of the sixty-two days of the siege and destruction by the Nazis. In fact, as Air Marshal Slessor was now forced to realise, Stalin had never intended at any point to assist Warsaw; his plan had simply been to hold the army back, waiting for the moment at which he could 'liberate' and occupy a broken city with minimum risk to his own forces. Only following the bitter Christmas of 1944 did the Soviet troops move forward, to take possession of Poland's devastated stronghold.

Slessor, by February 1945, had become filled with horror over the behaviour of the men he now spoke of as 'the brutes in the Kremlin'. (Slessor's unstinting support, after the War, for the cause of Florian Martini may – so Virginia believes – have served to ease his personal conscience.) Unfortunately, Jack Slessor's views carried infinitesimal weight compared to those of the Big Three, who would meet, that February, at Yalta. An ailing Roosevelt (he died later in 1945) rubber-stamped Stalin's right to occupy Poland. Churchill, after a few flowery speeches about the valiant hearts of the Polish, also bestowed his approval. Churchill, however, must have felt a twinge of concern about the consequences; returning home, he urged that those Poles who had fought for Britain's cause should become eligible for British citizenship.

POLES ARE BEWILDERED

In War—Heroes: In Peace—Unwanted

By A. NOYES THOMAS

THIS week-end, 108,000 Poles exiled in Britain are struggling to solve a great problem.

Before them, awaiting signature, is the piece of paper which will either send them back behind Europe's "Iron Curtain"—to an uncertain fate in Poland or keep them here in the newly-formed, Government-sponsored Resettlement Corps, training either industry in this country or overseas.

They are the most puzzled men in the land.

What is Forgotten

They do not speak of it, but clearly our easy forgetfulness—perhaps it is our ingratitude—leaves them bewildered.

For these are the same men who, early in the war, were welcomed here with town bands and who were proudly hailed as representatives of our "only and very gallant ally."

In their ranks are heroes of Norway, Dieppe, Arnhem, Falaise, Caen, Monte Cassino, Ancona, and many other campaigns. Among them are the fighter pilots who, in the Battle of Britain, shot down 220 German raiders, and in the whole war accounted for more than 1,000 enemy planes. Some are the bomber men who dropped on Germany over 14,000 tons of bombs and mines.

Another 92,000 Poles will arrive from Allied theatres overseas within the next few weeks. The total in Britain then will be 160,000. And now consider a few more figures.

Of the numerically tiny Polish Forces, approximately 21,000 became casualties, including 6,000 killed—a dreadful percentage.

Nearly 700 earned British decorations, including more than 50 D.S.O.s, nearly 30 D.S.C.s, about 50 M.C.s, and nearly 200 D.F.C.s.

It is not surprising that these magnificent warriors were welcomed as co-belligerents and accepted as friends.

What is their position now, after little more than a year of peace?

In many parts of the land they are met with open hostility. On walls in our streets they see the chalked signs: "Poles—Go home. You are not wanted here."

In reports of the recent T.U.C. conference at Brighton they see themselves described as "the most unpopular visitors Scotland ever had."

They are told that they "strut about like arrogant Fascists, as if they owned the place and had fought for it, instead of against it." They find that even their hard-won Polish decorations and prized regimental insignia, centuries old, are mistaken for "Nazi medals."

For the past week I have been investigating these allegations. I have talked to hundreds of Poles and to British officers and men who work with them. I have visited their camps and experienced their living conditions.

Most of the present ill-feeling, I find, is caused by the facts (1) that a large proportion of the Poles now in Britain served for a time in the Nazi forces, and (2) that a number of those now likely to seek training for employment in Britain did not take any useful part in the war.

About 59,000 of the Poles who joined the Polish forces serving with British or American formations after 1940 had previously served with the German armed forces.

Most of them were natives of Western Poland. All were forcibly conscripted into the German army or the Todt labour organisation.

All Were "Screened"

For this purpose the Germans divided all Poles conscripts into three categories: (a) "Reliable," (b) "Doubtful," (c) "Unreliable." The "unreliables" became slave labourers. They, it is true, are wearing the Nazi sign in Britain. I have seen it—branded by hot irons on their flesh.

Twelve thousand from this and the second ("Doubtful") categories deserted and crept out of Europe by the Underground route. Thousands more came over to the Allied lines in battle.

All these, and the Poles who joined our forces from the prisoner-of-war cages, were passed through an Allied (British-U.S.A.-Polish) security screen.

In this way the Polish forces grew to their present size.

If there are now among them any who did not take part in the fight, it is because they were then too old, too sick, too young, or still under training when the war ended.

Why, then, do these men not return to their native land?

The answer is that those who will apply to remain here—an estimated 80 per cent—are as reluctant to embrace the Russian brand of Communism as they were to tolerate the Nazis.

No Bitterness, Yet

Many of them have already sampled life under Russian rule—some in Russian concentration camps. They realise that service with the Western Powers has marked them as being essentially "undemocratic," from the Russian point of view.

They regard Poland as being still an occupied country—a battered land, torn within by an unending, secret war; terrorised by guerrillas and bandits seething with revolt.

In Britain they were promised refuge and new hope. They accepted eagerly and gratefully, never dreaming that a change of heart among some of our people was so soon to make their lives here, too, a misery.

I have watched their reactions closely these past few days.

As yet, they do not show bitterness. If they comment at all, it is usually to express the opinion that when a large number of foreigners congregate in a land—the British in India, Americans in China, or Poles in Britain—inevitably such outbursts will occur from time to time.

They do not complain of the injustice of accusations of luxury living when (at least in the camps I visited) they are in fact putting up a brave effort to make the very best of a bare minimum of creature comforts.

They do not openly resent the inference of idleness, which at present is due to the necessity of learning our language, in which task all are now engaged, and in many cases of mastering new trades.

They do not even point out—I had to discover it for myself—that the widely publicised "battle" incidents in Scotland did not involve these Polish would-be workers, but others awaiting repatriation to Poland.

Five months later, the War was over and Churchill had been replaced as Britain's Prime Minister by Clement Attlee. Voted in as the champion of a new Welfare State (viewed as essential for the survival of an exhausted and impoverished country), Attlee had no time for charity. The contributions of the Polish pilots towards saving the country of Britain were played down; instead, the airmen began to be characterised as burdensome immigrants, a drain upon the economy. To those who wished to stay in Britain (rather than be condemned to death as traitors in their newly brutalised homeland), Attlee offered a drastic change of lifestyle. The high-flying pilots, he proposed (and some 2,000 took up the offer), should go to work down the coal-pits – or go home to whatever fate might there await them.

'And they weren't even allowed to march in the victory parade!' exclaims Virginia, her voice rising. 'After all they'd done! Stalin announced that he didn't want any Poles to take part – and that was that.'

Florian, she adds, had stayed away from the parade; a few members of his squadron went along to watch the great march pass them by; some couldn't hold back their tears of bitterness and shame.

By mid-1946, memories of Polish heroism were being replaced by a new and more vicious image: the former airmen were now identified in the press as drunks, wife-stealers, work-poachers – in a word, trouble. Reports of violence began to surface: of Poles who had been ostracised, jeered at, beaten up. This much was clear: they were no longer welcome in England.

'And everybody loved the Soviets,' Virginia adds. 'There was even an issue of *Time* magazine that had Stalin on its cover as "Man of the Year". Nobody believed General Sikorski when he claimed that Stalin had ordered the Katyn massacre. Everybody felt that it had to have been the Germans. The General tried to set up an inquiry. It didn't do any good. Sikorski was killed soon after that in a plane crash. A lot of Poles I spoke to thought it was Soviet sabotage.'

And how had Florian taken all this? Teresa quietly asks.

'We never spoke about it,' the old lady murmurs. 'He couldn't bear it. There was too much pain.'

Grieving for the man with whom she was now deeply in love, Virginia remained cautious about allowing her love-affair to emerge into the light. In 1944, Florian accompanied her to the wedding of Diana Barnato, a fellow-pilot; a newspaper item shows him, looking both pleased and shy, standing beside Virginia at the 1944 London première of a film called *Cover Girl*. For the most part, however, the lovers remained discreet.

'I knew by then that I wanted to marry Florian,' Virginia confirms. 'But I had no idea how Grandy would take it. It wouldn't have done for him to find everything out while he was still away in camp, and he was hardly ever home. I told Florian that I wanted to choose the right moment to tell my husband, face to face.'

Grandy's memoirs suggest that he felt a keen admiration for the Polish airmen ('They were wonderful pilots, wonderful men,' he wrote). Did Virginia hope that such an enthusiasm as this might temper his response? To be honest, she tells Teresa, she had no idea.

'I never could tell what Grandy thought. Nobody could.'

The Child Villiers clan, swelled by members of Margaret Jersey's own extensive family, gathered in May 1945 to pay their last respects to Grandy's mother before her burial at Middleton; a month later, Virginia revealed her intentions to her husband.

Love-affairs had never troubled Grandy; the prospect of a divorce dismayed a man who still longed to father a male heir, and who had come to depend upon Virginia as his loyal ally and friend, the enhancer of his muted life, the chatelaine of the homes he could not – without her – envisage himself struggling to maintain.

Grandy asked for time too late: whispers of a rift in the Jerseys' marriage had already begun to circulate.

In October 1945, the New York columnist Cholly Knickerbocker broke the news that Virginia Cherrill was planning to leave her English husband's privileged world and return to her native land. The Earl was said to be devastated and so (Cholly had heard), were the blue-blooded throng who had once sworn to humiliate an American upstart. Lady Jersey, he told his readers, 'had captured a solid place in hard-to-crack London society'.

'People were very kind,' Virginia concedes.

London friends showed support by keeping her busy, during the months leading up to the divorce, with a flood of distractions: invitations to preside over committees, to raise money for worthy causes, to open charitable events, to attend fund-raising balls. Slight though the available information here is, it confirms that Virginia's English friends were ready to make a public show of their affection and respect.

Such a show of solidarity should not surprise us. The image of the gold-digging Hollywood blonde had seldom received such a knock. A beautiful former film-star might be expected to have an affair with a maharaja, and then to marry a rich aristocrat. But to give up wealth, status and security, simply for love: this was an act of pure romance. Who among her smart social friends, in such an instance, could feel they would do as much? Which of them would dare?

A more surprising glimpse into how the Jerseys were being viewed back then comes from an entry (touched upon here in an earlier chapter) in the diary of James Lees-Milne.

Brooks's Club, one of the most conventional and respectable of London establishments, let it be known to Lees-Milne in 1947 that, should he be rash enough to present his new friend Lord Jersey's name for election, it would be rejected. The intriguing reason given to Lees-Milne was that Grandy was judged to be 'a pleasurer', and that he had behaved badly towards his second wife. Were the members of Brooks's Club recalling Grandy's published announcement, back in 1936, that he would not be responsible for his first wife's bills, or did they know things (things that she herself chose not to discuss, even with Teresa) about Grandy's treatment of Virginia?

Both are possible. Virginia had been reticent, in the past, about Cary Grant; loyalty may have prompted her to be equally discreet about Grandy Jersey.

'Grandy never forgave me for leaving him,' is all that Virginia is prepared to tell Teresa. 'He took it very hard indeed.'

Nevertheless, however reluctantly, the Earl was prevailed upon to consent to a divorce. As was required by the old-fashioned law of the time, requiring the evidence of violence or sexual misbehaviour, Grandy once again went through the motions of adultery with a hired companion. The decree nisi was awarded on 31 July 1946 (the ninth anniversary, strangely, of the Jerseys' marriage).

Grandy's swift abdication from his habitual way of life was sufficiently radical to suggest that Virginia's departure had, in some sense, broken his spirit. Middleton was sold ('too big for modern times', he explained in his memoirs); Osterley, still occupied after the War by the employees of Grandy's own bank, was given to the National Trust in 1949. By then, following the local council's compulsory purchase of Tudor Lodge, his temporary dwelling near Osterley, Grandy had left England. In June 1947, he purchased Radier Manor on the isle of Jersey. There was no family connection to the island; what Grandy liked about Radier, he wrote in his memoirs, was simply its proximity to the sea.

It would be a mistake, however, to place too much responsibility upon Virginia for her husband's defection from his traditional role as a landowner, employer and maintainer both of a splendid modern house and an eighteenth-century masterpiece. The private houses that were occupied by troops, schools, hospitals and even – as in Osterley's case – by civilians, during the War years, were returned to their owners in a much diminished state. The outlook for their restoration to glory, and even for their survival, was bleak. Domestic service, in a newly egalitarian society, attracted few recruits; men ready to take up farm work, maintain large gardens, and carry on the general maintenance work essential to the upkeep of a large estate were in short supply.

Undoubtedly, Grandy's commitment to his old, pre-war role in society was weakened by the loss of an energetic helpmate; nevertheless, in a house – Osterley – of which he had once remarked that it took twelve people to bring a boiled egg to the breakfast table, it was unlikely that even the combined energies of Grandy and Virginia could have enabled the old way of life to continue. Osterley, derelict even before the outbreak of war, had offered an almost insuperable challenge to its owners; Middleton, ill-served by its use both as a school and a hospital, now presented similar problems.

Rather than ascribing the fate of Middleton and Osterley to the end of a marriage, it seems, then, that Virginia's departure – when combined with the death of old Lady Jersey, Grandy's last significant link to his family's social role – provided the final impetus towards an inevitable conclusion.

And did Grandy ever try to contact you again?' Teresa asks the old lady.

'I had a message from his daughter Caroline about thirty years later. She told me Grandy wanted to convey his good wishes. But our deal had never allowed for the fact that I might fall in love. He never forgave me.'

Virginia is probably right. The children of Grandy Jersey's third marriage (to a young Italian girl who became his wife in 1947) never heard their father mention Virginia during their years of life with him at Radier Manor. At Middleton, long since converted into individual apartments, it is asserted that Virginia Jersey disliked the house, and spent only a single night under its roof. At Osterley, a National Trust property, her existence is scarcely acknowledged.

Virgina, until she met Florian, had led a life that was dictated by the strokes of good fortune that befell a beautiful woman possessed of unique charm. Her character, once she had taken the decision to leave Grandy for Florian, seemed transformed. The initiative now flowed from her.

'Florian needed to get his mother out of Poland,' she explains to Teresa. 'He wanted her to come along with us to live in America. I couldn't tell him that I was having a hard enough time arranging for *him* to go and live there. He thought it was so easy. He told me he was going to be a cowboy. I said: "Fine. But first let's see about getting you into the country." I had ambassadors coming out of my ears! And all Florian worried about was whether his mother would mind that I wasn't a Catholic!'

Faced with trouble, Virginia pulled every string within reach. Jack Slessor wrote supportive letters; Clifton Daniel volunteered to visit Poland, in order to assist in the release of Florentyna Martini. Even Winston Churchill, so Virginia tells Teresa, sent ideas for possible ways around the problematic fact that Florian, as a youth, had suffered from TB. (America welcomed the needy and oppressed, but never, knowingly, the diseased.)

'I was worried to death about where we were going to live,' Virginia tells Teresa. 'I worried about what we were going to live on, and what work Florian could find. I worried all the time.'

'So did you begin to think twice about the marriage?'

'Never!'

Florian, she adds, was dimly conscious of the endeavours that were being made on his behalf; he understood that this was Virginia's way of testifying to her commitment. In January 1947, having gone ahead to America to further work on her lover's entry papers, she received a frantic call from London.

'Danny (Clifton Daniel) had tracked down Mrs Martini in Poland and gotten her a place on a British courier plane – God only knows how he did it. Florek wanted me back in time to greet her – you know – a proper daughterly welcome, everything nice and respectable. So I had to turn right around from visa-fixing and home-hunting and come straight back.'

Virginia had always hated flying. The plane that brought her home – she says it was the only flight she could find – came down for fuel in Iceland, and flew up again into a storm.

'I've always been a white-knuckle flyer: this was bad. It didn't stop. The steward said there might be a little problem. Then the plane lost height, and he said it wasn't so little but that we'd passed the point of no return. We finally bumped down in a field in Ireland. Worst flight of my life. And then, soon as I was back to greet Mrs Martini, the officials packed poor Florek off to Dunholme.'

Eleven thousand demobilised Poles, during the harsh winter of 1947, were shuttled into 'resettlement' camps; Dunholme Lodge was a low grim building on the fringe of what had formerly been an airfield for Bomber Command, just north of Lincoln. Here, while Florian was given intensive training in English and the basic skills intended to equip former pilots for civilian employment, Virginia did her best to reassure a fearful and antagonistic Florentyna Martini.

'All *she* wanted was for her son to come back to Poland. She didn't like England. She wasn't too sure about me, and she certainly didn't want to come to America. And Florian kept writing from Dunholme to ask when we were all leaving. It was difficult.'

Perseverance won through. In April, the month in which she turned thirty-nine, Virginia, together with Florian, Mrs Martini and Liesl Dietrich (Virginia's devoted maid), boarded the SS *America*, a liner bound for New York. Their accommodation was not elegant; the three women were ushered into a tiny cabin containing three narrow canvas berths.

'The ship was still kitted out for the troops. And all the way across, Florian's mother was crying and telling everybody she could find on board to listen that her darling son had taken up with an adventuress. She hated the fact that we weren't married, and she hated it even more that I wasn't Polish. It was a shame, because Florian was the most devoted son. Perhaps we shouldn't have taken her with us. She never settled down.'

I'm curious to know whether it was this awkward relationship with her prospective mother-in-law that caused Virginia, now a free woman again and passionately in love with Florian, to wait for a full year before committing herself to a fourth marriage. I'm intrigued, too, by her one furious outburst (the single occasion during the many hours of her taped conversations with Teresa). The target of the old lady's anger is not Mrs Martini, but the couple's first and nearest neighbour at their new home in West Hollywood.

'Max Ausnit was back in business, and set up in New York,' explains Virginia. 'Max had always been a good friend. He loaned me enough to rent a place to live, and to cover the cost of shipping over the furniture that Grandy let me have by way of a settlement. I rented a cottage on Fountain Avenue, near my mother. Unfortunately, we had the neighbour from hell.'

The neighbour, it transpires, was beautiful Loretta Young, an actress about whom Virginia, a woman renowned for her generous nature and forgiving tongue, has strong views. Young's sisters, Virginia declares, were good friends of hers, and 'darling girls'; Loretta was not.

'I do think Loretta Young was the most manipulative bitch I ever met. She'd slept with everybody, since she was about fourteen, and she had two illegitimate children, one by some big producer, and another by Clark Gable, and she took her husbands – well, she robbed the last one blind, even took his clothes and his dogs . . .'

Such a diatribe is not typical of Virginia; what has prompted it? Could Florian – he was, back then, a spectacularly handsome young man – have succumbed to a predatory and glamorous neighbour?

'Florek?' Teresa exclaims, and then, laughing, repeats herself: 'Loretta Young and *Florek*?!'

'What would I know?' Teresa's scepticism is probably well founded.

The delay in the date of the Martinis' wedding can best be explained by the bride's wish to choose a significant day for a union that she wanted to last for the rest of her life. The twelfth of April 1948 marked Virginia's fortieth birthday; that morning, dressed in a simple knitted suit, the former Countess of Jersey married her quietly adoring Polish airman at the Santa Monica Courthouse. Following the brief private ceremony, the couple drove back to West Hollywood and reported the news to their respective mothers.

Blanche evinced little surprise. Glancing up from a pile of ironing, she muttered only that nobody ever told her anything any more. Florentyna Martini was less stoical.

'She just started yelling,' Virginia informs Teresa. 'She was mad! She'd wanted her son to have a big wedding – and of course, she still wanted a Polish daughter-in-law. So we took the two ladies out to supper and Florian ordered me a birthday cake, but his mother still kept on crying. So Florian had to go to a motel for the night – and I stayed back at home.'

I can hear Teresa's gasp. Is Virginia saying that she spent her wedding night with her husband's *mother*?

'Well,' Virginia mildly responds, 'what else was I to do? She was so upset, poor woman, and she had to yell at *somebody*! I thought it might as well be me.'

Mrs Martini's distress did not diminish; six months later, she went home, at her own request, to Poland. Virginia (dipping into some more of Max Ausnit's loan) paid for a first-class passage on HMS *Batory*. Mother-in-law and daughter-in-law never met again.

'And then . . . ?' Teresa asks. Well, then, Virginia sighs, then times got tough.

'Although you might not have guessed that was how it was going to be. You see, when the divorce came through, Grandy was generous – in his way. He told me to take what I wanted, as long as it wasn't – so typical of Grandy – money. I could take any furniture, and even any of the paintings, that I liked. So I picked some things out at Osterley, and I asked for the contents of Richmond and Farm Street. I took just what I thought Florek and I could manage to live on, if we didn't have much else, for the next forty years. Max's money helped cover the shipping costs, but I had no idea how to go about selling things and that was a worry. We needed the money.'

In fact, as Virginia readily admits, she had been looked after for most her adult life. Nothing had equipped her to survive unaided – and Blanche, ageing, now also looked to her daughter for support. Florian, abandoning his dream of becoming a cowboy, finally secured more sober employment – as an engineer, out at Lockheed.

'It worked out pretty well,' Virginia announces. 'Every morning, I'd be up at dawn to make sandwiches for Florian to take to work. I'd clean, and I'd wash clothes, and I'd cook, and back he'd come for supper at seven, and we'd sit together in the little kitchen and talk about the day. And, you know what, Teresa . . . ?'

'No, I *don't* know what.' Teresa laughs, catching the lightness, and the quaver, in Virginia's tone.

'I think that I was never – and I mean, *never* – so happy in my entire life.'

And listening to that tremulous declaration, I find myself smiling as I realise how absurdly perfect this is, that a cattleman's daughter should end up with a husband who wanted to be a cowboy (and who did – thanks to Virginia – get to meet his hero, John Wayne).

And I think how, when the glamour fades from the story, what's left here is a simple Cinderella tale of the girl who came from out of nowhere, embarked on grand adventures, and married the mythical prince.

But there's a difference. This is a story in which Cinderella wakes up and discovers that – despite all the fame, honours and riches that have come her way – all she really wants is love. So Cinderella leaves the palace and travels back home, to the world where she was born; to where (back at the beginning of these interviews with her friend Teresa) Virginia declared that she truly, in her heart, belonged.

EPILOGUE: A SONG AT TWILIGHT
CALIFORNIA
(1948-1996)

I ought, by now, to be able to guess that Virginia's version of the past will always be a little brighter than the truth.

'She had no time for regrets,' says Father Virgil Cordano, the brown-robed friar who converted Virginia to Catholicism, her husband's faith, back in 1952. 'Virginia was very much a realist, but she never cried about what went wrong. And not everything went right.'

The young Slessors, visiting California shortly after Virginia's marriage to Florian in 1948, carried away happy memories. Henry was thrilled to be introduced to the celebrated American news reporter Edward R. Morrow, who had broadcast from London throughout the Blitz; Dinah, years later, recalled that she had almost fainted when Cary Grant, who had taken Virginia and herself out to supper – 'they were on the best of terms' – gave her a call at her London home. ('He said: "It's Cary Grant." Of course, I didn't believe him. So I said: "And this is Greta Garbo", and put down the phone. Virginia had to explain to him that I hadn't meant to be rude.')

The Slessors were too young – and probably too wrapped up in the very recent deaths of both of their parents, Ronnie in 1946, and Cynthia in 1948 – to register the worries going on behind this aura of glamour. Florian, a trained aeronautical engineer who had fought for Britain, and who, in 1949, still awaited the final papers that would enable him to live and work in America, was under investigation. Suspicions had been aroused, as Virginia explained in a frantic appeal for help, sent to the Polish Ambassador to Canada, 'owing to the misfortune of [Florian] having been born in Russia (his father was a Polish engineer working for the Imperial Russian Government at that time)'. In the eyes of American officials, in the early stages of the Cold War, few recommendations for working in aeronautics could have seemed more off-putting than birth in the Soviet Union.

I ask Teresa if she thinks that Florian was aware of just how hard his wife worked behind the scenes on his behalf: Teresa doubts it.

'She would never have let him know how worried she was. Still, Virginia managed to pull it off. When my own family came out here from England, back in the early Fifties, Florian was already working on missile programmes at Lockheed. They were up in Santa Barbara by then, running a little avocado ranch with two young Polish boys, the twins that Virginia had taken under her wing during the War. She managed to get the papers to bring them in. They were at the ranch for quite a time.'

Driving me up to see what remains of the ranch on Featherhill Road, Teresa tells me that Florian himself worked at planting the trees, and at building the modest guesthouse where the Martinis put up the steady flow of visitors from England.

'The people who came to the guesthouse were all old friends of Virginia,' Teresa explains. 'They didn't see much of Florian. He was always out at the factory.'

Looking up Florian's obituary, and noting that he worked upon the development of both ballistic missiles and nuclear weapons systems (Titans 1 and 2; the Polaris submarine and the Sidewinder rocket), it occurs to me that Lockheed was fortunate; few men could have worked with more dedication upon a programme designed to combat Soviet power than an exiled Pole.

By 1951, the last of Virginia's shipment of possessions had arrived; slowly, she began the tricky business of seeking out willing buyers. A few loyal chums made purchases. But it wasn't easy, as Virginia admitted only to her closest English friends, to find people during those post-war years who wished to expend substantial portions of their limited resources upon Old World paintings and European antiques. An antique shop in Santa Barbara was a short-lived venture; Virginia soon decided to cut her losses and sell her possessions instead, for whatever she could get, through a variety of hard-nosed dealers.

'But – as you can see – she didn't sell everything,' Teresa states, as she guides me around Virginia's last Santa Barbara home. The little hillside house on Pomar Lane, now owned by Bruce Wilcox, Virginia's favourite relative, still exudes the charm of her personality. Evidence of her life in England is abundant. A low table, supported by a crouching figure, once adorned Lady Jersey's Farm Street drawing-room. Two delicate looking-glasses may have come from Osterley; framed prints of a Tudor building beside the Thames, link Santa Barbara to wartime Richmond. Even the books that dominate the well-stocked shelves are by English authors on English subjects.

'She loved English history,' Teresa explains. 'Those were her favourite books.'

Neither the Glinskis nor the Martinis were living in luxury at the time when the two families became reunited in California, in the early Fifties. Virginia and Florian were still ranching (the nearest poor Florian came to his wistful dream of becoming a Western cowboy) at Featherhill Road, helped by the Polish twins. Tomasz, Teresa's father, the elegant Polish Count who had won prizes at the Warsaw Conservatory, now played jazz (for hip audiences that sometimes included a young Leonard Bernstein), at the Plow and Angel, on the Pacific Coast Highway; less frequently, he entertained a more conservative audience, guests at the Biltmore Hotel.

'And Virginia was always giving my mother lectures about where to get all the cheapest cuts of meat,' Teresa says. 'She hated to spend money on herself; she thought other people should act the same way. My mother adored Virginia, but she liked to shop where she wanted, and to get food we liked to eat.'

If Virginia scrimped at home, she made up for it elsewhere. Grateful friends in deprived and heavily rationed post-war England wrote to thank their Californian benefactor for hampers of delicacies (dates, chocolates and sweet biscuits were especially well received); a rapturous god-daughter wrote to tell her that 'there could not be a fairy godmother to equal you anywhere in the world'.

'Do write, Lily darling,' scrawled one of several London friends who used that tag – the punning allusion was to beautiful Jersey-born Lillie Langtry – as their pet name for Virginia. 'Why don't you ever write?' moaned another. Yet another friend became accusing: 'Lily! You are the worst correspondent that I ever knew!'

'I always hated writing letters,' Virginia had once confessed to a British interviewer, back in the early Thirties. 'I'm an American: I like the phone.'

Dinah Slessor's daughter, Basia Martin, visiting Virginia's Santa Barbara home as a young girl, during the early Seventies, confirms the truth of this declaration.

'I used to sit on the end of her bed in the morning. Virginia would be beautifully made-up and smiling, and chatting to friends on the telephone. That was her morning routine; all the rest of the time, she'd be taking me around places, or opening up cupboards, finding wonderful presents for me among her possessions. Virginia was so generous: she simply loved to give.'

'She never stopped,' says Teresa. 'She couldn't leave the house without buying somebody a present. Once, when I was eighteen and needed fancy-dress for some party, she even gave me the gown she wore for the Georgian ball at Osterley.'

I've become familiar with this aspect of Virginia's personality; it surprises me more to find how many of Lord Jersey's family kept in touch with Grandy's ex-wife. The playwright and poet Lord Dunsany (Grandy's uncle) was one of the first of the family to seek her out when he visited California in the early Fifties; Dunsany, who died in 1957, was followed to California by Jack Slessor (Ronnie's brother), Sally Colville (a niece), Ann Elliot (a former sister-in-law) and a throng of godchildren. Such demonstrations of loyalty and affection, in turn, startle me less than the discovery that the Duchess of Argyll, smarting from the humiliation of her widely publicised divorce case in 1960, headed straight for recuperation to the avocado ranch. (A photograph shows the former Margaret Whigham sitting upon a small and somewhat shabby sofa at Featherhill Road, sipping an evening cocktail and flanked by Florian and a smiling Virginia.) It's easier to understand why Virginia's friend Rosie d'Avigdor-Goldsmid, devastated after the accidental death by drowning of her older daughter, Sarah, left her husband's great Jacobean mansion of Somerhill to spend a fortnight in the tiny Santa Barbara guesthouse. Lady Cromer, crossing the continent during her husband's service as British Ambassador to the US, looked in on a retirement home in California and learned – without surprise – that Virginia was a regular and well-loved visitor to its aged inhabitants.

'That was so like her; she never mentioned it in her letters. Virginia always did good quietly. She didn't make a fuss.'

The sense of enduring friendships – maintained, with some difficulty, across oceans and continents – runs like a bright thread through the piles of correspondence that Teresa, after Virginia's death, took care to preserve. Sifting through these old missives together, Teresa and I come across a melancholy letter from Jai, written back in 1953, lamenting the fact that he had failed to track down his old friend ('I asked everybody!') during a brief jaunt to Hollywood. Another 1953 letter that surfaces in these heaps of closely written notes and scrawls is from Bhaiya, recalling old times and still unashamedly envying Jai (because Jaipur, unlike Cooch Behar, so it seems to the jealous Bhaiya, still operates as before the birth of Indian independence, in 1947 'just like the old states'.)

Virginia's last home still bears witness, when I visit it, to her own enduring love for her Indian friends. The bronze cast of Jo's arm has left its place of honour beside the bed. Near by, however, photographs of Jo, Jai and their children still perch among the pictures of cousins, friends and godchildren that cover every available surface.

They seem always to have been in her mind. In 1969, sending a birthday present to her old friend Mrs Blazier (formerly Anita Blair), Virginia accompanied it with a picture of Indrajit ('Digga'). 'In all my life, I never saw such a sweet person as Digga,' Anita wrote gratefully back from her home at Long Beach. 'Little did we know what fate had in store for him.' (Indrajit had recently died, as both women were aware.) Wistfully, Anita recalled the days 'such a short time ago [when] all of us were together: Digga, Jai, Jo and Bhaiya'. It comforted her, she told Virginia, to know that her own son was out in Delhi, working upon an American-funded programme to help hard-pressed Indian farmers.

Anita's appreciative letter was written shortly after its author had paid a rare visit to her former travelling-companion Blanche Cherrill, up at the Featherhill Road ranch. Blanche's health had begun to decline in 1961; for the next nine years, until her death in 1970, she was cared for by her daughter. The task, to judge from the cautiously phrased letters of condolence to Virginia, had not been an easy one: 'I know how difficult she was, even to you, who were angelic to her', wrote one sympathetic friend. Virginia, characteristically, declined to be drawn into complaints.

'I never,' Teresa tells me, 'heard her speak a word against her mother.'

Blanche's death grieved Virginia. The news, transmitted three years earlier, by his second wife, that Jim Cherrill was dead, prompted only feelings of obligation: the need for a daughter to oversee and attend the burial of her father's ashes in the family plot at Carthage. A greater source of sadness, as Virginia herself began to grow old, was the lack of any children of her own.

'Virginia never cried about what went wrong,' Father Virgil Cordano assures me; I'm not so sure.

Leafing through the piles of old photographs, I'm struck by how blissful Virginia looks when she is holding a baby or talking to a

Virginia with one of her many god-children.

child. Throughout her life, she had longed for motherhood. Three miscarriages are identified in her letters; one during the marriage to Cary Grant; two during her life with Grandy Jersey. The possibility of others should not be ruled out. In 1954, six years after her marriage to Florian, Virginia was still hoping – and still failing – to conceive. Father Virgil, newly arrived at the mission church of Santa Barbara in 1952, had overseen Virginia's conversion to Catholicism. Three years later, sympathetic to her longing for motherhood, he assisted her application to adopt a child through the Catholic Relief Agency.

'One year too late,' Teresa sighs. 'She was forty-seven – and the rules, back then, wouldn't allow anyone over the age of forty-six to adopt. Poor Virginia: she was heartbroken.'

Teresa believes – and her intuitions about Virginia usually prove correct – that this defeat of her hopes caused the trauma that led Virginia, on 30 July 1959, to write what appears to have been a suicide note. Begging her mother not to do anything foolish 'in the first shock', Virginia asked Mrs Cherrill to try to love Florian as her own son, and to be patient with him, 'as you've been with me . . . he deserves it more'. Poignantly, Virginia also confided to Blanche that she wanted Florian to find another woman: 'the sooner the better – and marry, and have children . . .'

This mood of despair was overcome and suppressed; to her friends, as always, Virginia maintained a cheerful exterior. The stories I hear – from Teresa, from Virginia's English visitors, from William Ducas (Virginia's godson who first encouraged me to write this book) – all testify to the sense of happiness that she unfailingly communicated. Jotting down these cameos and fragments of recollection, I'm struck by the fact that Florian remained an outsider – by choice – to the glamorous Hollywood world where his wife remained welcome and at her ease.

'Except for John Wayne!' Teresa reminds me. 'Meeting him really did give Florian a thrill. Mostly, though, he kept away. He liked staying up at the ranch. Virginia loved people, but Florek was never a social man.'

I've found an undated newspaper item, probably from the late Fifties, that confirms Teresa's claim. Headed 'Town

Chatter', it informs us that Virginia Martini is a former star of the screen who has also (news to me) often graced the London stage.

> She and Florian, an engineer, have an avocado ranch, and Florian loves it, so he hates to come to town. Virginia says he is the only Polish cowboy, so he only comes in to see Western movies. They have an agreement, that for every two Westerns, they have to see one other kind . . .

'Virginia hated Westerns,' Teresa smiles. 'But she loved Florian.'

Following the deaths of both her parents in the 1960s, Virginia's own life, although still rich in famous names and smart occasions, began to dwindle. Later photographs offer poignant glimpses of a charming, ageing woman, moving (inexorably, and without much show of vanity or distress about it) towards an end.

'Look what I've found for you!' Teresa has retrieved a photograph of the ABCs – the Ageing Beauties Club – to which Virginia Cherrill once belonged.

As she had hoped, I'm charmed.

Eight splendid old ladies (beauties still, if jauntily past their prime) all behatted and kitted out for the camera, face their photographer with expressions that range from the flirtatious (Barbara Strauss, whose husband owned Macy's) to the aloof (Maychka de Peyster, a former member of the Romanoff family). Virginia was never vain. An orange straw hat does her as few favours in this photo as does her brown flowery dress, and her trademark red spectacles have become tinted and thick-lensed; I'm just pleased to see that she's evidently happy and enjoying herself, out with the girls, remembering old times.

'They'd meet up for drinks and lunch, once a month; it was a real get-together,' the daughter of one former ABC member tells

The ABC (Ageing Beauties Club). Standing left to right: Barbara Strauss; Virginia; Eleanor D'Arrast; Maychka de Peyster; Peggy Carter; unidentified. Sitting: Lenore Adams; Lulu Anderson.

me; the group (she adds) resembled the heroines of *The Golden Girls*, that famous American sit-com of the mid-1980s, to which these spirited old ladies were addicted.

Listening to Teresa's stories of the past, I find myself confronted by the biographer's eternal dilemma: what to exclude, and what to retain? I like her account of Virginia's late-flowering friendship with the outspoken – and often fairly drunk, even on stage – Dame Judith Anderson, the actress she first saw in the Twenties, back in Chicago, on her first schoolgirl date with Irving Adler. I'm enthralled to hear of the occasion when Virginia took a very young Teresa to Hollywood, to meet Hal Wallis, and to try out for a film. ('Elvis Presley was auditioning at the same studio, along with his mother,' Teresa recalls. 'I didn't get my part, but Elvis started a new career. He was pretty sweet, that day, very shy and polite.')

Breakfasting at a café beside the ocean, I watch a gull deftly swoop for pickings from the bread-basket on a newly abandoned table, and listen as Teresa describes a chance encounter of her own with Cary Grant, late on in Virginia's life. Cary, she tells me, lit up at the mention of his former wife. He took down her telephone number and promised to visit.

'Only he wanted to fly up to Santa Barbara, courtesy of the Fabergé business jet, and Virginia told him to take a taxi. (She was bedridden during her last ten years, and Florian wasn't well; she didn't want the kind of publicity that came with Fabergé.) 'So Cary said: "You always were a bitch," and put the phone down,' Teresa remembers. 'And he never did come to visit her.'

The stories fascinate me, but they amount only to a string of disconnected episodes. After noting them down, I go to seek out Father Virgil Cordano. A handsome old man, nearing his ninetieth year, he receives me in his office at the Franciscan mission in Santa Barbara.

'*If* I could ever have married,' Father Virgil sighs. '*If* Mr Martini hadn't been around –' He winks as I take out my notebook. 'But why marry one and disappoint fifty!'

It's a line, I'm convinced, that he has used before. This warm-faced priest is an urbane communicator; he knows just how to deflect any questions that may threaten his privacy. He'll reveal no secrets.

Instead, placing his palms flat on the desk, he offers a tribute.

'Virginia,' he says, 'was a real lady, and she had a God-given faith. No hidden agenda; no guile. You'll smile at this, but she had the purest spirit that I've ever known. I'm not saying that she was perfect, or that she lived like a saint, in her early years. But Virginia never nursed a grudge, and she was never unfair.'

I watch as he looks down at his hands, considering.

'And she was funny! I visited her every week after she got sick. I gave her Mass, and then we'd just tell jokes and laugh; that's what she liked to do. I'd forget she was ill; we'd be sitting there, the tears running down both our faces. I was paying those visits for ten years. I was always sorry when the time came to leave.'

Teresa has told me that Father Virgil himself took the service at the Mission for Virginia's funeral.

'I did. I wanted her friends to know about all the work she did for us at the Mission. And it turned out to be the first time in my life I couldn't say a word. I choked up.'

'It's true,' Teresa later confirms. 'He tried to speak. And then he just sat down on the altar steps and put his head in his hands and wept.'

'She did have an easy death, didn't she?' I ask Father Virgil.

He tells me that it was one of the most tranquil that he's seen.

'I went to the Mission hospital to give her the last rites. And afterwards, she put up her poor, thin little arms to give me a hug, and she said: "Father Virgil, I love you." That was the last thing I heard her say.'

'The first thing she said to *me* when I came to the hospital was: "You bitch!"'

A love that lasted: Virginia and Florian.

(Still in Santa Barbara, I've arrived back with Teresa at the simple house up above the town, where Virginia and Florian spent the closing decades of a marriage that endured for fifty years.)

Still under the spell of Father Virgil's emotional account of Virginia's final moments, I express prim shock.

'But it was *funny*!' Teresa attempts to hide her impatience with my slowness. 'Listen, she was eighty-eight, and she was still putting on a show. She was dying, and she knew it, and so did we. Florian wasn't well enough – he was suffering from dementia by then – to visit more than every three days or so. I'd brought her cousin Bruce Wilcox – she adored Bruce – along to the hospital, and William Ducas was there, her favourite godson. And she was being funny – just to keep our spirits up.'

'You bitch, Teresa!' Virginia said. 'You come in here, bringing two handsome men, not a word of warning – and I haven't even got my lipstick on!'

'I told you how she wore that bright red lipstick, even when she went to sleep. So I found her bag, and I painted it on – awful, sticky stuff, but it always did look good on her – and the three of us sat around the bed. We had a hard time finding anything to say; we all knew that she was on the way out. I could see Virginia fretting for us, trying to rescue the situation.'

'You three look famished,' the old lady announced. 'Take something out of my purse and go treat yourselves to some dinner down the street. And don't you come back here until you've had some decent food and a nice bottle of wine.'

Teresa pauses. 'Of course, we did what she wanted us to do. We hadn't even reached the end of the corridor when a nurse came running up behind us. Soon as we were out of the room, Virginia had turned her face to the wall and died. I couldn't believe it. Gone – just like that.'

'It was time,' she adds, after a pause. 'She'd been failing for years.

I was sad for us, not for her, but I kept thinking how glad I was that we'd done those tapes . . .'

'And do you think she *knew*?'

Teresa hesitates. 'Sometimes, I thought she did, and that she liked the idea. Other days, we'd have the maid going around with the vacuum and the dog yapping, and Florek calling out about one of his cowboy programmes on television, and she'd just keep chatting quietly along. I couldn't tell. It seemed, sometimes, as if she wanted me to record everything *but* the sound of her voice.'

I look up from my note-taking, to catch her expression.

'Drove me crazy,' Teresa says, but she's smiling.

Teresa looks back at me now. 'So there she is. What do you think? Can you make a book out of it?'

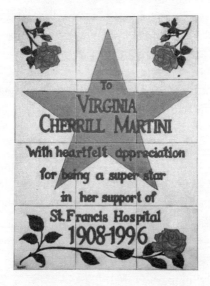

I didn't, back then in 2005, know quite what answer to make. Virginia had entranced me (along with a few million others) from the first time I saw her glow out of the screen in *City Lights*. Since then, I have listened to the tapes, and shared Teresa's recollections of a woman whose personality still seems radiantly alive to everybody who knew her. A biography, for this fortunate group, seems gratuitous; I can only dot the i's and cross the t's; I can't match their fond memories. What's the value of a reported life to those who were able to experience and savour the pleasure of knowing Virginia Cherrill?

And for those – like myself – who didn't know her: what does she have to offer?

Virginia strikes me, firstly, as a woman of her own time in whom – doubtless instilled by her mother – an oddly old-fashioned set of high principles survived. I am struck by Father Virgil Cordano's emphasis on his friend's rare combination of gaiety of heart with purity of spirit. Virginia, as everybody who knew her confirms, was without guile or ambition. Her naturalness, the spectacle of a beautiful young woman peering eagerly but short-sightedly at the combatants in a boxing ring, was what first caught Chaplin's eye; her naturalness is what communicates itself so powerfully to viewers of *City Lights*.

Virginia's one great role came about by happenstance: by the simple fact of being in the right place (the audience for the Friday-night fight) at the right time (as Chaplin sought a beautiful girl who could act blind). It was Virginia's good fortune that her first director was a man who could choreograph everything but the look in her eyes: that – which was everything – was all her own.

Virginia chose to pursue her subsequent film career with a light heart and no ambition. She cannot, with the sole exception of her astonishing performance for Chaplin, be regarded primarily as a film-star. What, then, does she offer us?

Grandy Jersey, like Jai, like Cary Grant, and like Florian Martini was attracted, not by the nature of Virginia's celebrity, but by her beauty and, beyond that, her spirit. Whatever company Virginia appeared in – and the company she kept was often raffish, cold and not very scrupulous – her spirit shone out. Her personality enchanted her friends; her integrity commanded their respect.

Consider, to take an example, the fact that both the Maharaja and Maharani of Jaipur never failed, when writing to Virginia, to send their regards to her mother and to invite Blanche Cherrill (not the most exciting of women) to join their gatherings. Virginia's priorities were clear; she owed everything to her mother. She wished her mother to be honoured. Her friends did not fail her.

I admire Virginia Cherrill for – at last – taking charge of her destiny and choosing love above circumstance. I cherish her, for her faith in the human spirit, for her love of life and for her clear values.

'She changed us,' says her cousin, Bruce Wilcox, a financier. 'She never changed. Virginia was the catalyst. We were – all of us – better for knowing her.'

His words remind me of what was said, after her death, about Lady Ottoline Morrell, by one of the young writers who benefited from knowing that much misunderstood woman as a friend: 'no one can ever know the immeasurable good she did.'

Yes, I answer Teresa's question. I do think Virginia Cherrill's life deserves to be told.

I hope I've done her justice.

Miranda Seymour
September 2008

ACKNOWLEDGEMENTS

For unfailing support and kindness, my gratitude to Teresa MacWilliams, without whose enthusiasm and long friendship with Virginia Cherrill this book could not have been written (and whose company, hospitality and friendship added much to the pleasure of the project). I also owe many thanks to Bruce Wilcox, who allowed me to make myself at home in Virginia's house, and gave me the run of everything that remains there. Unfettered freedom of access is a rare privilege for a biographer; I have never known it to be offered in such generous measure.

William and Sarah Ducas first set me on the trail, back in 2006; they provided the key introductions, and offered support throughout. Again, I can't imagine how I could have written the book without them.

The thanks I offer below are not perfunctory. Everybody I have approached has gone out of the way to do more than was expected; they did so, I am sure, because of the way they felt about Virginia herself, but it was wonderful for me, the vicarious beneficiary of their recollections and observations. I hope that anybody whose name has inadvertently been omitted will accept my heartfelt apologies and thanks, but it has not been possible to identify the names of everybody to whom I spoke at public libraries, record offices and archives.

For Virginia's early life:
Edie Blender; Sandy Callaway (at Carthage Public Library); Ruth Covington; Jayne Eckhardt (for information about the Wilcox family's life at Durham, which now has a population of just three); Alice and Mary Agnes Habben; Franklin Hartzell; Sydney Hosford.

For Virginia in England
Michael Barker; Liz and Simon Bonham; Mary Bowden; Mark Bristow (RAF Northolt); John Burn; Colin Campbell; John and Celia Child Villiers; the Countess of Cromer; Gilbert Elliot; Bamber and Christina Gascoigne; Margaret Goddard (RAF Northolt); Isabella Harrison; the Earl of Jersey; Patricia Leckie; Alex Liddell; Candia Lutyens; Basia Martin; Ann Marks; Simon and Marion Marks; Caroline Ogilvy; staff at the Orchard Pub; Sally Pigot; Jane Ridley; Henry Slessor; Nancy Spufford; Chloe Teacher.

For Virginia in India
William Dalrymple; Lucy Moore; members of the family of Man Singh, the late Maharaja of Jaipur; co-ordinators of the Jaipur Literary Festival and tour guides provided with the help of Faith Singh.

For Virginia in the US (later years)
Peter Bogdanavich; Sarah Ferguson; Geraldine Chaplin; Sam Kashner and Nancy Schoenberger; Justin Manask; Elizabeth Skene; Stephen C Shafer; the San Simeon Trust; Sandra Tyler; Bruce Wilcox; Elizabeth Wilcox.

It would be nice to see a little more acknowledgement of Virginia at Osterley, where (on my last visit) it was hard to glean more than the fact that Lord Jersey had once married an American actress; a little of her glamour, warmth, and charm might help brighten the personality of one of the National Trust's most icily un-atmospheric properties. I wish I could have established more comprehensively the degree of Virginia's input at Middleton, the English country house which Sir Edwin Lutyens designed (in collaboration with his son, Robert) for the Jerseys in the 'Thirties. I'd love to know more exactly the degree to which Virginia influenced Lord Jersey in his creation of what was then, among the aristocracy, a pioneering collection of modern paintings (his fellow peers remained, at that time more conventionally wedded to the idea of cloaking their walls with watercolours, prints, and Old Masters). I'd give much to know what really happened between Virginia and Chaplin to inspire such a powerful mutual hostility – and such discretion.

The debt I owe to the British Library and to my own wonderful local library, at Swiss Cottage, is immense, both for providing work refuge, and for the books they have enabled me to read. My agents, Anthony Goff and George Lucas, have been terrific; so has my editor, Mike Jones, helped by his wonderful team (Rory, Hannah, Joe: I hope you do know just how grateful I am) at Simon & Schuster. Alan Hollinghurst's generosity in reading (once again) the text is appreciated more than I can say to that most consummate of stylists, and kindest of friends. It's with a full heart that I add to these cherished names that of my beloved husband, Ted Lynch, most patient, understanding and astute of readers, advisors, and allies. Thank you, Ted. And above all, once again, thank you, Teresa.

PICTURE CREDITS

I would like to acknowledge with gratitude the following picture suppliers:

Teresa MacWilliams
Esme Countess of Cromer
Lady Caroline Ogilvy
John Child Villiers
The family of the late Man Singh, Maharaja of Jaipur
Chloe Teacher
Simon Marks
Mark Bristow (Northolt)

Thanks also to:

Chicago History Museum
Country Life Magazine
Getty Images
Los Angeles Public Library

My apologies to anybody who has been inadvertently omitted from the above list.

INDEX

(the initials VC in subentries refer to Virginia Cherrill)

353

ABOUT THE AUTHOR

Miranda Seymour, author of the award-winning *In My Father's House* has written many acclaimed novels and biographies, including lives of Mary Shelley, Robert Graves, Ottoline Morrell and Helle Nice, the Bugatti Queen.